EXPLORING KANTŌ

EXPLORING KANTŌ

Weekend Pilgrimages from Tokyo

MICHAEL PLASTOW

WEATHERHILL
New York & Tokyo

First edition, 1996

Published by Weatherhill, Inc.
568 Broadway, Suite 705
New York, NY 10012

Protected by copyright under the terms of the International Copyright Union; all rights reserved. Except for fair use in book reviews, no part of this book may be reproduced for any reason by any means, including any method of photographic reproduction, without permission of the publisher. Printed in the United States of America.

All photographs by the author.

Library of Congress Cataloging-in-Publication Data
Plastow, Michael, 1959–
    Exploring Kantō: weekend pilgrimages from Tokyo / by Michael Plastow.
       p.   cm.
    ISBN 0-8348-0332-1 (soft)
    1. Kantō Region (Japan)—Guidebooks. 2. Temples, Buddhist—Japan—Kantō Region. I. Title.
DS894.43.P53 1996
915.2'130449—dc20   96–4410
                                                                                       CIP

CONTENTS

Acknowledgments   9

INTRODUCTION   11

TEMPLES AND WALKS

1. SUGIMOTODERA   31
   Tsurugaoka Hachiman Shrine and Yokohama Nature Sanctuary

2. GANDENJI   41
   The Zushi Hills and Asahina Pass

3. AN'YŌIN   49
   Kamakura from South to North

4. HASEDERA   58
   The Great Buddha and Zeni-Arai Benten

5. SHŌFUKUJI   66
   Ashigara Pass and Hakone

6. HASEDERA   77
   Nanasawa Hot Spring and Hinata Yakushi

7. KŌMYŌJI   80
   Mount Kobo and Tsurumaki Hot Spring

8. SHŌKOKUJI   83
   The Zama Kite Festival

9. JIKŌJI 86
Mount Kasa

10. SHŌBŌJI 89
Woods and Warlords

11. ANRAKUJI 98
Ancient Graves and Ponpon Mountain

12. JIONJI 106
In the City of Dolls

13. SENSŌJI 114
Tokyo's Shitamachi

14. GUMYŌJI 124
The Port of Yokohama

15. CHŌKOKUJI 127
*Minowa Castle, Mount Haruna,
and Ikaho Hot Spring*

16. MIZUSAWADERA 138
Mount Mizusawa and Ikaho Hot Spring

17. MANGANJI 141
Mountain Priests and Neanderthals

18. CHŪZENJI 150
Picturesque Nikko

19. ŌYAJI 159
Stone Country

20. SAIMYŌJI 169
Mashiko Pottery

21. NICHIRINJI 178
Mount Yamizo—The Hard Place

22. SATAKEDERA *In the Steps of Mito Kōmon*	186
23. KANZEONJI *Azaleas and Modern Art*	196
24. RAKUHŌJI *Mount Kaba*	199
25. ŌMIDŌ *Mount Tsukuba*	209
26. KIYOTAKIJI *Pigs, Paddies, You and Moi*	212
27. ENPUKUJI *Cape Inubō*	215
28. RYŪSHŌIN *In the Plain of Bandō Tarō*	224
29. CHIBADERA *City Parks and Museums*	233
30. KŌZŌJI *Port and Tidal Flats*	236
31. KASAMORIJI *The Chiba Hills*	240
32. KIYOMIZUDERA *Deep in the Country*	243
33. NAGOJI *Tateyama Bay*	246
INDEX	255

ACKNOWLEDGMENTS

I would like to thank everyone who contributed to the writing and production of this book. I regret that I do not know every name, but I am indebted to them all. Special thanks are extended to Michi Ishijima for his generous loan of the camera, and to my friends at NHK International and NHK Science and Technical Research Laboratories for their invaluable assistance with the software. I am also grateful to my editor, David Noble, and to all at Weatherhill for producing such a handsome volume. Finally, I wish to thank my parents, Arthur and Mary Plastow, for teaching me the joys of the journey.

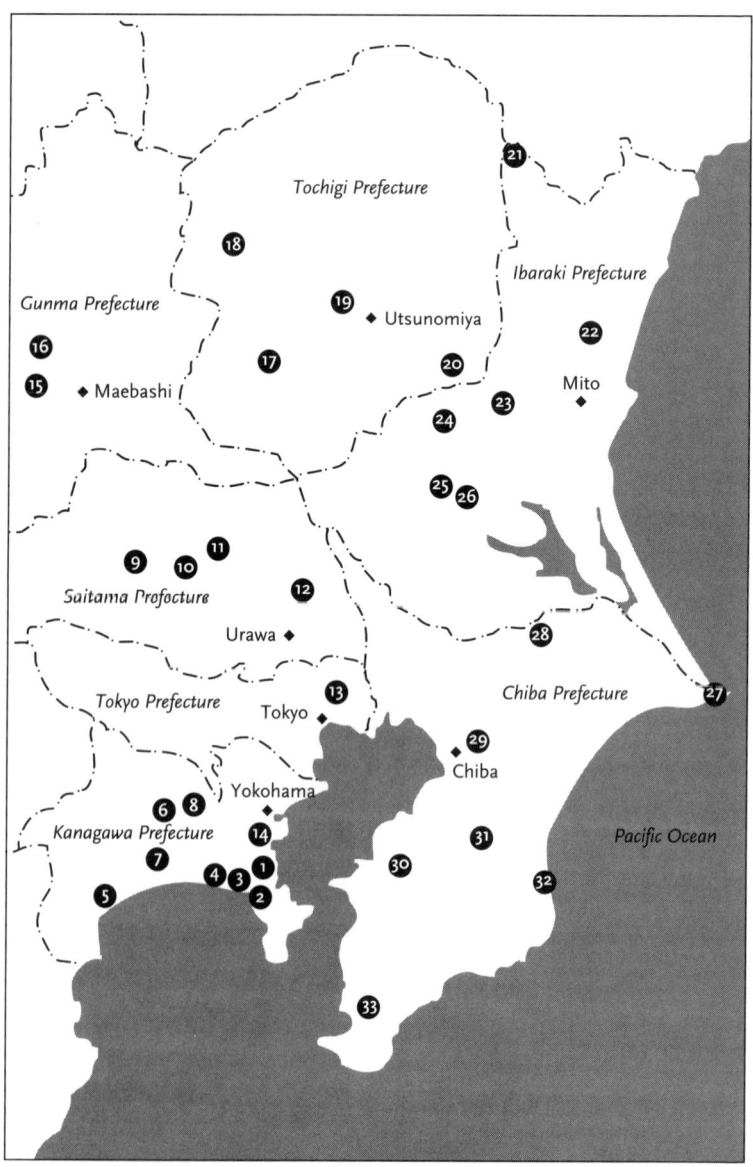

THE THIRTY-THREE TEMPLES OF THE BANDŌ PILGRIMAGE
The thirty-three chapters of this book correspond to the traditional number and sequence of the Bandō temples shown above.

INTRODUCTION

A pilgrimage is a journey. Some go for religious reasons and others to enjoy the trip. This book was planned as a respectful day-trippers guide to an ancient pilgrimage route. For those who want to know more about Japanese Buddhism and religious culture, the sights and history of the temples on the route are described in some detail. For those who simply want some rewarding day walks near Tokyo, this guide is intended as a key that may open many pleasant and interesting doors. In addition to the temple art and architecture and the people who you will meet on the way, you will find scenery that ranges from the urban to the rural and mountainous, and attractions that run the gamut from kilns and doll factories to hot springs, zoos, and holiday beaches. The walks introduce areas and aspects of the region surrounding Tokyo that might be difficult to discover in any other way.

As the title *Exploring Kantō* suggests, the main emphasis is on these acts of discovery. For those unfamiliar with the geography, Kantō is the name of the region centered on Tokyo. It is formed by the Kantō Plain, Japan's largest, and the surrounding mountains, and serves as the center of the modern nation's politics, culture, and economy. Kantō has the population of a medium-sized country (thirty-five million people) and plenty of variety to match. Some of its cities are internationally renowned tourist resorts, such as Kamakura, capital of the medieval shoguns, and Nikkō, site of the famous Tōshōgū Shrine. But you will also find quiet plains, valleys, and mountains that only half belong to the modern era. You will walk among ancient burial mounds, remains of old castles, lovely lakes and marshes, and many legends from the distant past.

INTRODUCTION

The region today includes the prefectures of Tokyo, Saitama, Kanagawa, Gunma, Tochigi, Ibaraki, and Chiba. In terms of the old provinces of Japan, whose names appear often in this book, Kantō is normally taken to include Musashi (corresponding to parts of present-day Tokyo, Kanagawa, and Saitama Prefectures), Sagami (part of Kanagawa), Kōzuke (Gunma), Shimotsuke (Tochigi), Hitachi (Ibaraki) and Shimōsa, Kazusa, and Awa (all in Chiba). Do note, however, that the overlap between the traditional provinces and the modern prefectures is only approximate.

Kantō was considered semi-barbaric in ancient times. The name literally means "the land to the east of the gate," referring to the many checkpoints on Japan's old highway system. The connotation is rather like that of the land to the north of the Watford Gap in England, as viewed from the supposedly civilized south; or to the west of the Cumberland Gap in America, seen from the original thirteen colonies to the east.

Kansai, "the land to the west of the gate," centered on the ancient capitals of Nara and Kyoto, but just where the barbaric east began was a moot point which shifted depending on the era. The earliest usage referred to areas east of Ōtsu near Lake Biwa, which is now considered well inside Kansai. The term now indicates regions to the east of the former gates at Hakone and Ashigara near Odawara, plus the one at Usui Pass between Gunma and Nagano Prefectures.

The pilgrimage is called the Bandō Sanjūsansho, "the thirty-three sites of Bandō." Bandō, too, is an old name for the land to the east. Bandō literally means "the eastern slope," referring to the eastern side of the passes at Hakone, Ashigara, and Usui. The thirty-three sites are temples linked into a circuit pilgrimage; when visited in order, they connect in a loop. The pilgrimage, as its name suggests, leads right around the Kantō region.

Japan has countless circuit pilgrimages. The Bandō circuit is dedicated to Kannon, (Avalokitesvara in Sanskrit), a merciful bodhisattva who is supposed to have thirty-three separate manifestations (hence the number of temples on the circuit). Another famous circuit pilgrimage of Kannon temples, called the Saigoku Sanjūsan-sho, is found in the Kansai area.

There are many others. Some seventy Kannon circuit pilgrimages were founded in the Edo era alone. You will also find circuits for other buddhas, bodhisattvas, and Buddhist teachers. There are thirty-two-temple routes dedicated to Sakyamuni; twenty-four and one-hundred-eight-temple routes for Jizō; six and forty-eight-temple Amida pilgrimages; thirty-six Fudō, forty-nine Yakushi, and sixty-six Enma circuits; and then there are a variety of non-Buddhist pilgrimages like those for the Shichifukujin (Seven Gods of Good Fortune). The most famous circuit pilgrimage of all is the eighty-eight-temple circuit in Shikoku, which follows in the steps of Kūkai (Kōbō Daishi).

The walks presented in each chapter of this book are mostly easy. A system of stars is used to indicate difficulty. One star indicates that the walk is very easy. A three-star walk may not be suitable for everyone. *The times given in the chapter headings are direct point-to-point, start-to-finish walking times, not the actual time you are likely to spend on the course. In fact, the typical walk, including sightseeing, represents a full day of six to eight hours on your feet.*

Travel information is given at the end of each chapter. Those using JR (Japan Railway) trains may wish to check the schedules with the JR English-language information service (☎ 03-3423-0111). Another useful English-language telephone service is the Japan Travel Phone run by JNTO (Japan National Tourist Organization), which is available to answer a wide range of questions (including ones about accommodations; they do not make reservations, but will help) from 9:00 am to 5:00 pm daily (In Tokyo , call ☎ 03-3503-4400; free numbers for eastern Japan are ☎ 0088-22-2800 or ☎ 0120-22-2800).

When seeking reservations anywhere in Japan, the most useful network of hotels is the Welcome Inn group, which goes out of its way to cater to foreigners. A directory of Welcome Inns (all priced under ¥8,000) is available from the JNTO tourist information centers at Narita, Yurakuchō, and elsewhere. The main office is in the

Kōtsu Kaikan building outside the Yaesu exit of Tokyo station. Members include business hotels, *ryokan*, *minshuku*, pensions, and youth hostels. Many are located in Tokyo. The Welcome Inn reservation center may be reached at ☎ 03-3211-4201.

The Bandō Pilgrimage and the Kannon Faith

The Bandō pilgrimage is dedicated to Kannon. Before we talk about the pilgrimage itself, we must explain who Kannon is, and give some background to the Kannon faith.

The name, Kannon, tells part of the story. It means "the one who hears the cries of the world," and suggests Kannon's role as the personification of infinite compassion. Kannon is a bodhisattva, a Buddhist term which refers to a person who vows to achieve enlightenment through a long series of rigorous practices, but to postpone his or her own entry into buddhahood in order to help all other beings to attain enlightenment as well. Kannon, like Jizō, Monju, and Fugen, is one of these embodiments of the Mahayana Buddhist ideal of universal enlightenment and compassion for all sentient beings.

The pilgrims are looking for this help, which has both practical and spiritual aspects. Concerning the practical side, the best-known passage is found in section twenty-five of the *Lotus Sutra*, which tells how Kannon saves humanity from seven fearful afflictions and the three poisons of greed, anger, and ignorance. The spiritual side of the Kannon faith is uppermost in the *Heart Sutra*, the other key text for Japanese Kannon pilgrims, whose message is that we see the truth when all sensation, thought, desire, ignorance, and even wisdom have been transcended. Pilgrims accordingly seek not only relief from suffering, but also enlightenment beyond the turbulence of the physical world.

Pilgrimage circuits typically consist of thirty-three temples because Kannon is believed to have thirty-three distinct manifestations, as mentioned above. You will not, however, see thirty-three different types of Kannon image on any circuit I know. The most popular forms in which Kannon is represented in Japan are Shō Kannon (the original form), Senju Kannon (the thousand-armed Kannon, whose many hands can help multitudes at once), Jūichimen Kannon (the eleven-headed Kannon, who sees and hears all that is going on) and Batō Kannon (the horse-headed Kannon, savior of animals). The thirty-three Bandō temples have, as their main images, fourteen Jūichimen, twelve Senju, six Shō, and one Enmei Kannon (the Kannon of longevity).

The Kannon faith was already very old when introduced to Japan, probably in the sixth or seventh centuries AD. The original Sanskrit version of the *Lotus Sutra* appears to have been written at about the time of Christ, and archaeological finds suggest that the Kannon faith was already old in India by that time. The first mention in Japan is the dedication of a Kannon statue by Shōtoku Taishi at Hōryūji in Nara in the early seventh century. Kannon images were consecrated all over Japan at officially established provincial temples (*kokubunji*) during the Nara period.

Kannon may have entered Japan as the object of an independent tradition based on the *Lotus Sutra*, or perhaps as an attendant to the buddha Amida in the Amida Sanzon trinity. In any case, the Kannon faith certainly arrived as a faith for the favored few, for the early statues at temples like Hōryūji were only displayed to the aristocracy. Prayers in those days were typically made to save the emperor from sickness and quell disturbances.

The faith appears to have become more popular beginning in the late seventh century. On the Bandō pilgrimage, the temples at Hasedera (in Kamakura), Chūzenji, and Ōyaji have great statues and carvings from this period. Kannon worship in Japan now expanded beyond the confines of the imperial court to become closely associated with the esoteric Buddhism of mountain ascetics and itinerant priests. The name of one, Gyōki (668–749), an ascetic priest of Korean extraction who taught the importance of good works to atone for past and present sins, appears in many of the founding legends of the Bandō temples.

The legend of the origin of the pilgrimages also comes from that period. It concerns not Bandō but Saigoku (Kansai), the land in the west. The story is told of how Tokudō Shōnin, the priest who founded Hasedera at Yamato around 720, fell sick and descended to hell. Enma, the lord who sits in judgment on new arrivals, told him to save sinners from hell by selecting thirty-three holy places in Japan for worship. Enma gave Tokudō thirty-three seals for the temples and sent him back to the land of the living, where unfortunately no one believed his story. He buried the seals at Nakayamadera, the place that later became the first temple of the Saigoku pilgrimage.

The legend then leaps to the late tenth century in the time of Emperor Kazan (r. 984-986), who is said to have revived the Saigoku pilgrimage and founded the Bandō circuit. We are told that Kazan was persuaded to embark on a pilgrimage by Butsugen Shōnin of Kawachi (present-day Osaka) and dug up the seals buried by Tokudō in order to travel the Saigoku course in the prescribed order (though, in fact, several of the Saigoku temples had still not been founded at the time).

The early legends of the circuits are questionable but the idea of journeying to the paradise of Kannon is old. The *Lotus Sutra* tells that Kannon lives on a mountain named Potalaka off the southern coast of India. Soon, the Japanese were finding representations of Potalaka everywhere. Shōdō Shōnin, for example, appears to have been seeking Kannon's paradise when he founded the temples of Nikkō. Fudaraku (Futara) the old name for Mount Nantai, is a Japanese reading of Potalaka. Other priests set sail for Potalaka, notably from Kumano, which later became the start of the Saigoku Kannon pilgrimage.

The first historical hint of pilgrimages around Kannon circuits comes in the tenth century with the emergence of a six-Kannon faith in esoteric Tendai Buddhism. The six Kannons were thought to save souls in the six lowest realms of existence: those of hell, ghosts, beasts, warring spirits, men, and devas. Another six-Kannon faith was developed by the esoteric Shingon sect, and soon the two archetypes gave rise to some seven-Kannon circuits. This appears to have happened because one of the six manifestations of Kannon on the Shingon list was different from the six of the Tendai list, making a combined total of seven between the two. A seven-Kannon course was already established in Kyoto in the Heian period. All thirty-three of the Saigoku Kannons in fact belong to those seven types: Shō, Senju, Jūichimen, Batō, Fukū, Kenjaku, Juntei, and Nyoirin.

Saigoku was the first thirty-three Kannon pilgrimage to appear in the historical record. The first account of the Saigoku pilgrimage concerns Gyōson (1055–1135), the abbot of Miidera, but this seems dubious, not only because it was added to the record later but also because one temple, Imagumano Kannonji, was only founded in 1160. The earliest convincing story tells of how Kakuchū, also a Tendai priest of Miidera, completed the course in seventy-five days in 1186. This was probably an ascetic practice not intended for ordinary people.

It was perhaps only natural that the people of the east should soon want a pilgrimage of their own. The Bandō *musha,* the warriors of the Kantō region, had acquired a strong Kannon faith. We know, for example, that Minamoto Yoritomo, the first Kamakura shogun, was a fervent believer who always fought with a tiny Kannon in his hair. Kannon probably provided the warrior class with a welcome safety-net for avoiding hell. It has also been suggested that temples of the old esoteric Tendai and Shingon sects saw in such pilgrimages a way to restore their fortunes against the rise of the new popular forms of Buddhism preached by Hōnen, Nichiren, and Shinran.

Besides, the founding of the Bandō pilgrimage was related to new political realities. On the one hand, the new political stability in the east with the rise of the Kamakura shogunate made travel easier. On the other, the pilgrimage may have been devised as an instrument of political control. Temples and shrines have always served as both source and evidence of power. They are territorial markers. The promotion of pilgrimages possibly helped to forge the new political stability of the Bandō region by building bridges between the territories of the local warlords and thereby helping to impose the ideology of the ruling elite.

Some say that the Bandō course was fixed by Sanetomo, Yoritomo's son. At the very least, the fact that the Bandō course starts in Kamakura and ends in Tateyama, a short boat ride from the Miura Peninsula below Kamakura, is strong circumstantial evidence for the importance of the shogun's capital.

The first definite record of a Bandō pilgrim dates from 1234. This particular pilgrimage was slow: the priest Jōben spent three-hundred days at Nichirinji, Temple 21. The historical record then leaps across two hundred years to *fuda* (votive plaques) from the 1470s that survive at Bannaji in Ashikaga. These show that ordinary people were now taking part.

It should be noted that although the Saigoku pilgrimage appears earlier in the historical record, its course, too, is suggestive of the influence of the Bandō *musha*. Put simply, the Saigoku course both starts and ends in the east, implying that it was devised according to the convenience of people coming from the east and not, for example, from Kyoto and Nara.

However the traditions began, the Japanese eventually took to the idea of Kannon pilgrimages with energy. The Bandō course was already popular with lay people by the Muromachi period, when the thirty-three-Kannon pilgrimage of Chichibu was also started. Someone, probably in the early Edo period, then had the bright idea of giving the Chichibu course a thirty-fourth temple. The Saigoku, Bandō, and Chichibu pilgrimages added together became the one hundred Kannons of Japan. You will also hear of the one-hundred-eighty-eight *fudasho*, a number achieved by combining the one-hundred Kannons with the eighty-eight temples of Shikoku mentioned above.

Needless to say, not all of the pilgrims had religion as their main aim. Travel was tightly restricted in the Edo period, but was permitted for pilgrimages, with the result that they developed a definite touristic tinge. More than two-hundred pilgrims' guidebooks were published in that era.

The Edo period ended on a difficult note for Buddhism as the Mito Tokugawa clan and then the new Meiji government separated Buddhism from Shinto and strove to establish a Confucian version of Shinto as the national faith. Many temples were abandoned or destroyed, including several on the Bandō circuit. The temples of Ibaraki, in the heart of the Mito domain, were the worst affected.

But the pilgrims were not to be denied. The circuits are popular again today, perhaps more so than ever. Besides the main courses, minor long-forgotten pilgrimages are now being revived all over the country. They offer an escape, solace, and an object for many who seek more from life.

Minamoto Yoritomo and the Bandō Musha

Besides its religious interest, the Bandō pilgrimage offers a fascinating glimpse of the political map of Kamakura-period Japan. So many stories are related to the wars of those times that a brief account of the political background must be given here.

The temples of the pilgrimage reflect the power structure of medieval Japan. Many are located close to the sites of great castles. Their histories are intertwined with those of the Bandō *musha* who fought for half a millennium across the plain. These warrior clans included the Hiki and Hatakeyama in Musashi, the Utsunomiya in Shimotsuke, the Hata around the Katori Inland Sea and Tsukuba, the Satake in Hitachi, the Chiba in Shimōsa and Kazusa, and the Satomi in Awa.

The Bandō *musha* were the rough diamonds of Japanese history. They were warriors who scorned the effeteness of the court and valued horsemanship, the bow, and the sword. They came to be known for their fearlessness, austerity, and loyalty, though some readers may wonder about the latter in view of the tales of treachery you will find in this book. The Bandō pilgrimage began in the world of the samurai.

The story of the founding of the Kamakura shogunate is a tale of rivalry between two warrior families, the Taira and Minamoto, who were both descended from the imperial line. The imperial family had grown too large by the Nara and Heian periods, so the custom arose of creating new aristocratic clans as offshoots of the imperial line. Although so many Taira and Minamoto branch families were created that it hardly makes sense to consider them unified clans, the labels somehow stuck and, with important exceptions, the families of the Taira and Minamoto clans soon became rivals of each other. The chief exceptions were in Bandō, where certain Taira families played a key role in bringing Minamoto Yoritomo to power.

Many of the Bandō clans were Taira descended from Emperor Kammu, who ruled Japan from 781 to 806. The first Taira ancestor to arrive in Bandō was Prince Takamochi, who was given an official post in Kazusa around 890 and later settled in Musashi. The Taira warriors of Bandō were descended from his fifth son, Muraoka Yoshibumi. They were the pioneers who developed the land and, once established, were determined to defend it against all comers. A major revolt against the central government was launched as early as the 930s by Taira Masakado. Another by Taira Tadatsune was put down by Minamoto Yoriyoshi in 1031.

The Minamoto were originally based chiefly in the west, but began to gain valuable allies and military influence in the east through two wars fought by Minamoto Yoriyoshi and Minamoto Yoshiie: the Earlier Nine Years' War of 1051–62 and the Later Three Years' War of 1083–87. Yoriyoshi was made governor of Sagami and founded Hachiman Shrine in Kamakura in 1063.

All briefly seemed lost for the Minamoto when Taira Kiyomori won outright control in Kyoto through victories in the Hōgen Disturbance of 1156 and the Heiji Disturbance of 1160. Many of the Minamoto were slaughtered during or after the fighting. But Kiyomori made the fatal mistake of sparing Minamoto Yoshitomo's young sons, Yoritomo, Noriyori, and Yoshitsune.

Yoritomo was exiled to Izu, where he was guarded by a Taira, Hōjō Tokimasa. Unfortunately for the Taira in Kyoto, Yoritomo and Tokimasa got on so well that Tokimasa even permitted Yoritomo to marry his daughter, Masako. When Kiyomori installed his own grandson as Emperor Antoku in 1180, Minamoto Yoritomo raised the standard of revolt.

Yoritomo was defeated at Ishibashiyama, but fleeing to Hakone and then across Tokyo Bay to the Bōsō Peninsula, he was able to regroup with the support of Chiba Tsunetane, Taira Hirotsune and other Bandō *musha*. Yoritomo then established his military base in Kamakura and won the battle of Fujigawa. That produced a stalemate until 1183, when the Taira attacked Minamoto Yoshinaka, Yoritomo's cousin in Shinshū (now Nagano Prefecture), and lost.

This victory placed Yoshinaka in charge of Kyoto but he showed no enthusiasm to follow up his success by chasing the Taira. It seems that he did not want Yoritomo to march into the capital in his stead. Yoritomo sent a force to Kyoto under his brothers, Noriyori and Yoshitsune, who defeated Yoshinaka in 1184. The brothers then continued westward to overwhelm the Taira at Ichinotani. The Taira escaped to an island off Shikoku, but were finally crushed at the naval battle of Dannoura in 1185.

Yoritomo now turned from cousin to brother. He outlawed Yoshitsune, who fled to take refuge with the Ōshū Fujiwara family of Hiraizumi in the northeast. Once there, however, Yoshitsune was forced to kill himself by the son of his treacherous host. This only served to precipitate Yoritomo's Ōshū campaign of 1189, which brought even the wild northeast under his control. Yoritomo then kept his capital in Kamakura in order to bypass the imperial court in Kyoto. The epic struggle between the Minamoto and the Taira, known as the Genpei War, is related in the military romance *Heike Monogatari* and a chronicle entitled *Azuma Kagami*.

Many tales especially are told of Yoshitsune, the victorious general who, betrayed by his brother, died by his own hand at the age of thirty. He is one of the perennial tragic heroes of Nō and Kabuki drama. Most tales also involve his faithful retainer, Benkei. But while Yoshitsune is recalled as a romantic hero, few remember poor Noriyori, who also died on Yoritomo's orders. On the Bandō pilgrimage, Noriyori is associated with the temple Anrakuji.

Yoritomo became shogun in 1192. He was now commander-in-chief of all Japan. As related in the chapters for the first four Bandō temples, that victory was to be short-lived. Yoritomo died only seven years later, after falling from his horse. His son, Yoriie, succeeded him but was then destroyed by Hōjō Masako, the boy's own mother, because he favored the Hiki family over the Hōjō.

Masako prevented her father, Tokimasa, from overthrowing Yoriie's little brother, thirteen-year-old Sanetomo, in 1205, but the "poet shogun" was never allowed to wield real power. Sanetomo, the last of Yoritomo's line, was assassinated by or on behalf of a nephew, the priest Kugyō, at Tsurugaoka Hachiman Shrine in 1219, apparently in revenge for Yoriie's murder.

A series of imperial princes now filled the puppet position of shogun, but the Hōjō *shikken* (shogunal regents) ran the country. We must be careful not to exaggerate the stability obtained by the Kamakura shogunate. The shoguns ruled the province of Sagami directly beginning in 1192, but other parts of Bandō stayed firmly in the hands of local warlords. Fighting continued throughout the region. Castles continued to be built and to fall, but at least the conflicts were mostly very local.

The real decline of the shogunate began with the Mongol invasions of Japan in 1274 and 1281. The Mongols were repulsed, but at the cost of allowing local warlords to build up military strength once more. Two warlords of Minamoto descent from northern Bandō, Nitta Yoshisada and Ashikaga Takauji, overthrew the Hōjō on behalf of Emperor Godaigo in 1333. The shogunal capital was moved back to Kyoto when Takauji established the Ashikaga shogunate in 1338.

The story of the Bandō *musha* was not yet finished, but most of the stories relating to the temples of this book come from the Kamakura shogunate, so the rest may be summarized very briefly. In the 1400s, a new Hōjō family, unrelated to the first, began to spread its influence across Kantō from its base in Odawara. The Hōjō won control of most of Kantō before their defeat at the hands of Hideyoshi at Odawara in 1590. The main exceptions were the territories of the Satomi in Awa, the Satake and Asahina in Hitachi, the Sanada in Kozuke, and various lesser warlords in Shimotsuke. It is noteworthy that Tokugawa Ieyasu, the founder of the Tokugawa shogunate, also claimed Minamoto ancestry.

The Modern Pilgrims

The Japanese themselves often say that they are not a religious people. Much depends on what is meant by religiosity. They certainly participate in many religious festivals and rites, and pray sincerely at ancestral graves, temples, and shrines. On the other hand, few Japanese want to talk about their faith with those who do not share it. The majority dislike rationalizing it even to themselves. Moreover, the typical Japanese has a very personal relationship with ancestors and gods of various traditions that does not lend itself easily to sophisticated theology.

It is easy to be cynical about Japanese religion. Most prayers, whether for money, health, success in examinations, or safety on the roads, can seem rather selfish, and Japanese often joke about priests who only go through the motions of religion. One young friend, when I mentioned the thousand-armed Kannon, made gestures to suggest that all of those thousand hands are imploring, "Money, please!" But it must be said that Japanese pilgrims are sincere. When you ask around, you will find a remarkable number of people who have been on a Kannon pilgrimage or dream of doing so in the future. Surveys by a research institute, the Tōkei Sūri Kenkyūjo, show that over seventy percent of Japanese believe that religious sensibility is important and over thirty percent profess to religious faith. That adds up to a lot of people in a country of 120 million.

The important point is that Japanese religions minister directly to both material and spiritual needs. Prayers bring safe births, rich catches, and abundant harvests, but are also good for the soul. Regarding pilgrims, Japanese religion has a long tradition of seeking to escape the world of mundane things through the physical displacement: of going on a journey.

Who are the pilgrims? The Bandō circuit pilgrimage was originally male-only, though women also prayed at many of the individual temples on the route. These days, women are in the majority. Most pilgrims are middle-aged or older, often setting out on pilgrimage when relieved of their everyday cares by retirement. But some are very young: a Japanese-language guidebook is being prepared for cycling the Bandō circuit.

In terms of mentality, the typical pilgrim feels that she or he has had a hard and restricted life and now seeks peace and fulfillment away from the daily routine. A pilgrimage is a way to find oneself. These days, the Bandō pilgrimage appeals to people who find that ordinary leisure pursuits still leave them empty. The Bandō circuit provides order, purpose, and a challenge, with a sense of achievement at the end. And the pilgrims have the added pleasure of making the trip with like-minded people. Another advantage is that it gets easier to pray as the pilgrimage advances. This is a benefit of repetition, relaxation, and familiarity.

In his book *Junrei no Kokoro* (The Heart of the Pilgrim), Kosho Shimizutani gives many testimonies by Bandō pilgrims. Here are the words of one housewife: "Going on the pilgrimage helped me to reflect on aspects of myself that I never usually think about.

Climbing the steep stone steps and walking the mountain paths strengthened my mind and body. It relieved stress and cleansed my life. I'll take my husband along, too, next time." Pilgrimages can also mend relationships and bring people closer together.

Many pilgrims take part with very specific motives. Some do the pilgrimage for the repose of lost relatives or to thank Kannon for relief from illness. Some make it on behalf of others who, for whatever reason, cannot do the circuit themselves. Some pilgrims hope to atone for past sins, or to learn how to die well. Some believe they travel not only with Kannon but also with dead children, spouses, or ancestors, and sometimes even take the ashes with them. These pilgrims have an especially heavy responsibility, for they must atone for two people instead of one. Pilgrimage is, at any rate, democratic: everyone can go for what they want or need.

The priest of Kōzōji tells this story in a book on the Bandō pilgrimage: "We recently built a parking lot because so many visitors come by car these days. One result is that we now get hot-rodders. I didn't like it at first, but at New Year's these youngsters came dressed up to pray to Kannon. I realized that they are yearning for something, too."

There was a time when youngsters did the pilgrimage as a kind of coming-of-age tour. Some communities even regarded completion of the pilgrimage as a basic condition for marriage. Stories are told of poor girls from farming villages racing around the circuit as fast as they could in order to keep their expenses as low as possible.

The Bandō pilgrimage was much harder in the Kamakura period than now, but it remains expensive and difficult to fit into the busy schedules of contemporary life. It now takes about twelve days by public transport and forty days on foot. If walked in order, the circuit is over 1,300 kilometers long. Modern pilgrims mostly use cars or buses. You see lines of pilgrims at the temples but not on the roads between. Individuals typically visit one temple at a time over a long period. But those who prefer can join guided tours which complete the entire pilgrimage with fantastic speed. Advertisements for the Bandō course offer temples one to fourteen in two nights; fifteen to twenty-six in three nights; and twenty-seven to thirty-three in two nights. Although this may sound punishing to the point of negating the value of the experience, pilgrims who take part would strongly differ. They are usually the most devout. The Bandō pilgrimage has always combined religious fervor with elements of both masochism and tourism.

Rest assured that you are allowed to do the Kannon course at your own convenience. The numbering of the temples has not changed since the pilgrimage began but you do not have to visit them in order. Different Chinese characters are used for *junpai*, the word for a circuit pilgrimage, depending on whether it is performed in the prescribed order or not. A pilgrimage performed in reverse order is known as *gyakuuchi*.

You will see many Japanese pilgrims at the temples, often in the full pilgrim's regalia. For the serious pilgrims, there are many things that ought to be borne in mind. The first requirements concern their state of mind. In *Kannon Fudasho Meguri no Subete* (Everything You Need to Know About the Kannon Pilgrimage), Ryoyu Hirahata specifies three basic conditions: a healthy heart and mind; no anxiety about leaving the family; and enough money for the journey. In addition, the following ten commandments used to be given at the first temple: don't kill any living thing; don't steal; don't commit adultery; don't deceive others; don't be frivolous; don't bad-mouth others; don't say anything that will harm others; don't be covetous; don't get angry; don't break nature's laws.

The most important accessory is the pilgrim's album (*nōkyōchō*) for receiving the seal of each temple they visit. These seals are said to before presentation to Enma at the court of the dead to prove the pilgrimage has been completed, but the album also serves as earthly evidence of absolution and achievement. The older practice was to receive seals on copies of the Buddhist sutras, but most pilgrims use the albums today.

Some group pilgrimages regulate clothing and religious observances strictly. The pilgrim wears white clothes and carries a staff (*kongōzue*) marked with Sanskrit characters for earth, water, fire, wind, and the void. The staff thus represents universal harmony. It can also double as a grave-marker for pilgrims who die on the road. Some even say that the white clothes started out as funeral garb. The pilgrim only returns to this world when he takes them off.

What do pilgrims do when visiting a temple? Here is the procedure prescribed by Shimizutani. First, rinse the mouth and wash the hands using the ladles at the water trough found in all temple courtyards. Ring the bell (if allowed). The bell should only be rung when entering, never when leaving. Visit the office (*nōkyōsho*) and ask the priest to enter the temple's seal in the album. Then, with the priest's permission, go to pray at the main image. Dedicate candles and incense sticks. Hold the hands together in prayer and recite a Buddhist text. Suitable texts are the *Kaikyōnoge* (Gatha on Opening the Sutras); the *Kannongyō* (section twenty-five of the *Lotus Sutra*); the *Hannya Shingyō* (*Heart Sutra*); and the *Ekōmon* (a verse for transferring personal merit to others). Then sing the *eika* (pilgrim's song) and chant *Namu Kanzeon Bosatsu* ("Hail to the bodhisattva Kannon!") three times. Lastly, return to the priest to receive the album. Give the temple a donation (*gohōzen*) when getting the stamp. On returning home, place the album on the family altar and give thanks to your ancestors. The pilgrimage is not the individual's achievement alone; it is due to their efforts as well.

Many pilgrims also dedicate *fuda*, the paper stickers or wooden plaques used throughout the Orient for warding off evil. Legend says that in Japan the practice began with Emperor Kazan when he visited Kokawadera on the Saigoku pilgrimage. Pilgrims used to hang wooden *fuda* around their necks for dedication at each temple. These days, however, they are requested not to stick or hang them directly on the temple walls, but to leave them in the care of the priest.

At this point, it must be firmly restated that no visitors to these temples, either Japanese or foreign, are required or even expected to do any of this. You are perfectly welcome just to go along as a tourist in the spirit of the walks described in this book. If, however, you do wish to take part in a genuine group pilgrimage, you can join the pilgrims' society, Junrei no Kai. Membership costs three thousand yen annually and you will receive a monthly Japanese-language newsletter. (Address: Manganji, 9822-1 Tennōdai, Chōshi-shi, Chiba-ken. ☎ 0479 24 8416. Expect to speak in Japanese.)

For the rest, who are using this book, the only things you will need are a pair of stout walking shoes and sensible respect for the beliefs of others.

A Note on the Maps

All thirty-three temples of the Bandō pilgrimage are introduced in this volume, with a chapter devoted to each of them and to walks in their vicinity, but only the twenty best day trips are described in full. You are encouraged to try the others too, for even the thirteen given briefer treatment make for a pretty enjoyable trip..

Each chapter is accompanied by a map showing the area around the temple. The maps are roughly to scale, but simplified; they should be sufficient to follow the walks described, but readers intent on fully exploring an area are advised to pick up local maps on the spot or to purchase them at one of the major Tokyo bookstores before setting out.

Major features common to all the maps are shown in the key on the facing page.

Key to the Maps

KŌMYŌJI ❼	Bandō route temple
卍	Other temple
⛩	Shrine
◆	Point of interest
△ 570	Mountain (elevation in meters)
👤	School
♨	Hot spring
〰	River or stream
⬭	Park
▬▬▬	Railway line
═══	Major road
———	Minor road
- - - - -	Footpath
⬡	Railway Station
⚲	Bus stop

SUGIMOTODERA — 1
Tsurugaoka Hachiman Shrine and Yokohama Nature Sanctuary

Sugimotodera stands in Kamakura, the city that Minamoto Yoritomo made the capital in 1185. The old temples and shrines of Kamakura hold a special place in the history, arts, and folklore of Japan, as do its personalities, who include warlords like Yoritomo and Yoshitsune; Yoritomo's strong wife Masako; Yoshitsune's loyal servant Benkei and lover Shizuka; and the poet-shogun Sanetomo.

The artworks of the Kamakura period (1185–1333) were fabulous. Unfortunately for the tourist, many are locked away in dark and very private temples. Always, however, a small selection of masterpieces may be viewed at the Kamakura Museum inside the grounds of the Tsurugaoka Hachiman Shrine.

The sights are so numerous that the almost rustic Sugimotodera, with its thatched roof and modest interior, becomes a minor stop along the way. But this first temple of the Bandō course is tasteful, unpretentious, and very much a part of the low-key atmosphere that sets Kamakura apart from other famous tourist spots of Japan.

Kamakura has had ups and downs in its long history. When Lafcadio Hearn visited at the turn of this century, he found a desolate, near-deserted town; his descriptions make Yoritomo's capital sound like the kingdom of Ozymandius. A 1956 guidebook to Kanagawa Prefecture called Kamakura the Nice of the Orient. Today, the whole fabric of the city creaks under the pressures of overdevelopment. The Kamakura of the 1990s is a plush commuter town.

The visitor who expects spectacular sights like those of Nikkō, Kyoto and Nara will be disappointed. But Kamakura, with its quiet

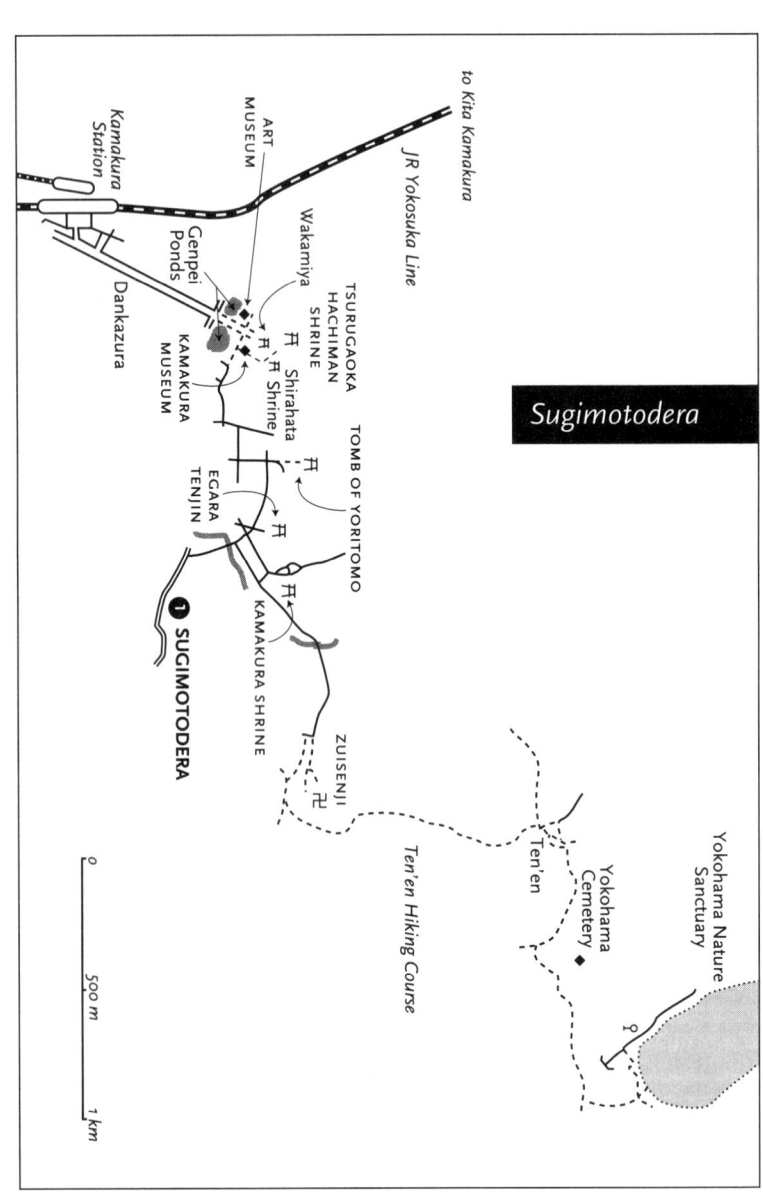

suburban atmosphere, is a wonderful place to live and to study. The visitor who comes prepared will find much to admire and enjoy.

The walk tours some of the main sites, including Tsurugaoka Hachiman Shrine, Yoritomo's grave, Sugimotodera, and the Zen temple Zuisenji, with its famous medieval garden. It then ascends the Ten'en Hiking Course to the wooded ridge above the city before winding up at the Yokohama Nature Sanctuary on the far side.

THE TEMPLE

Sugimotodera is not the kind of temple you might expect to start off the Bandō route. A grand edifice like Sensōji in Tokyo's Asakusa district might seem more suitable. But Sugimotodera is the oldest Buddhist temple in Kamakura, and Kamakura was the capital of Japan when the Bandō course began. The choice was natural all those centuries ago.

Sugimotodera was founded in 734 by Gyōki and an imperial minister, Fujiwara Fusasaki, at the order of Empress Kōmyō. Gyōki carved the first image, an eleven-faced Kannon, and Ennin added a second in 851. Finally, a third statue was carved by Genshin in 985. All three images miraculously survived a great fire in 1189 because the flames, it is said, would not touch the attendant who rescued them. Another story tells how the statues fled of their own accord and hid beneath a giant cedar; hence the name Sugimoto, which means "beneath the cedar."

Minamoto Yoritomo rebuilt the Kannon hall two years after the fire and held a ceremony for "miracles in all ages." The three older Kannons were enshrined at the back; a fourth large Kannon out front was donated by Yoritomo himself. You can enter and see the three older statues. Gyōki's statue is on the left, Ennin's in the center and Genshin's on the right. A fifth, very new statue was sculpted by a recent priest of the temple.

The Kannon carved by Gyōki also earned the appellation Geba Kannon—Dismounting Kannon—because all who tried to ride by without dismounting invariably fell from their horses. This punishment only ceased after intensive prayer by the Zen master Daikaku, the founder of Kenchōji (see Chapter 3). Admission is ¥200. Entering by the thatched *niōmon*, built in 1725, you will see banners beside the steps proclaim this to be a pilgrims' temple dedicated to Kannon. Halfway up, you come to a small Benzaiten shrine, pond, and cave shrine to the right. The old mossy steps to the top are barred off, but new steps go up the side.

The present main hall dates from the 1670s, with various renovations since. It could almost be mistaken for a country farmhouse. Yoritomo's eleven-headed Kannon stands in full view inside. You will also see many votive tablets left by Edo-period pilgrims. To the right of the hall there are a number of small pagoda-shaped graves from the middle ages. A path continues up the hillside to the left, but only leads to private houses. A Sugimoto Castle once stood at the top, but its site cannot be visited today.

THE WALK ** *(1 hour 30 minutes)*

Kamakura has many signs in English, starting inside the station itself. Leave Kamakura station by the exit for Tsurugaoka Hachiman Shrine. The tourist information office is outside on the right.

Cross to the broad main road on the far side of the square. The *torii* gate with two fierce guardians is the second gate leading up to the shrine from the beach. You approach the shrine through a tunnel of cherry trees that lines the raised path up the center of the road. Known as the Dankazura, this path was built by Yoritomo in 1182 to carry his baby son, Yoriie, for blessing at the shrine. Today, it is used by children going to school each morning. You will get some charming photos when the cherries are in bloom.

A drum bridge stands at the final gate. Tradition relates this bridge was reserved for the shoguns. Visitors are still not allowed to walk across (or rather, up and down) it, but the design was always more aesthetic than utilitarian. You are now inside the precincts of

Yoritomo's great Tsurugaoka Hachiman Shrine. Hachiman, the god of war, was the guardian deity of the Minamoto family. The shrine, founded near the beach by Minamoto Yoriyoshi in 1063, naturally became the centerpiece of Yoritomo's Kamakura.

The ponds on either side of the path are known as the Genpei ponds. The one on the right has three islands, three being a lucky number. It represents the Minamoto. The one on the left has four, the number for death, representing the defeated Taira. White lotuses are used for the Minamoto and red for the Taira, white and red being their respective emblematic colors. These devices are said to have been the idea of Yoritomo's wife, Masako. A Benzaiten shrine stands on the largest island to the right.

The shrine has a lovely peony garden, also on the right. The winter peonies flower from early January to late February and the spring peonies from mid-April to May. There are also cherries, hydrangea, camellias, sasanqua, azaleas, and bush clover.

Continuing up the broad approach to the Tsurugaoka Hachiman Shrine, you pass the Kamakura Museum of Modern Art on the left. *Yabusame* (horseback archery) is held on this concourse annually on September 16. Horseback archery contests date back at least to the Heian period, but Yoritomo is widely credited with establishing the official form in 1192. Contestants dressed in samurai armor shoot at wooden targets on the gallop.

At the end of the concourse, you reach an open-air stage and the Wakamiya Shrine, said to be the place where, in 1186, Shizuka performed her famous dance of defiance before Yoritomo. Shizuka, pregnant by Yoritomo's disgraced half-brother Yoshitsune, boldly sang Yoshitsune's praises when ordered to perform. One could hardly imagine a more dramatic gesture before a jealous and ruthless man like Yoritomo. She was spared but her baby was killed.

The enormous old ginkgo tree on the left at the foot of the long, steep staircase leading up to the main shrine also has a place in history. This is where Yoritomo's son, Sanetomo, was assassinated in 1219.

Reaching the main shrine at the top, the entrance to the right is for those who want blessings. To the left, for a fee of ¥100, you can view the shrine's treasures. They range from statues of Yoritomo and bows and arrows donated by him, to court clothing, armor, and Kamakura-period lunch boxes.

Return down the steps and go left across the red bridge by Wakamiya Shrine, following the sign to Kamakura Museum. You come to the black Shirahata Shrine, dedicated to Yoritomo and Sanetomo. Bearing right, Kamakura Museum is the white building on the left. Kamakura Museum is open from 9:00 to 4:00 daily except Mondays, the year-end holiday period, and days when the displays are changed. The museum exhibits Heian- and Kamakura-period masterpieces from the temples and shrines of Kamakura. All are labeled in English as well as Japanese. This small museum has some of the best statues, scroll paintings, and other religious relics on display in Japan. Admission is ¥150.

Exiting the museum, you are back at the Minamoto pond. Turn left and leave the shrine by the small gate. Go around the primary school, following Japanese signs to Kamakura Shrine, and soon English signs to the tomb of Yoritomo as well. You have entered residential Kamakura, with its quiet lanes, genteel atmosphere, and pensioners walking their dogs.

Turn left just before a second school (a shop stands on the near corner). Yoritomo's modest grave is at the end of the road. The great Kamakura shogun is commemorated by a simple five-story stone pagoda, each story representing one of the five elements that constitute the universe. Retrace your steps a few meters and take the lane behind the second school. English signs indicate Egara Tenjin and Kamakura Shrine. Keep straight for five minutes to the old cypress at the gate of the Egara Tenjin Shrine.

As with Tenjin shrines all over Japan, this is a place to pray for success in study, which in Japan means for success in entrance exams. The wishes of hopeful students are written on *ema* (votive tablets) and hung outside the main hall. Notice also the huge green writing brush covered with pictures of the goblins known as *kappa*. This is where students bury their trusty pens. This shrine, too, has a grand ginkgo tree which is thought to be nine hundred years old.

Continuing along the same road, don't follow the Japanese sign left to Kamakura Shrine, just a few steps later. Keep straight across the stream and go left at the T-junction. Sugimotodera lies three minutes along the main road on the left.

After viewing the temple, return to the English sign to Kamakuragū (Kamakura Shrine) at the stream. You reach the corner of a larger road in three minutes. The signs read 50 meters left to Kamakuragū and 850 meters straight on to Zuisenji. Visit the shrine first and then carry on up this road.

Kamakura Shrine is a nineteenth-century foundation from the era when the new Meiji government was instituting Shintoism and emperor-worship as the national religion. It is dedicated to Prince Morinaga, son of Emperor Godaigo, who was maligned and eventually killed by the shogun Ashikaga Takauji. Morinaga, who was steadfastly loyal to Godaigo, came to be regarded as a martyr to the imperial cause. The cave cell where he spent his final months may be viewed behind the shrine. Otherwise, the shrine has little of interest for the tourist, but you should look at the treasures. They include festival lion heads, portable shrines, bows and arrows, and a painting of the Meiji emperor.

Outdoor Nō plays (*takigi* Nō) are performed here each year on September 21 and 22. Admission is free but you must apply in advance. Send a stamped, self-addressed postcard to the Kamakura City Tourist Association (Kamakura-shi Kankō Kyōkai, 1-9-3 Komachi, Kamakura-shi; ☎ 0467-23-3050) between September 1 and 8. Seats are distributed by lottery.

Heading again towards Zuisenji, you pass some tennis courts on the left. This was the site of Yofukuji, a great temple built by Yoritomo in 1192 on the model of Chūsonji in Hiraizumi, which

Yoritomo had conquered during the Ōshū campaign of 1189. The land was reclaimed for paddies after the temple burned in 1492.

Zuisenji is approached through a huge garden of shrubs, flowers, and plum trees. Notice the white post pointing up a lane to the right just beyond the first small outer gate. This is the entrance to the Ten'en Hiking Course.

This Zen temple was founded in 1327 and flourished under the patronage of the Ashikaga shoguns. The rock garden by the caves behind the main hall is Kamakura's only surviving Kamakura-period garden. It was excavated and renovated in 1970. Admission to Zuisenji is ¥100.

Return to the entrance to the Ten'en Hiking Course. A second post on the left just behind the house on the corner points up a narrow path. It is an easy five-minute climb to the ridge. Turn left at the ridge, then left again soon after. The hiking course runs right along a low wooded ridge in the north of Kamakura. The walk is well-known and easy with only minimal ups and downs. It is pleasant after the temples and shrines to have such a gentle stroll through woods so near at hand. The views must have been better in the past, when the city was smaller, but give some idea of the topography.

There are several sights along the way. First, in a cave on the right, you see the five-story stone pagoda grave of a Kamakura warrior. Similar caves soon follow. These burial caves are found all over the hills of Kamakura, dug here because the shogunate forbade the digging of graves in fields on account of the shortage of good land.

Just below Mount Tendai, you come to the red-bibbed Kaifuki Jizō, the Conch-Blowing Jizō who, according to legend, warned regent Hōjō Takatoki of the approach of Nitta Yoshisada's forces in 1333. The warning was of no avail, for Hōjō was defeated anyway.

At Ten'en, about thirty minutes from the entrance to the course, you reach a couple of resthouses that serve hot food This is where I suggest turning right for the Yokohama Nature Sanctuary. If you prefer to finish the whole Ten'en course, you will find the latter part described in the walk for Chapter 3. It takes twenty minutes from here to the point where that walk reaches the ridge above Kakuonji. It is impossible to miss your way.

The route to the Yokohama Nature Sanctuary takes you along a second ridge away from the crowds. Take the path to the right behind the first resthouse and turn right at the junction at a fence. The huge Yokohama cemetery on the left is a blot on the landscape, but by some miracle the path mostly avoids that part of the view. The problem of where to put graves has returned with a vengeance in the modern era. At least in the Kamakura period only nobles could have them; these days, a grave is a virtual obligation for every family.

Take the left fork ten minutes from the resthouse, following the signs for Kanazawa Nature Forest and Mount Enkai. You reach the entrance to the Yokohama Nature Sanctuary (Yokohama Shizen Kansatsu no Mori; ☎ 045-894-7474) in four more minutes.

Climbing the short flight of steps to the sanctuary, you come to two large maps. Notice the third small map inset in the top right corner of the first. Yokohama Nature Sanctuary is shown in blue. Paths connect this with a series of other parks. It is unlikely that you will want to visit all of these right now but there is plenty of walking to be done in this part of Yokohama.

The nature sanctuary is sponsored by the Environment Agency. It has a nature center and a number of short paths for viewing birds, insects (including fireflies), flowers, and trees. The bird checklist includes 123 species. There is a pond for waterbirds. You can also have a bath (mixed; rental swimwear, ¥500) or meal and even stay the night at the Kamigo Mori no Ie (Kamigo Forest House).

Leave by the same steps and descend to the road. The bus stop is a short way down on the right. Buses on this side of the road go to Kanazawa Hakkei; those on the far side to Ōfuna.

TRANSPORTATION
Outbound:
JR Yokosuka line to Kamakura from Tokyo (¥880) or Shinagawa (¥680).

From Shibuya: Tōkyū Tōyoko line to Yokohama (¥260), changing there to JR Yokosuka line to Kamakura (¥320).

Return:

From Kanazawa Hakkei: Keihin Kyūkō line to Shinagawa (¥530).

From Ōfuna: JR Tōkaidō or JR Yokosuka lines to Shinagawa (¥610) or Tokyo (¥760).

ACCOMMODATIONS

Akiyama Minshuku (☎ 0467-22-3499). Five minutes from Kamakura Station.

Kamigo Mori no Ie (Information: ☎ 045-895-2211; Reservations: ☎ 045-895-5151). Adults ¥3,000. Near Yokohama Nature Sanctuary.

Komachi-sō (☎ 0467-23-2151). Five minutes from Kamakura Station.

Ryokan Komatsu (☎ 0467-22-2902). Between Kamakura Station and the beach.

USEFUL KANJI

Egara Tenjin	荏柄天神
Kamakura	鎌倉
Kamakura Museum	鎌倉国宝館
Kamakura Shrine	鎌倉宮
Kanazawa Nature Forest	金沢自然の森
Mount Enkai	円海山
Sugimotodera	杉本寺
Ten'en Hiking Course	天園ハイキングコース
Tsurugaoka Hachiman Shrine	鶴岡八幡宮
Wakamiya	若宮
Yokohama Nature Sanctuary	横浜自然観察の森
Zuisenji	瑞泉寺

GANDENJI ⬤2
The Zushi Hills and Asahina Pass

Gandenji is a beautiful hillside temple; or rather, the hill itself is the temple, right up to the Kannon statue at the top. The extensive grounds are a short hike in themselves, with excellent views of Kamakura and Zushi Bay.

The temple was much beloved of both Yoritomo and Sanetomo. Although it lies only two kilometers from Sugimotodera, Gandenji is located in Zushi. The walk climbs to the hilly border between Zushi and Kamakura via Lake Hisaki, then takes a little-used trail along the edge of a former U.S. Army ammunition depot. You have the wooded ridge to yourself, with only a rusting fence to show that there used to be something unpleasant below the trees.

In truth, the unpleasantness is not over yet. A huge row has raged since 1984 about whether to develop this land for housing or conserve it as a nature reserve. Despite strong local resistance, the developers appear to have won. The compromise is that some of the housing to be built on the eastern side will be multistory, thereby minimizing the area of woodland destroyed.

The path comes out at an orchard of plum, cherry, chestnut, and other ornamental trees, and then descends to the entrance of the Asahina Pass, the most beautiful pass in Kamakura. Turning right, it follows the ravinelike cutting across the border into Yokohama.

THE TEMPLE

Leave Zushi station by the west (rear) exit and turn left down the road beside the tracks. You reach a right turn for Gandenji, by a

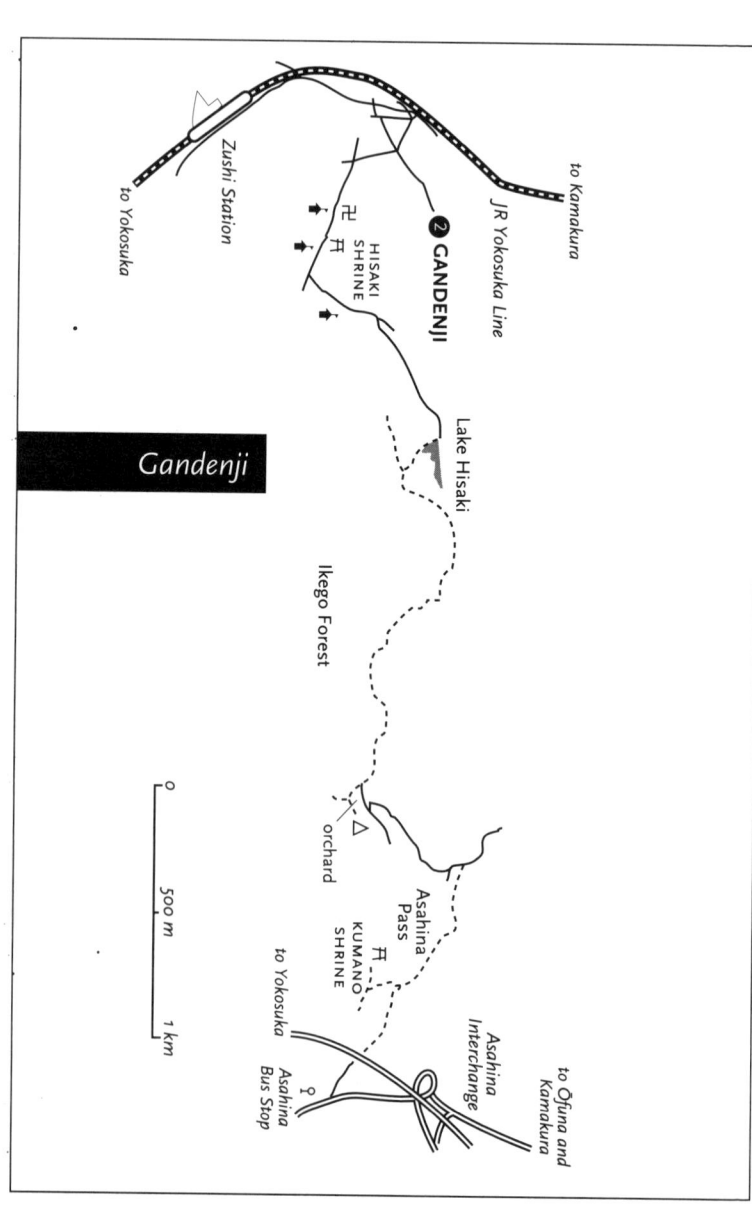

mailbox and a pedestrian crossing, in about eight minutes. There is a sign to the temple facing the other way. Turning here, follow a sign to the left a minute later (remember this junction for the walk), and you will reach the steps up to the temple in another two or three minutes. The gate is open from 8:00 AM to 5:00 PM.

The stones lining the final stretch of the path up to the steps are dedicated to the thirty-three Kannons of the Bandō pilgrimage. Ascending the steep steps towards the belfry, you pass a couple of Jizōs. Legend has it that Kūkai carved the roughly-hewn Tsumebori Jizō with his fingernails. The Edo-period Kannon hall stands at the top, beside a pond donated by a modern writer, Izumi Kyōka.

The main image is hidden, but don't miss the Kannon in the cave behind the hall, which tradition attributes to Gyōki. The stones around the courtyard are for the thirty-three Kannons of the Saigoku pilgrimage.

Gandenji traces its origins to a visit by Tokudō Shōnin, the priest of Hasedera in Yamato who received the seals for the Saigoku pilgrimage from Emma, the lord of the dead. When Tokudō came here, a strange light in the sky illuminated this spot and a venerable old man appeared beside the cliff. Tokudō recognized him as the deity Kumano Gongen, and told the villagers that in future this place would be a pure land of great compassion.

It was left to Gyōki to found the temple a few years later, after a similar set of experiences. He carved and dedicated the eleven-faced Kannon in 721. In the twelfth century, Minamoto Yoritomo made a habit of praying here every month. Sanetomo often came here, too. Yoritomo had special cause to be thankful to the Kannon of Gandenji, for the statue transformed itself into a sailor and assisted Yoritomo's flight to Chiba in 1180.

Take the path up from the left side of the Kannon Hall. The small cave shrines are dedicated to two Shinto gods, Inari and Sarutahiko. Turn left at the top to see a little statue of Shōtoku Taishi dedicated to world peace, or right to reach the Kannon statue at the peak. Shōtoku Taishi (574–622) was the imperial regent who did so much for the spread of Buddhism in ancient Japan. He also issued a famous Seventeen-Article Code of political ethics. His qualifications as a pacifist are somewhat questionable, however; while it is true that he entered into diplomatic relations with China, he did so only after his military expeditions of 595 and 602 to the Korean peninsula had failed.

The stones beside the Kannon are for the thirty-four Kannons of Chichibu. Continue around from the Kannon along the ridge to descend to the other side of the Kannon hall. Kumano Gongen is enshrined in the hall at the foot of the steps by the pond.

THE WALK ** *(2 hours)*

The first fifteen minutes of the walk will take you to Lake Hisaki. Returning to the temple gate, retrace your steps to the second sign for Gandenji noted above. Turn left here (the second left from the temple) and left again at the crossroads a couple of minutes later. This road takes you past a small temple, a shrine, and a school. Go left at the crossroads soon after the school. Continue past a second school and straight across another crossroads. Just a few meters beyond, there is a turning to the right signposted for Lake Hisaki Park. Turn right here and follow the road (which becomes an unpaved path) to the lakeside park at the end.

The lake is pretty, with carp, ducks, and trees all around. Take the promenade to the right. You might want to walk all the way around the lake, but you will have to return here afterwards because the path to the ridge ascends from the near right-hand corner of the lake (from behind the second bench). It is unmarked but easy. Take the gulley to the left. You reach the ridge in four or five minutes. Turn left at the fence. There is no sign, so don't expect to find this path if coming in the other direction.

The path on the ridge is broad and firm. The fence does spoil it a little but is often invisible in the trees. The route leads through pretty mixed woods far from the nearest roads. You would be hard-pressed to find a better nature trail in this part of Kanagawa, excluding the woods to the right, which are out-of-bounds.

It is a curious but understandable irony that weapons of destruction have here conserved the natural environment. While developers built large housing projects and cemeteries—all too visible on this walk—on neighboring hilltops, they were denied access to Ikego Forest, which surrounded the U.S. munitions dump. Because of the ammunition buried in tunnels underground, the forest on top was hardly disturbed.

Quite a few archeological discoveries have also been made on this site, including Jōmon-period items from five thousand years ago and wooden carvings from around the time of Christ, as well as giant white clam fossils some three million years old.

Today, it is not local Japanese but Americans who want to use this land for housing. The U.S. forces, backed by the Japanese central government, are building new accommodations for military personnel. They were opposed for twelve years by the city government and a powerful citizens' movement that wanted to turn the forest into a Life Science Park. It was an ugly dispute, for the Japanese proved keener to protect nature from American housing than they ever were to stop projects of their own. The fact is, however, that citizens had belatedly realized how little of the natural environment remained.

One qualification should be made to that statement about local residents. A protest in the 1960s against housing development on the hill behind Tsurugaoka Hachiman Shrine in Kamakura (see Chapter 1) led to the hill's designation as Japan's first National Trust property.

Construction of the first set of apartments at Ikego commenced in May 1993 over the strong opposition of the mayor and citizens of Zushi. A total of 854 housing units are scheduled for completion by the end of fiscal 1996.

It takes around twenty-five minutes to reach the orchard shown on the map, the Junisō Kajuen, which has zones for chestnuts,

GANDENJI

pines, cherries, plums, and citrons (yuzu). You quickly reach a sign at the top of a path up through the orchard. You should descend by this path but first follow the sign along the ridge to the peak, turning left at the next sign a couple of minutes beyond your present position. The benches and table in the clearing at the top are an ideal spot for a picnic.

You may wander around the orchard but be sure to stick to the paths. Then return to that first sign and descend to the gate (going left a minute below the ridge). The gate may be a problem: it is only open from July 1 to August 20 and from October 21 to May 10. If you have come out of season, the only way out is to climb over the top, which happily is not hard.

Descending the rough track, in five minutes you reach the highlight: a pass that is also a designated National Treasure. You cannot miss it in its setting beside a small waterfall. The mansion of Taira Hirotsune, medieval overlord of Kazusa in what is now Chiba Prefecture, once stood here, for this was the pass leading toward his domains. Despite being a Taira, Hirotsune sided with Yoritomo in the war of 1180. His great military strength was a key factor in Yoritomo's success. That, of course, also made Hirotsune a danger to the government, and with the complicity of Yoritomo, he was murdered close to this spot in 1183. His domain was divided between Chiba Tsunetane of Inohana Castle (see Chapter 29) and the Wada clan.

The waterfall, and the pass itself, are named for the legendary figure who supposedly cut the pass in a single night: Asahina Saburō. The history books tell us that the cutting was actually undertaken by the regent Hōjō Yasutoki some sixty years after Hirotsune's death. It is deep and narrow to facilitate the slaughter of unwanted visitors.

The walk up through the cutting is wet underfoot, but utterly unique. The path is like an old railway cutting with clifflike walls and deep shade. It takes about ten minutes to the top. Two great caves have been hewn into the cliff. The little piles of stones inside are a form of prayer found throughout the Buddhist world. A Buddhist image is carved into the rock face. Also notice the little modern marker stone; you are now entering Yokohama. You would hardly believe it in this verdant, historic location, but the hum of vehicles from nearby Route 16 helps keep your mind on present reality.

The path down to Yokohama is firmer and drier. First, however, turn right up to the Kumano Shrine from the gate a minute below the pass. Tradition tells that the shrine was founded by Yoritomo to protect the entrance to the city. Keeping straight at a four-way junction, you reach the shrine in five minutes. Then return to the main path down into Yokohama.

The old road passes under Route 16 and comes out on a vehicular road just the other side. The wayside stones at the entrance include a *dōsojin*, some Jizōs, and Kōshin stones with their images of monkeys and the six-handed god Shōmen Kongō. Also notice the grand old *kaya* tree (*Torreya nucifera*) fifty meters further on the left. It is a designated Natural Treasure of Yokohama City.

Turning right at the T-junction just beyond, you come out at a bus stop. Buses on the right go to Ōfuna or Kamakura stations; those on the left to Kanazawa Hakkei station.

If taking the bus in the direction of Ōfuna and Kamakura you might like to get off a few minutes later at the Yokohama Reien Mae stop (just after the tunnel) for the Yokohama Nature Sanctuary (Yokohama Shizen Kansatsu no Mori). The Nagakura stop just after is beside the heated Sakae swimming pool.

TRANSPORTATION

Outbound:
JR Yokosuka line to Zushi from Tokyo (¥880) or Shinagawa (¥680). The trip takes a little over an hour.

Return:
Buses run from Asahina to Kamakura and Ōfuna stations on the JR Yokosuka line and Kanazawa Hakkei on the Keihin Kyūkō line

(for Shinagawa). The bus to Kamakura also stops outside Sugimotodera (see Chapter 1) on the way.

ACCOMMODATIONS

Shindōtei Ryokan (☎ 0468-71-2012). Three minutes from Zushi Station.

USEFUL KANJI

Asahina Pass	朝比奈切通し
Gandenji	岩殿寺
Lake Hisaki Park	久木大池公園
Kamakura	鎌倉
Kanazawa Hakkei	金沢八景
Ōfuna	大船
Tsumebori Jizō	爪堀地蔵
Yokohama Nature Sanctuary	横浜自然観察の森
Zushi	逗子

AN'YŌIN — 3
Kamakura from South to North

With An'yōin, you return to Kamakura. An'yōin is called after the posthumous name of its founder, Hōjō Masako, wife of Minamoto Yoritomo, who did so much to establish the line of Hōjō regents. Her grave is at the rear of the temple. An'yōin is small, and seldom visited except by Bandō pilgrims, as befits a woman, for female status was generally low in traditional Japan. But Masako was no ordinary woman, and this temple with its beautiful azaleas also has a prime location in southern Kamakura.

The walk visits nearby temples and a shrine in the south, then heads north across the wooded hills of Gion to Hōkaiji, Kamakura Shrine, and Kakuonji. It climbs to the latter part of the Ten'en Hiking Course (the first half was described in chapter 1), reaching a lookout point with a panoramic view of Kamakura to the sea, then finally descends to the Zen temples of Kenchōji and Engakuji near Kita Kamakura station.

Switching between quiet wooded paths, residential streets, and famous temples—from squirrels in the trees at one moment to statues or gardens at the next—this course offers a well-rounded view of Kamakura. It also takes you to the sites of some of the bloodiest incidents in Kamakura's turbulent history.

THE TEMPLE

Masako, Yoritomo's widow, founded An'yōin in March 1225 to commemorate her husband. However, she died herself just four months later, on July 11, at the age of sixty-eight. Records indicate that she was buried at An'yōin the following day. This temple, as

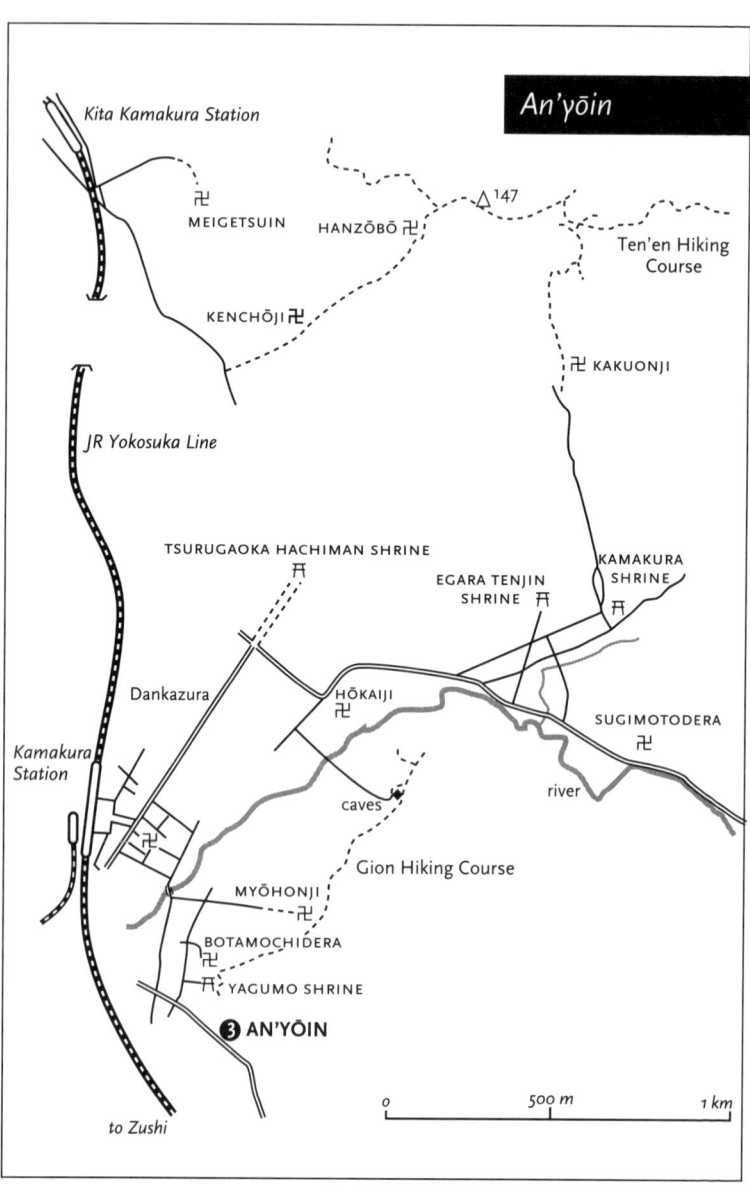

noted, is small. The gate is so modest that most motorists on the busy modern road surely don't see it at all. Even the walker is uncertain until just a few yards from the entrance. This does not look like a popular pilgrims' temple. Admission is ¥100.

Passing through the gate, a Jizō image and an old *maki* (a Chinese black pine) stand on the left. The tree is said to have been planted by the priest Ryōben Songan, the son of Hōjō Tomotoki. Also notice the giant footprints of the Buddha, a legacy of the earliest days of Buddhist iconography, when complete physical representations of the Buddha were avoided. An Amida, a thousand-armed Kannon, and other Kannon statues stand inside the main hall. The temple also has a small image of Masako herself, her head shaven as a nun.

Various stones are ranged behind the temple, including a row of Jizōs, Kōshin stones, and two old graves. The one on the right is the grave of Songan, erected in 1308. The smaller one on the left is said to be the grave of Masako. It should be noted that another Kamakura temple, Jufukuji, also claims to have Masako's grave. The most unusual stone is the Migawari Jizō (Surrogate Jizō) on the other side of the path. It looks exactly as if it is sleeping in a futon. This is no doubt intended, for a *migawari* is a substitute who endures sorrows on another's behalf. The most typical prayer is for relief from sickness. An'yōin, by the way, has a little shrine for curing syphilis.

THE WALK ** *(1 hour 30 minutes)*

Leave Kamakura station by the exit for Tsurugaoka Hachiman Shrine and cross the square to the main road. Crossing the road, turn right towards the gate of Daikōji, a Nichiren temple founded by Nitchō in 1274.

Nichiren (1222–82), the founder of the Nichiren sect, preached for many years in this part of Kamakura. He was a religious and political radical who taught that recitation of the title of the *Lotus Sutra* was the only true path to salvation in a degenerate age. Much

AN'YŌIN

of Nichiren's career was spent in exile, first in Izu and then on Sado, but he left a deep imprint on Kamakura. Several temples on the left side of this road still belong to his sect.

Daikōji has little for the casual visitor, but the next temple, Honkakuji, is rather special. Turn left immediately after the post office. The side entrance to Honkakuji is a hundred meters up the lane. This austere temple has a large main hall, a Nichiren hall, and several small ginkgos and pines within the broad precincts. The green-tiled Ebisu hall by the main gate is an eye-catching example of twentieth-century innovation in Buddhist architecture.

Leaving Honkakuji by the main gate, cross the bridge and turn left towards the gate of Myōhonji, Kamakura's biggest Nichiren temple. Myōhonji is a pretty temple with a striking steep roof. It was founded in the mid-thirteenth century by the only surviving son of Hiki Yoshikazu. The graves of the Hiki, whose mansion once occupied this site, stand in a row to the right of the main hall.

These graves bear witness to the ghastly incident that secured power for the Hōjō after Yoritomo's death. Hiki Yoshikazu was a nephew and adopted son of Yoritomo's nurse. His daughter, Wakasa no Tsubone, was the mother of Ichiman, shogun Yoriie's son. Connections of that sort were dangerous in the murderous world of the Minamoto. For a time, favored by Yoriie, the Hiki were in the ascendant. But when Yoriie fell suddenly ill in 1203, the Hōjō moved swiftly to undermine the three-year-old boy's claim to the shogunate.

The boy's maternal grandfather, Hōjō Tokimasa, proposed that since Ichiman was so young, the shogunal powers should should be shared with Yoriie's younger brother, Sanetomo. Yoshikazu was furious and refused, but Tokimasa was the swifter to act. First, he informed the emperor that Sanetomo would be heir. Then he had Yoshikazu assassinated and ordered the massacre of the Hiki family near this spot. Tokimasa made himself regent and banished Yoriie to Izu. When Yoriie was murdered the following year, apparently at the order of his mother, Hōjō Masako, Sanetomo was installed in his stead.

CHAPTER 3

Yoshikazu's son, Yoshimoto, who survived to found Myōhonji, was a two-year-old boy in Kyoto at the time of the massacre. He was able to return to Kamakura after Ichiman's sister, Yoshiko, was married to the fourth shogun, Yoritsune. Yoshiko died in childbirth. Climb up the steps to the left of the main hall. Yoshiko's simple grave may be found at the end of the graveyard.

Returning from all that distant bloodshed to the gate, turn left along the lane at the foot of the hills. You pass the colorful little Botamochidera in a couple of minutes, then Yagumo Shrine a minute after that. *Botamochi* is the name of little cakes traditionally made from pounded rice (*mochi*) and sweet bean jam at the time of the spring and autumn equinoxes. Here, however, the annual Botamochi Festival is held on September 12. It commemorates Nichiren, who was executed on that day. This is where he was given the *botamochi* that he ate as his last meal.

Yagumo Shrine is the start of the Gion Hiking Course. You will come back here after An'yōin, so save the sightseeing for a moment. Continue another fifty meters to the T-junction and turn left. An'yōin is a short way down this bigger road on the left. Then return to Yagumo Shrine, a quiet enclave at the foot of Mount Gion noted for exorcism. See the foxes on the left, messengers of the harvest god Inari. Through the windows of the treasure house, you can glimpse old *mikoshi* (portable festival shrines), equestrian equipment, various utensils, and old tiles. There are burial caves behind the shrine.

The Gion Hiking Course starts from the steps on the right. Take the left fork half way up. You reach the top in five minutes, with some lovely views of the bay on the way. The Gion course is short, but sufficient to leave the city behind for the pleasures of a quiet woodland path. The footing is a little rough in places, but the walk is basically easy. It is also less crowded than the better-known Ten'en course.

Turn left at the top and follow the ridge north for fifteen minutes, ignoring various paths off to either side. Two paths to the left are signposted for Myōhonji. Finally, the main path veers sharply

AN'YŌIN

down to the left. A Japanese sign for the Gion Hiking Course points back the way you came. Descend here and immediately turn left to reach a cave with a wooden shrine gate.

Having witnessed the cruel birth of the Hōjō regency, now we reach the spot where it died. In 1333, as the forces of Emperor Godaigo under Nitta Yoshisada pressed in on Hōjō Takatoki, the last Hōjō regent, Takatoki and 837 followers committed *harakiri* on this spot. Takatoki himself is said to have died in the second large cave a minute further down the path. That terrible day marked the end of the Kamakura period in history.

Continue down the path across the stream to the T-junction at the end. Turning right, you reach the entrance to Hōkaiji at the corner of the next main junction. Godaigo, too, was shocked by the bloody end of Takatoki and his followers. The emperor ordered the founding of this temple that same year, 1333, for the repose of the Hōjō souls. It stands on the site where nine generations of the Hōjō had their Komachi residence. The main image is a Jizō carved in 1365. Admission is ¥100. The grounds of Hōkaiji are beautifully maintained. The benches in the courtyard are a good place for a short rest. Come in early September when the white bush clover is in bloom. The flowers are said to represent the souls of the Hōjō. The temple also has camellias, plums, and cherries.

Restarting in the same direction, the now broad road bends around to the right. Turn left onto a road that veers off diagonally about five minutes from Hōkaiji. Look for a Cosmo petrol station on the other side of the road and a small bakery on the corner. This road leads directly to the *torii* of the Kamakura Shrine. The many restaurants along the way make it the ideal place to stop for lunch.

After viewing the shrine, follow the English sign left (when facing the shrine) to Kakuonji (700 meters). Once again, you leave the crowds as the narrow lane climbs gently past the houses. A post on the right at the 250-meter sign marks the entrance to the Ten'en Hiking Course, reading 2.2 kilometers to Ten'en. Return here after seeing the temple.

Kakuonji only lets tourists enter five times daily at 10:00 AM, 11:00 AM, 1:00 PM, 2:00 PM and 3:00 PM. It is closed in bad weather, in August, and from December 20 to January 7. You are shown around and have to stay with the group. Admission is ¥300. Kakuonji has no gate. The first building you come to is the main hall. You will not be allowed inside. The highlight of the tour is the thatched Yakushi hall, said to have been rebuilt by Ashikaga Takauji in 1354. Yakushi, the Healing Buddha, is flanked by Nikkō and Gakkō (deities of the sun and the moon), the Junishinshō (Yakushi's twelve warrior attendants), an Amida image, and other figures. The temple itself was founded in 1218 after the second regent, Hōjō Yoshitoki, had a bad dream.

Now return to the entrance to the Ten'en Hiking Course. Once again, you climb swiftly away from the houses onto gentle woodland paths. It takes about ten minutes to reach the ridge. There are more burial caves with stone buddhas about fifty meters from the pass. Turn left at the pass, and left again two minutes later, following the English sign directing you to Hanzōbō Temple and Meigetsu Valley. You pass more caves in a rugged outcrop, then reach a magnificent lookout point with a view of all Kamakura. Mount Gion, the station, the sea, and Wakamiya Ōji, the broad road leading from the beach to Tsurugaoka Hachiman Shrine, are all clearly visible. This view that explains why Yoritomo chose Kamakura as his capital. The square plain is embraced on three sides by hills and on the fourth by the sea. Kamakura offers the perfect natural fortification.

The junction above Kenchōji is reached in five more minutes. A large English map of the temple is posted beside the path. Turn left to reach the Hanzōbō hall a couple of minutes away. Kenchōji is a huge temple complex, extending from the head to the foot of the valley. It is a practicing Zen temple, and most of the halls are closed to the general public. However, a walk through the grounds is still impressive because of all the lovely maples, ginkgos, and flowers.

Hanzōbō, the hall at the top, is notable for the long-nosed and beaked *tengu* statues that surround it. Their faces, wonderfully expressive, perfectly catch the proud, impish, schoolboy nature of these mythical mountain goblins. You will want to photograph every single one. As is often the case with *tengu* temples and shrines, Hanzōbō is a place to pray for protection against fire and other disasters. Fishermen also used to pray here for good catches and safety at sea. It is a five-minute walk from Hanzōbō to Kenchōji's main buildings. The cherry blossoms are wonderful in early April, the maples in early December. Take your shoes off and walk around the outside of the first big hall, the Ryūōden, to see the garden at the back.

Kenchōji was built in 1253 by the fifth regent, Hōjō Tokiyori. It was Kamakura's first big Zen temple, founded here in part as a counterweight to the older sects of Kyoto. The first abbot was a Chinese priest, Dao Long. At its height, the temple had forty-nine halls. All, however, were lost in fires.The present buildings date from the Edo period or later. The huge Sanmon gate, built in the mid-eighteenth century, is one of the grandest buildings in Kamakura, yet still blends perfectly with the modest thatched belfry at its side. The bell was forged in 1255. Pay the ¥300 admission charge at the bottom on your way out.

You are now just a short walk from Kita Kamakura station and face a dilemma. Most visitors will feel that they have seen enough temples for one day. But for those made of hardier stuff, two of the great foundations of Kamakura still stand between Kenchōji and the station. In the normal way, they have to be seen. Whatever you decide, turn right out of the gate of Kenchōji and right again at the railway line. Don't cross the railway; follow the road along the tracks.

First, on the right, you reach Meigetsuin, which was founded in 1160 by Yamanouchi Tsunetoshi for the repose of his father, who died in the Heiji Disturbance. Meigetsuin, too, is huge with glorious verdure. It is most famous for the hydrangeas of mid-June and the grave of Hōjō Tokiyori. The thatched Kaizandō and burial caves also make a lasting impression.

Then, just a few steps before the platforms of Kita Kamakura station, there is the entrance to the other great Zen temple, Engakuji.

CHAPTER 3

Like Kenchōji, this is a fully functioning temple which takes many trainees. It was founded in 1282 by the eighth regent, Hōjō Tokimune. The Shariden, the hall at the top of the compound, was erected by Sadatoki, the ninth regent, in 1285, with various renovations since. It is only open to the public January 1–3. Most of the other buildings are new and closed off. The garden at the top is pretty but, in terms of attractions for the tired visitor, Meigetsuin is the better place to visit at the end of a long day.

TRANSPORTATION

Outbound:
From Tokyo: Same as in Chapter 1.
Return:
From Kita Kamakura: JR Yokosuka line to Shinagawa (¥680) or Tokyo (¥760).

USEFUL KANJI

An'yōin	安養院
Botamochidera	ボタモチ寺
Daikōji	大巧寺
Engakuji	円覚寺
Gion Hiking Course	祇園山ハイキングコース
Hōkaiji	宝戒寺
Honkakuji	本覚寺
Kakuonji	覚園寺
Kamakura	鎌倉
Kamakura Shrine	鎌倉宮
Kita Kamakura station	北鎌倉駅
Kenchōji	建長寺
Myōhonji	妙本寺
Ten'en Hiking Course	天園ハイキングコース
Yagumo Shrine	八雲神社

HASEDERA — 4
The Great Buddha and Zeni-arai Benten

Hasedera is one of the liveliest pilgrims temples on the Bandō route. It could hardly provide a more striking contrast to the quiet of An'yōin. This is a place to observe popular faith at its most colorful and attractive.

As befits this tourist temple, the Kannon of Hasedera is huge. At nine meters and eighteen centimeters, it is the largest wooden image in Japan. The view of the bay from the main courtyard is also one of the best in Kamakura.

The walk starts on the grand scale with Hasedera, then grows grander still with Kamakura's famous 120-ton copper Great Buddha, erected in the thirteenth century. From there, it crosses the hills to Zeni-arai Benten, the "money-washing" temple where worshipers pray to double their money, and the beautiful Zen temple of Jōchiji.

You finally emerge at Tōkeiji, the former nunnery to which wives once fled from unbearable husbands. The extensive grounds of Tōkeiji, with mossy graves and magnificent, towering trees, are a tranquil spot to wind up a day of famous sights.

THE TEMPLE

Hasedera's pretty hillside location recalls Gandenji. Admission is ¥200. The temple claims to have been established by Tokudō Shōnin, the priest to whom legend also attributes the founding of the Saigoku pilgrimage. The story of the temple's founding tells how two statues were made from the same great tree. One was consecrated at Hasedera in Yamato and the other cast into the waves.

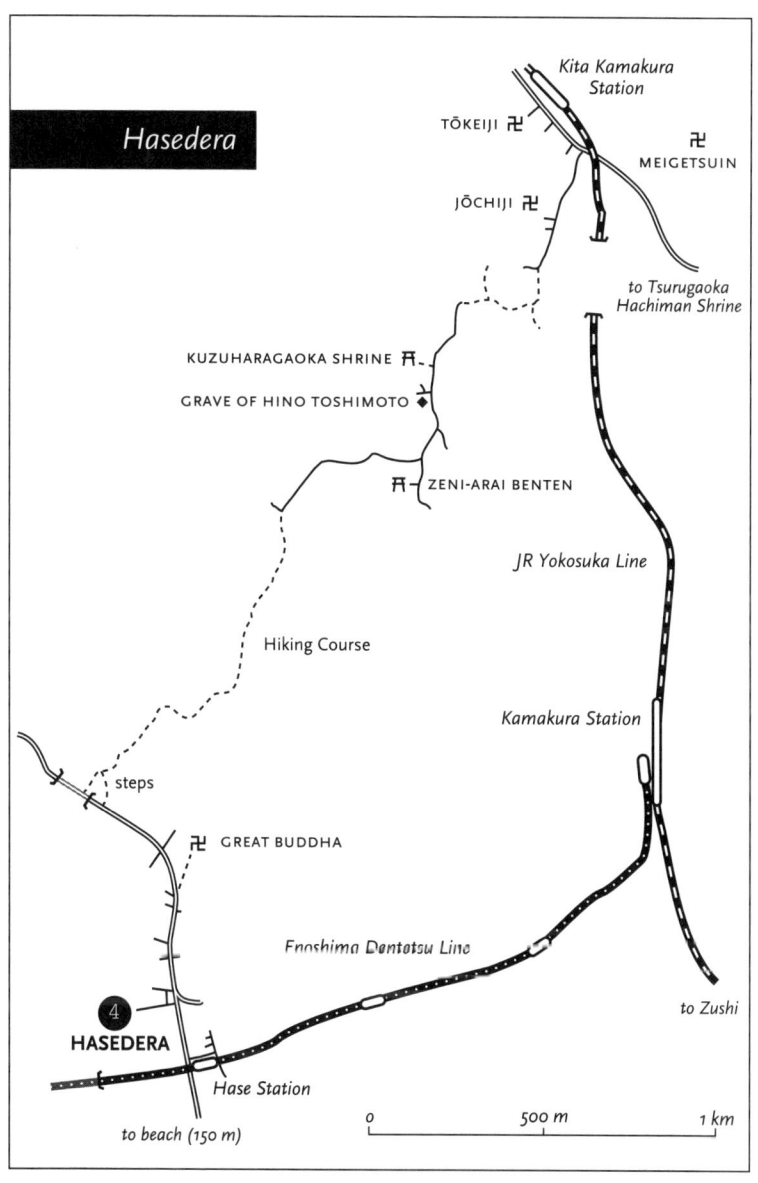

That was in 721. It washed up at Nagai on the Miura Peninsula in 736 and Tokudō Shōnin built this temple in the same year.

The first sight is a pretty garden on the right as you enter the gate, with carp and a small waterfall. You will notice racks of the votive offerings called *ema* and two statues of Fudō Myōō just beyond. Enter the small group of connected caves behind the statues.

The first cave has carvings of Benten and sixteen child-attendants, called Benten Dōji, sunk into the wall in a style reminiscent of an old Christian crypt. Worshipers light candles in front of each. Benten, the largest carving at the rear, known in Sanskrit as Sarasvati, is goddess of music, eloquence, wealth, and wisdom. Originally a river-goddess, she remains closely associated with water.

The second cave has another Benten, an Amida, and a Mizuko Jizō, to whom mothers pray for the repose of stillborn and aborted children, an important task in a country in which the dead are normally prayed for by their descendants. The third cave is filled with tiny Kannon statues. You may dedicate one yourself for ¥300.

Returning to the garden, the hall on the left of the gate is for Daikokuten, a god mainly associated with the harvest and prosperity. Daikokuten and Benten are both members of Japan's Shichi-fukujin, the Seven Gods of Good Fortune, and hence extremely popular. They have come to represent Japanese religion at its most material.

Climbing the steps, you reach a Jizō hall surrounded by hundreds of little Jizō statues. These are the physical representation of people's prayers for lost children. In the popular mind, they serve as both models of the god and effigies of the children. More than fifty thousand Jizōs have been placed here since World War II. You get some idea of the frightful turnover from the fact that most are kept here for only one year.

The final flight of steps brings you to the main courtyard and a magnificent view of the bay. You see the belfry; a large Amida statue in the hall on the right, commissioned by Yoritomo in 1194; and the huge Hase Kannon itself in the modern main hall. Happily, for a change, the main image is well-lit and on full view. Try imagining the size of the tree it came from.

To the right of the Kannon, there is a very lifelike and venerable statue of Tokudō Shōnin beside a seated Jizō. On the left, you see Binzuru (in Sanskrit, Pindola), one of the Buddha's disciples. The Japanese believe that touching Binzuru cures disease. He is a common fixture in the main halls of temples.

A treasure hall with old bells, gongs, stones, ema, coins, statues, and scrolls is attached to the hall. Especially interesting for the Bandō pilgrim are the fourteenth-century statues of four of Kannon's thirty-three incarnations, showing fierce, wise, and merciful aspects of the deity. There are plenty of English labels. Admission is ¥100.

Continuing past the treasure house, you reach the Mawaridō, a rotating repository of Buddhist sutras, and then another multitude of Jizōs. A rest house with refreshments is located inside the precincts.

THE WALK * *(1 hour)*

Take the road to the right from Hase station. You reach a left turn for Hasedera (the Hase Kannon Mae junction) in a couple of minutes. There is an English sign on the corner.

After viewing the temple, return to this junction and continue along the same road following signs to the Daibutsu (Great Buddha). The entrance is five minutes up the road on the right. Admission is ¥150.

Few visitors to Japan can fail to have heard about and seen photos of the Daibutsu. The greening copper Buddha is so serene, and blends so harmoniously with the courtyard and hills, that you almost neglect to realize its gigantic size. It belongs to a dimension where a colossus is at home.

The statue represents Amida, the royal prince of India who became a Buddha and established a paradise for the dead in the

West. He vowed that all who called his name could join him, thus becoming the one to rescue those without the strength to save themselves. The Kamakura Daibutsu personifies this spirit of mercy on a scale that impresses believer and non-believer alike.

It seems strange, given that the Daibutsu looks so appropriate in the open, to learn that it once had a roof over its head. The hall was destroyed by a tsunami in 1495. Besides the elements, the statue is also exposed to tourists clambering around inside. You may, too, for a small fee. The Kamakura Daibutsu inevitably draws comparisons with the Daibutsu that Gyōki built at Tōdaiji in Nara. Gyōki's statue is still housed under a roof, which possibly detracts from its power to impress, but few would dispute that the Kamakura statue is the finer work.

The name of Minamoto Yoritomo also figures significantly in the story of the Daibutsu. Yoritomo and other Bandō *musha* were heavily involved in the reconstruction of Tōdaiji, which was burned by Taira Shigehira. Utsunomiya Tomotsuna, for example, funded the Kannon image beside the Nara Daibutsu. We know that Yoritomo visited Tōdaiji in 1195, just four years before his death, and it has been suggested that the sight inspired him to build a Daibutsu in Kamakura, too. He wanted his capital to be as grand as the cities of western Japan.

Yoritomo died before work could begin but Masako and others continued to promote the project. Construction of a wooden Daibutsu commenced in 1238 only to see everything lost in a storm. The present bronze Buddha was completed in 1252. Behind the Daibutsu, you will also discover a hall with a Kannon image. This is number twenty-three of the thirty-three Kannons of Kamakura.

Returning to the gate, turn right and continue a few minutes up the same road to the mouth of a tunnel. The hiking course starts up the steps to the right. Take the steps on the left side of a private house (but not the path over the top of the tunnel). The route is clearly signposted from the top.

CHAPTER 4

You reach the ridge in less than five minutes. Turning right at the top and right again at a junction soon after, you find yourself on a quiet wooded path. Look for occasional views of Mount Fuji on the left. If you are sharp, you might catch a glimpse of the Daibutsu, too.

As the path eventually turns into a lane, the whole bay appears on the right. Keeping straight for five minutes more, ignoring occasional paths down, you reach the steps down to Zeni-arai Benten at an English sign. The entrance to the shrine, a tunnel dug in 1958, lies two minutes down from the ridge.

Zeni-arai Benten is literally the "Money-Washing Benten." This watery hollow in the hills is filled with tiny cave shrines to water gods and the Seven Gods of Good Fortune. The main cave has a spring where worshipers wash their money (paper money as well as coins), for all cash washed here is supposed to double in value. There is some debate about the odds; optimists expect it to increase ten- or a hundred-fold. Votive miniature shrine gates are hung inside the cave. You will be lucky to see the Benten statue at the rear because the view is usually obstructed by the gates. This Benten has the body of a snake, Benten's usual intermediary.

Not surprisingly, this curious, fabulous shrine owes its origin to a dream. In 1185, when the Japanese state was still chaotic, the harvest god Ugajin appeared to Yoritomo while he slept and told him of a spring in the western hills with waters pure enough to appease the gods. Yoritomo was told that this spring would make the people religious and bring peace and prosperity to the nation. Yoritomo ordered a search and built the shrine here upon its discovery.

The money-washing tradition is attributed to Hōjō Tokiyori, who was regent from 1227 to 1263. The many large shrine gates in the compound are donated by worshipers who have struck it rich thanks to the efficacy of their prayers.

Now return to the ridge, and continue straight across the path you came along from the Daibutsu. The broad unsurfaced lane leads through parkland. You soon reach the grave of Hino

Toshimoto on the left, just before the gate of Kuzuharagaoka Shrine. Toshimoto, a court official loyal to Emperor Godaigo, was executed in 1332, just before Nitta Yoshisada defeated the Hōjō and won Kamakura for the imperial cause.

Kuzuharagaoka Shrine has only a simple building, but the benches might be a good place for a rest. The path to Jōchiji continues straight from the shrine gate. You now re-enter the woods. Look for the roof of Kaizōji below on the right. Soon after, you reach the stone pagoda at the top of Tenja Pass and start the descent to Jōchiji. Jōchiji was founded in 1281 by Hōjō Murotoki. It is a pretty hillside temple with cedars, cherries, many old graves against the cliffs, and also a formal garden. The thatched roofs add to the general serenity. Don't miss the fine statue of Hotei, another of the Seven Gods of Good Fortune. Jōchiji is a stop on the Kamakura Shichifukujin course. The main hall houses images of Amida, Sakyamuni, and Miroku, representing the past, present, and future.

Continue downhill from Jōchiji and turn left at the bottom. You reach the entrance to Tōkeiji in another couple of minutes. Tōkeiji was founded as a nunnery in 1285 by the widow of Hōjō Tokimune. Men were banned. Accordingly, in a society where women had little other recourse, it became a sanctuary for abused wives. The nunnery functioned until 1902. Today, strangely, Tōkeiji is a Zen temple for men. Admission is ¥50.

The buildings of Tōkeiji are not so interesting, but the grounds are beautiful. One could hardly imagine a more splendid place for a grave than beneath the giant trees in the valley at the rear of the compound. Many famous people are buried here, including Suzuki Daisetsu (better known as D.T. Suzuki), who did so much to popularize Zen in the West. Two statues of Kannon are designated National Treasures. You should also visit the treasure house with its diverse statues and scrolls (admission ¥300).

Turning left out of Tōkeiji, you reach Kita Kamakura station in two minutes.

Chapter 1. *The ancient steps leading to the main hall of Sugimotodera, adorned with banners proclaiming the eleven-headed Kannon enshrined within.*

Chapter 2. Pilgrims descending the steps beside the belfry at Gandenji.

Chapter 3. The graves of the Hiki at Myōhonji.

Chapter 4. The Great Buddha of Kamakura, made from 120 tons of copper.

Chapter 5. Bathers at Yūhi Falls.

Chapter 6. *The precincts of Hinata Yakushi, dedicated to the Buddha of Healing.*

Chapter 7. *Seen from Mount Kōbō, Mount Fuji rises over the city of Hadano.*

Chapter 8. *Preparing a giant kite for flight at the Zama Kite Festival.*

Chapter 9. *Tea fields at Nanae.*

Chapter 10. *Stone images of Kannon nestle in the cliff face at Shōbōji.*

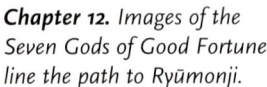

Chapter 11. *An artist sketches the pagoda of Anrakuji.*

Chapter 12. *Images of the Seven Gods of Good Fortune line the path to Ryūmonji.*

Chapter 13. Kaminarimon, the outer gate of Sensōji, and the shopping street known as the Nakamise.

Chapter 14. View of Yokohama harbor from the top of Landmark Tower, the tallest building in Japan.

Chapter 15. *Outdoor bathing at Ikaho Hot Spring.*

Chapter 16. *Seventy-two-meter Funao Falls.*

Chapter 17. *Guardian king in the niōmon at Manganji.*

Chapter 18. *Lake Chūzenji and Mount Nantai.*

Chapter 19. *The main hall of Ōyaji, beneath a massive stone outcropping.*

Chapter 20. *A Mashiko potter working at her wheel.*

Chapter 21. *Gate at Yamizomine Shrine.*

Chapter 22. *The thatched main hall of Satakedera.*

Chapter 23. *Sculpture garden at Nichidō Museum of Art.*

Chapter 24. *Procession of Buddhist clergy at Rakuhōji.*

Chapter 25. *Nantai Shrine, atop one of the twin peaks of Mount Tsukuba.*

Chapter 26. *Rice growing in the vicinity of Kiyotakiji.*

Chapter 27. The fishing port of Tokawa.

Chapter 28. Guardian figures at Ryūshōin perch above a plaque inscribed with the temple's name.

Chapter 29. *Sunset at Chiba Sculpture Garden.*

Chapter 30. *Interior of one of the halls at Kōzōji, plastered with stickers left by pilgrims.*

Chapter 31. *The veranda at Kasamoriji, overlooking lush forest land.*

Chapter 32. *The belfry at Kiyomizudera, seen from the main hall.*

Chapter 33. Main hall of Gake Kannon, set into a cliff high above Tateyama Bay.

CHAPTER 4

TRANSPORTATION
Outbound:
Tokyo to Kamakura: same as in Chapter 1.
Kamakura to Hase: Enoshima Dentetsu (Enoden) line (5 minutes, ¥190).
Return:
Kita Kamakura to Tokyo: JR Yokosuka line.

ACCOMMODATIONS
Kamakura Kagetsuen. Youth Hostel. Seven minutes from Hase Station.
Taisenkaku. Traditional inn by entrance to Hasedera.
Hase Ryokan. By Hase Station.
BB House Inn (women only). Two minutes from Hase Station.
Minshuku Ai (women only). Three minutes from Hase Station.

USEFUL KANJI
Daibutsu (Great Buddha)	大仏
Hase	長谷
Hasedera	長谷寺
Jōchiji	浄智寺
Kamakura	鎌倉
Kita Kamakura	北鎌倉
Tōkeiji	東慶寺
Zeni-arai Benten	銭洗弁天

SHŌFUKUJI — 5
Ashigara Pass and Hakone

With Shōfukuji, the pilgrimage moves to the western edge of Bandō, the land to the east of Ashigara Pass. Shōfukuji stands near the foot of the pass in Odawara. The walk leads to the top for a glorious view of Mount Fuji, then continues along the ridge to Mount Kintoki and the beautiful caldera of Hakone. This is the back door to Hakone, which avoids all the crowds.

When the Ashikaga shoguns established their capital in Kyoto, Kamakura became a backwater. Many blacksmiths and other military suppliers relocated to Odawara, the gateway to the Kantō Plain. Odawara flourished as a castle town, especially for the century from the entry of Hōjō Soun in 1495 till the city fell to Toyotomi Hideyoshi in 1590. The castle was badly damaged by the earthquakes of 1703 and 1782 but survived, with successive restorations, through the Edo period. It was only demolished in 1870, in the course of the early Meiji-era reforms. The present reconstruction was built in 1953.

A very early start is required to combine the temple and walk in a single day. If possible, save the hike for the next day and combine visits to the castle, museum, and park, all a five-minute walk from Odawara station. The park is at its best around the last week of March and first week of April, when the cherries are in bloom. The new Odawara Castle, like the view of Mount Fuji from Ashigara Pass, is pure picture-book Japan.

THE TEMPLE

The bus from Odawara station stops right outside Shōfukuji's early-eighteenth-century *niōmon*. On the left, as you enter the gate,

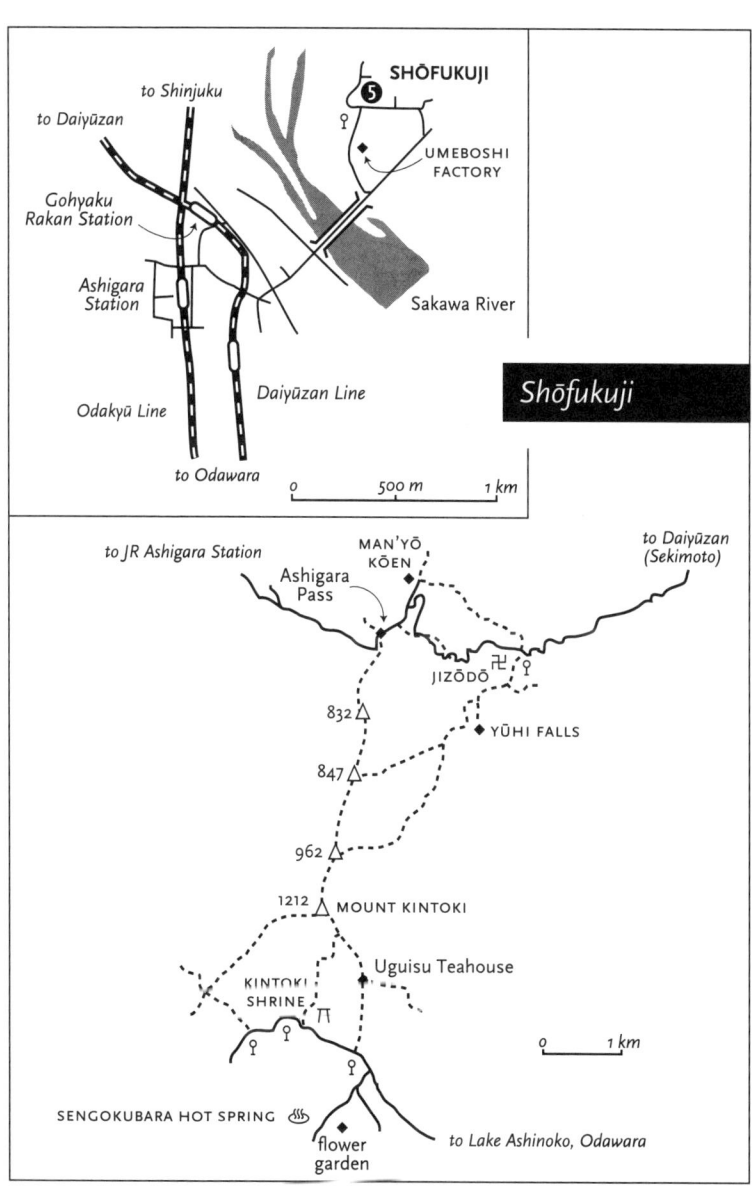

you see a statue of Kūkai in pilgrim's garb; a large ginkgo tree, thirty meters high and seven hundred years old; and a hall dedicated to Dainichi. The lone Kannon beyond is a Migawari Kannon. Like the Migawari Jizō at Anyoin, this is a substitute or scapegoat Kannon that suffers sorrows, especially disease, on behalf of those who pray to it.

The earthen platform on the left of the main hall is for *sumo* wrestling, for Shōfukuji is also an old *sumo* temple. Notice the handprint of the great champion, Raiden, perhaps the most renowned wrestler in *sumo* history. The twenty-two-year-old Raiden, who won the title of *ozeki* in 1796, fought a great bout at this temple in 1789, five years after entering his stable in Edo. Raiden had a career record of 254 wins against only ten losses, the highest-ever percentage of wins. One story of his extraordinary strength tells how he lifted his horse to clear the road for the procession of the lord of Kaga.

Moving back to the center of the courtyard, notice the boat-shaped bronze hand-washing trough. It has a dragon figurehead and an eleven-headed Kannon in the stern. The trough was made in the Kanda district of Edo, now Tokyo, in 1704. The bronze bell was cast locally in 1629. As noted above, many blacksmiths moved to Odawara after the fall of Kamakura. The city long maintained some of the finest forges in the Kantō area.

Statues for the eighty-eight temples of the Shikoku pilgrimage stand around the rim of the courtyard on the right. Perhaps the most distinctive statue, however, is that of Ninomiya Kinjirō kneeling in abject piety in front of the main hall. The statue recalls a story in which young Kinjirō was deeply moved by a recital of the *Kannon Sutra* by the priest of Shōfukuji.

Ninomiya Kinjirō (1787–1855), known in his adult years as Ninomiya Sontoku, was a local boy who lost his parents while young, but through diligence and study got on in the world as a highly efficient estate manager for the lord of Odawara. He is still regarded as a paragon of thrift, endeavor and virtue. Statues of him, reading a book as he carries a load of firewood on his back, have been erected in primary schools throughout Japan.

Sontoku served the common people as well as the lord of Odawara. Notably, it was he who persuaded local officials to open the castle granary during the terrible famine of 1836. His technique was simplicity itself. When the officials refused to act until they had word from their master in Edo, Sontoku replied, "So be it. But while we wait, let us abstain from food ourselves, in order that we may share the suffering of the people." The granary was opened at once. Today, Sontoku's work lives on in the activities of the Hōtokusha (Moral and Economic Association), which has branches in hundreds of farming villages throughout Japan. They teach Confucian ideals of duty, sincerity, and selflessness. "Think not," said Sontoku, "that you get anything but a cucumber when planting cucumber seeds. What you plant is what you reap."

Legend tells how the temple was founded in 770 by a priest named Dōkyō. He dedicated an eleven-headed Kannon that had been brought to Japan by Jianzhen in 754 and presented to Empress Kōken. The temple was moved to its present location in 830. The name Shōfukuji (Victory Temple) was chosen in the early fifteenth century when the temple was appointed to protect the gateway to Odawara Castle. The main hall was rebuilt in 1706. The present Kannon image appears to date from the twelfth century. It is only revealed to the public once in thirty-three years.

Shōfukuji has a *toshi no ichi* (year's end market) on December 17 and 18. The market features red *daruma* dolls, a traditional good-luck charm. The original Daruma (in Sanskrit, Bodhidharma) was the Indian priest who brought Zen Buddhism to China and, according to tradition, meditated so long that his legs withered and his eyes were plucked out by crows. In the case of the dolls, the eyes must be painted back in. Insert one when you make your wish for the New Year and the other when the wish comes true.

After viewing the temple, those not planning to do the hike should visit the *umeboshi* factory fifty meters back from the bus stop. Hikers may also drop in but time may be short.

Umeboshi are the pickled plums eaten with rice and *sake*. They are not to everybody's taste, and neither is the stench of the factory, but those with hardy noses can enjoy a guided tour between 9:00 am and 7:00 pm daily. You should book the tour in advance, but may also ask in the shop to be shown around. (Kamio Shokuhin Kōgyō; ☎ 0465-47-7141). The *umeboshi* were the food of warriors in battle and travelers along the old Tōkaidō road. They might also make the ideal supplement to your picnic on Mount Kintoki or in Odawara's castle park.

THE WALK *** *(3 hours 20 minutes)*

For the walk, follow the bus route back three stops across the broad Sakawa River to the Iizumi Iriguchi junction (there is a sign in English). Turn right to reach Gohyaku Rakan station in a couple of minutes. Take the train to Daiyūzan and the bus from there to Jizōdō, as described below.

Daiyūzan station stands at Sekimoto, site of the Sakamoto (later Sekimoto) post station on the Tōkaidō in the days when the great east-west road crossed the Ashigara Pass. Outside the station, note the statue of the nude boy, wearing only a bib, riding on the back of a bear. This is Kintarō, the little hero of Ashigara. Kintarō was the childhood name of Sakata Kintoki, one of the four trusted generals of Minamoto Yorimitsu (968–1021) under the Fujiwara regents.

Kintoki lived in an era of great deeds. *Konjaku Monogatari*, for example, tells how Yorimitsu slew the ogre Shuten Dōji. Kintarō, for his part, was raised by a witch on Mount Ashigara and lived as a wild boy wrestling bears and wolves. As Kintaro, he joined Yorimitsu in battle with enemies both human and supernatural. His hatchet suggests connections with the thunder god.

Alighting at Jizōdō, the little Jizō hall stands at a fork in the road. Here you have several options. One is to take the connecting bus from here to Ashigara Pass and Man'yō Kōen, the botanical garden at the top. There are also four ways to walk up.

If you take the left fork from Jizōdō, you reach the campsites at Yūhi Falls in about fifteen minutes. The path divides soon after, but both routes ascend to the ridge between Ashigara Pass and Mount Kintoki. Turning right at the Jizō hall, you can either continue up the road to join the path directly to the pass, or take the family hiking trail to Man'yō Kōen.

Taking the direct route, notice the stone male and female *dōsōjin* (gods of the road) in a little thatched shelter on the left just past the hall. Stay on the forest road for the first fifteen minutes, with the tall, pudding-shaped peak of Mount Yagura dominating the scenery. You soon come to the old path to Ashigara Pass. The road crosses this path several times but the path keeps straight up. Each junction is marked with the sign Ashigaradō Iriguchi ("entrance to the Ashigara Road"). Here you will also catch your first views of the striking peak of Mount Kintoki over to the left. It takes about forty minutes from Jizōdō to the pass.

The family hiking trail starts down a narrow concrete lane to the right between the houses just a few meters past the Jizō hall. It crosses a river and climbs through tea fields and then a forestry plantation. The scenery is mostly obscured by trees, but there are some attractive spots. The path gets a little confusing halfway along: keep straight up, following the red and white ribbons on the trees. This route also takes forty minutes to the ridge, but then allow an extra fifteen minutes along the ridge to reach the pass.

The view of Mount Fuji from Ashigara Pass is breathtaking. To the left, between Fuji and Hakone, you also see the volcanic peaks of Echizen, Ihai, and Ashitaka. As related in *Hitachi Fudoki*, a premodern gazetteer, you now stand at the barrier, at the *kan* of Kantō and Kansai, the lands to the east and west of the gate. Before returning to Kantō, the walk now winds along the ridge for some of the most dramatic views from any low mountains in Japan.

Ashigara Pass was the main pass from Kansai to Kantō in the Nara and Heian periods. The first official road across it was designated in 645. The Hakone route became more popular from around the time of Minamoto Yoritomo, but Ashigara continued as a well-trodden alternative at least until 1321, when the road was closed by a major eruption of Fuji. Although reopened the following year, the pass never regained its former popularity.

Turning left along the road at the ridge, you reach some teahouses, a Shōten hall for the gods that unite couples in wedlock, more statues of Kintarō, and then the border gate itself. The first gate was built in 899 on account of brigandry in the lands to the east.

Climb to the lookout point above the junction where the road turns down into Shizuoka Prefecture. This was the site of Ashigara Castle during the days of the Hōjō. The castle finally fell to the forces of Tokugawa Ieyasu when Odawara was being taken by Hideyoshi. The peak provides the most famous view from Ashigara of Mount Fuji, Gotenba, and Mount Kintoki. There are benches, so you may as well sit down for a while. Fuji is all yours.

Returning to that junction, follow the unpaved track along the ridge towards Mount Kintoki. The trip will take about ninety minutes. The route is flat and easy, but at first the views disappear. It takes about twenty minutes to reach the parking lot at the end of the vehicular road, where the first of the two paths comes up from Yūhi Falls. The sign here indicates sixty minutes to Mount Kintoki.

Now the path climbs gently towards the extraordinary pinnacle of Kintoki itself. Kintoki has the alternative name of Mount Inohana (Mount Boar's Nose), supposedly on account of its shape. The thirty-minute sign and the second path up from the waterfall are reached in another twenty minutes. This was the site of a medieval fort, also named Inohana.

The serious climb now begins. Kintoki is very steep. In the past, hikers used ropes and chains to get over some of the rock faces but these days life is made simpler by the introduction of metal staircases in the trickiest places. The danger is gone but nothing can be done about the gradient. Take it very slowly. The rewards are fully commensurate with the effort. The views are great at the foot and get better all the way up. Allow twenty-five minutes to reach the summit.

Here, at the highest point of the old rim of the Hakone caldera, the view of Mount Fuji meets competition from that of Hakone on the other side. The craggy peak of Kintoki looks across over the plain of Sengokubara towards Lake Ashinoko. Further off, you can make out the Tanzawa Mountains and the southern Japan Alps. The hiking courses around the rim of this gigantic caldera are all clearly visible, so this is the place to plan your next hike. The peak also has the small Inohana Shrine. Refreshments are available at the Kintoki and Kintarō teahouses.

There are various ways down. The quickest is to follow the sign to the left for Sengokubara (55 minutes) and Mount Myōjin (2 hours 5 minutes). The path descends steeply on a boulder-strewn slope. Go right twenty minutes from the peak for Kintoki Shrine, or left if you want a hot-spring bath at the bottom or the bus to Odawara. The bus to Shinjuku station in Tokyo stops at the foot of both paths. The path to the left brings you to the road in about forty minutes at the Kintoki Tōzanguchi bus stop. Go right at the rest house halfway down. Just after the path reaches a road of pleasant villas, look for a couple of small wooden signs for the Kenkō Sansō Kutsuwaya Bekkan hot spring pension. Go right at the crossroads after the second sign. The pension is on the right soon after. You can bathe in the small open-air bath for just ¥500.

Return to the crossroads and continue down to the Kintoki Tōzanguchi bus stop at the bottom. If going to Odawara, turn left a few hundred meters along the road to the Sengoku bus stop, where the service is more frequent. The hotel information center (*ryokan annaijo*) for Sengokubara Hot Spring is close to this second bus stop.

Returning to that junction below the peak, the path down to Kintoki Shrine is easy, with broad views at first, followed by a stretch in the woods. Even if the peak of Mount Kintoki was crowded, you are unlikely to see many others on this path. A giant, split stone stands twenty-five minutes from the junction and is known as Kintoki Yadoriishi. This is the place where, according to legend, Kintarō was raised by the crone. The path crosses a road and reaches the shrine some fifteen minutes from the stone.

Kintoki Shrine is, of course, dedicated to Sakata Kintoki. A Kintoki festival is held on May 5 each year, with a footrace on Mount Kintoki from 10:20, lion dances from 11:00 until just after noon, and children's sumo wrestling from around 12:30. The *koinobori* (carp streamers) displayed on this day express the wish that modern little boys will grow up as brave and sturdy as Kintarō.

The bus stop is directly below the shrine: left for Lake Ashinoko and connections to Odawara, and right for Gotenba and Shinjuku. Those taking the bus in the Gotenba/Shinjuku direction may wish to alight fifteen minutes down the road (the fare is ¥440) for a bath at Gotenba Onsen Kaikan (Gotenba Hot Spring Hall). The bath is indoors but the big windows give a panoramic view of Mount Fuji. Admission is ¥500 for two hours; ¥800 for six. Also look for the tall white pagoda in Heiwa Kōen (Peace Park) on the left. This houses some of the ashes of the Buddha, presented by Jawaharlal Nehru.

TRANSPORTATION
Outbound:
From Tokyo or Shinagawa: JR Tōkaidō line to Odawara (¥1,420). Or Tōkaidō Shinkansen from Tokyo to Odawara (¥3,070).
From Shinjuku: Odakyū line to Odawara (¥830 plus ¥730 express surcharge).
From Odawara to Shōfukuji: Bus for Iizumi Kannon from stand number 11 (15 minutes, ¥230), alight at Iizumi Kannon Mae (Note: this is three stops after Iizumi Iriguchi).
From Gohyaku Rakan to Daiyūzan: Daiyūzan line (14 minutes, ¥210). 5 trains per hour. If not going from Shōfukuji, take the Daiyūzan line from Odawara.

From Daiyūzan to Jizōdō: Bus stand number 4 around the corner to the right from Daiyūzan station (20 minutes, ¥420). Buses run weekdays at 7:15 am, 9:05, 9:22 (to Man'yō Kōen at Ashigara Pass, ¥540), 9:50, 10:15, 10:50, 11:50, 12:25 pm, and 1:25 (to Man'yō Kōen). On Sundays and holidays there are more frequent departures, starting at 8:10 am. For further information contact Hakone Tōzan Tetsudō Bus Lines (☎ 0465-82-0382).

From Jizōdō to Man'yō Kōen: Buses at 9:00 am (Sundays and holidays only), 9:47, 10:23, 11:20, 1:50 pm, 2:25, 3:05.

A frequent bus service also runs between Shin Matsuda on the Odakyū line and Sekimoto (Daiyūzan). The trip takes 15 minutes. Some buses continue to Jizōdō (¥610).

Return:

From Kintoki Shrine (Kintoki Jinja Mae) or Kintoki Tōzanguchi: Odakyū highway bus to Ikejiri Ōhashi on the Hanzōmon subway line and Shinjuku (2 hours 10 minutes, traffic permitting. ¥1,750). You can usually pay on the bus, but it is sometimes full. Hourly service at 40 minutes past the hour till 5:40 pm, with last bus at 6:10. Reservations available from Odakyū outlets.

ACCOMMODATIONS

Near Daiyūzan station:
Shirasagi Ryokan (☎ 0465-74-0114).

Near Jizōdō:
Yūhi no Takishita Bungalow (☎ 0465-74-4512).

Near Kintoki Tōzanguchi:
Kenkō Sansō Kutsuwaya Bekkan (☎ 0460-4-7776). Hot spring pension.
Minshuku Yamaboshi (☎ 0460-4-7228). Hot spring pension
Minshuku Asahiso (☎ 0460-4-9213).

Sengokubara:
There are fourteen hot spring hotels in Sengokubara.

Near Gotenba Onsen Kaikan:
Otome Shinrin Kōen Kampujo (☎ 0550-82-2090). Campsite with

bungalows (¥10,000) and rental tents (¥2,000). Own tent ¥1,000.

Near Odawara station:
Odawara Station Hotel (☎ 0465-22-6222).
Koshimizu Ryokan (☎ 0465-24-0336).

USEFUL KANJI	
Ashigaradō Iriguchi	足柄道入口
Ashigara Pass	足柄峠
Lake Ashinoko	芦ノ湖
Daiyūzan	大雄山
Gohyaku Rakan	五百羅漢
Gotenba	御殿場
Iizumi Kannon	飯泉観音
Jizōdō	地蔵堂
Kintoki Shrine	金時神社
Kintoki Yadoriishi	金時宿り石
Man'yō Kōen	万葉公園
Mount Kintoki	金時山
Mount Myōjin	明神岳
Mount Yagura	矢倉岳
Odawara	小田原
Sekimoto	関本
Sengoku	仙石
Sengokubara	仙石原
Shinjuku	新宿
Shin Matsuda	新松田
Shōfukuji	勝福寺
Yūhi Falls	夕日の滝

HASEDERA — 6
Nanasawa Hot Spring and Hinata Yakushi **
(1 hour 10 minutes to Nanasawa; 2 hours to Hinata Yakushi)

The second Hasedera of the Bandō circuit is located above the hot spring resort of Iiyama in the foothills of the Tanzawa range. The temple claims to have been founded by Gyōki in 715. A separate legend attributes it to Kūkai. See the *niōmon*, built at the order of Minamoto Yoritomo; the main hall, over five centuries old; and the little statues around the courtyard that represent the entire Bandō circuit in miniature. The day to visit is April 8, when the hundreds of cherry trees are in bloom and the eleven-headed Kannon is revealed to the public. Young couples also visit the husband-and-wife pine trees in the courtyard on that day to give thanks for arranged marriages. For the walk, I suggest you ascend the low wooded hills to little Hakusan Shrine (famous for its dragon rain dance), Kōtakuji (another hot spring resort), and Mount Hinata, to finish at Hinata Yakushi, another temple founded by Gyōki, and now one of the great temples of the Kantō Plain. The main hall has a lovely thatched roof and the precincts have many ancient cedars. Be sure to visit the treasure house for the statues of Yakushi, Amida, the Shitennō, and the Jūnishinshō. The main Yakushi image is revealed on January 1–3, January 8, and April 15.

TRANSPORTATION
Outbound:
Tokyo to Hon Atsugi: Odakyū line express from Shinjuku (50 minutes, ¥470). Bus from Hon Atsugi stand number 4 to Miyagase, Susugaya, or Kami Iiyama, alighting at Iiyama Kannon Mae (17 minutes, ¥420).

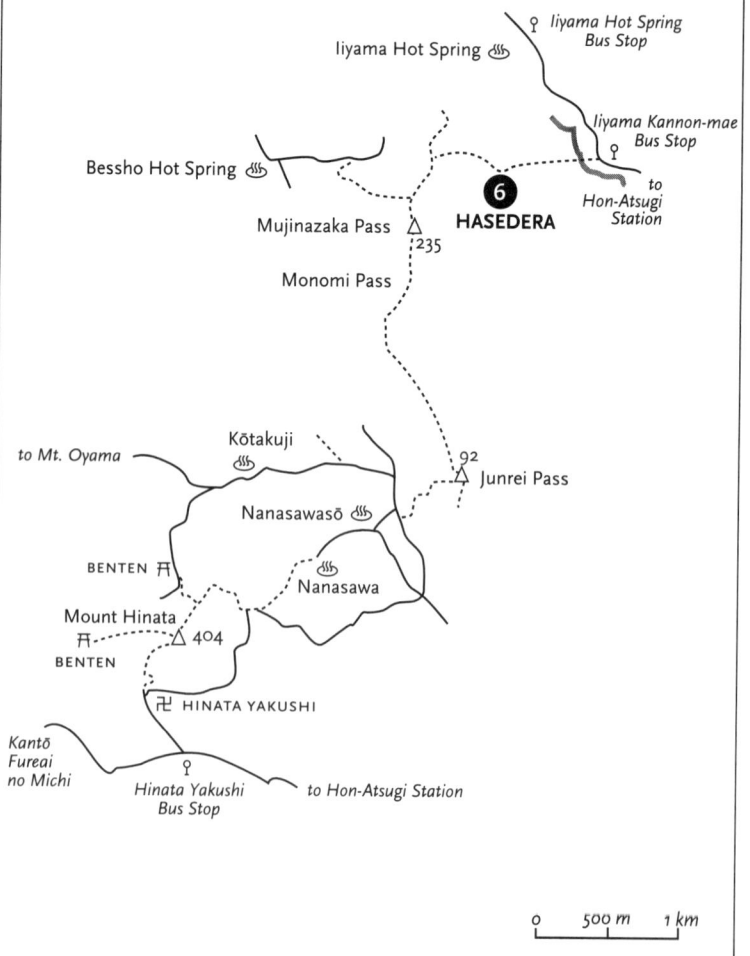

CHAPTER 6

Return:
   Bus from Hinata Yakushi to Isehara (20 minutes, ¥240).
   Odakyū line from Isehara to Shinjuku: (1 hour, ¥550).

ACCOMMODATIONS

Iiyama Hot Spring:
   Yamatoya (☎ 0462-41-1654).
   Motoyu Ryokan (☎ 0462-42-0008).
Nanasawa Hot Spring:
   Nanasawaso (☎ 0462-48-0236).
   Fukumatsu Ryokan (☎ 0462-48-0324).
   Seirakuen (☎ 0462-48-0101).
   Sansuiro (☎ 0462-48-0025).
   Fukumotokan (☎ 0462-48-0334).
   Nakaya Ryokan (☎ 0462-48-0008).
   Tamagawakan (☎ 0462-48-0002).
Kōtakuji Hot Spring:
   Gyokusuiro (☎ 0462-48-0011).

USEFUL KANJI

Hasedera	長谷寺
Hakusan Shrine	白山神社
Hinata Yakushi	日向薬師
Hon Atsugi	本厚木
Isehara	伊勢原
Junrei Pass	順礼峠
Kami Iiyama	上飯山
Kantō Fureai no Michi	関東ふれあいの道
Kōtakuji	広沢寺
Miyagase	宮ヶ瀬
Mount Ōyama	大山
Nanasawa	七沢
Nanasawa Benten no Mori	七沢弁天の森
Susugaya	煤ヶ谷

KŌMYŌJI — 7

*Mount Kōbō and Tsurumaki Hot Spring * (1 hour 30 minutes)*

Kōmyōji is located in the plain just beneath the peak of Mount Ōyama. Legend tells that the first Shō Kannon was discovered on Koiso Beach at the mouth of the Kaname River in 702. A priest identified it as a carving by Shōtoku Taishi, the early seventh-century regent. Gyōki carved and dedicated a second Shō Kannon in the mid-700s, placing the original inside its womb. The tradition thus arose that Kōmyōji was a place to pray for safe birth. Yoritomo's wife, Masako, came here before giving birth to Sanetomo. Experts judge that the statue really dates from the eleventh or twelfth centuries. The present main hall was built in the 1490s but looks perfectly new, following a renovation in the mid-1980s. The main image is only revealed once in sixty years. You can ask to be shown the statues of Kannon's thirty-three embodiments. There is little else to see, apart from glimpses of Mount Fuji on the horizon, and the plain once swept by warlords' armies is now awash with automobiles. You can walk directly from the temple past historic sites to Tsurumaki Hot Spring, but it is better to take the bus and start the walk at Mount Kōbō. This trek across low hills is a popular family hiking course.

TRANSPORTATION

Buses run between Hiratsuka (JR Tokaidō line) and Hadano (Odakyū line). For the temple, take bus number 71, 74, or 75 and alight at Kaname station (20 minutes from Hadano, 25 from Hiratsuka, around ¥300). For the walk, take bus 71 or 74 (not 75) from Kaname station in the Hadano direction and get off at Kawaramachi (12 minutes, ¥220).

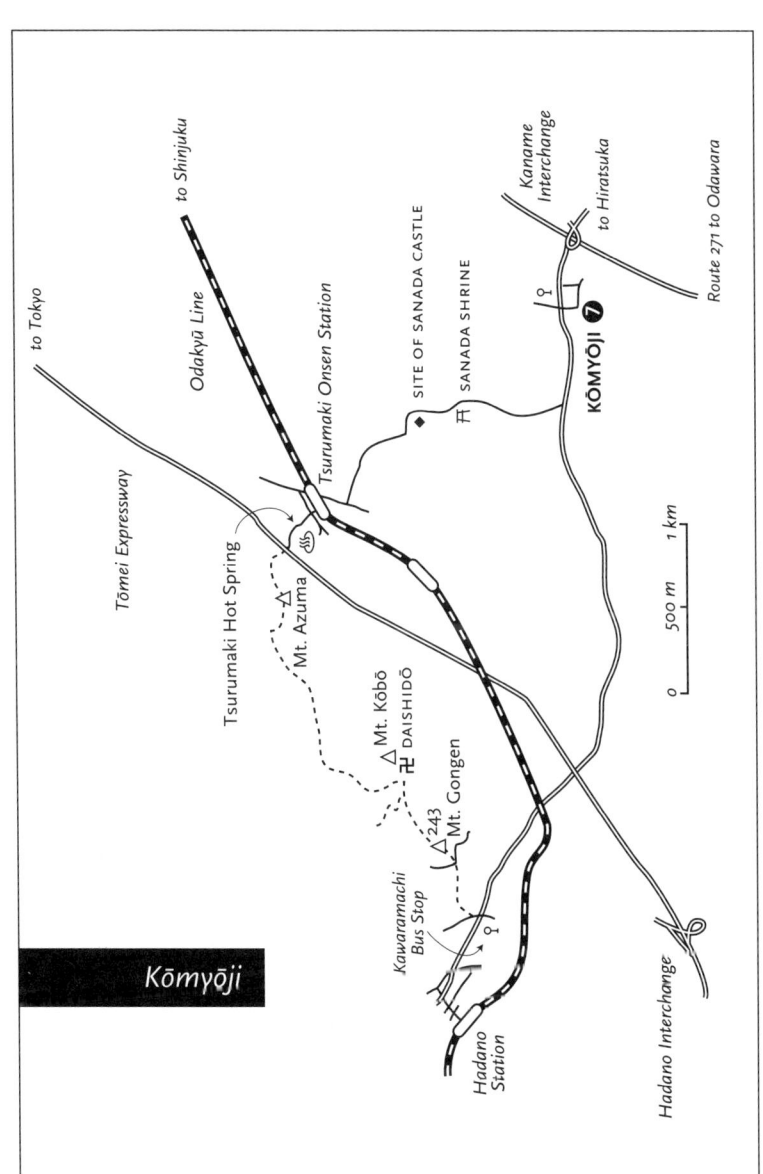

KŌMYŌJI

ACCOMMODATIONS
Tsurumaki Hot Spring:
   Hotel Kokakuen (☎ 0463-77-1500),
   Yamato Ryokan (☎ 0463-77-1222),
   Miyuki Ryokan (☎ 0463-77-1230),
   Tsuruyoshi (☎ 0463-77-1270),
   Shinobu (☎ 0463-77-1250),
   Bontensō (☎ 0463-77-1719)
   Tsurumakien (☎ 0463-77-1565),
   Tsurumaki Onsen Kaikan (☎ 0463-77-1339),
   Yutaka (☎ 0463-77-1778),
   Fukuzuru (☎ 0463-77-1348),
   Jinya (☎ 0463-77-1300).

USEFUL KANJI

Hadano	秦野
Hiratsuka	平塚
Isehara	伊勢原
Kaname	金目
Kawaramachi	河原町
Kōmyōji	光明寺
Mount Azuma	吾妻山
Mount Kōbō	弘法山
Tsurumaki Hot Spring	鶴巻温泉

SHŌKOKUJI — 8
*The Zama Kite Festival * (Walking distance: 2 hours)*

Shōkokuji, too, is a Gyōki temple. Legend tells how Gyōki heard Kannon chanting the *Lotus Sutra* just north from here and carved and consecrated a Shō Kannon. That Kannon statue later escaped from a fire by flying to the south and the temple was rebuilt where it landed. Shōkokuji is small, but it does have several notable sights, starting with the two great *niō* statues in the open at the entrance. The bell, forged in 1227, is the second oldest in Kantō. See also the statue of Kūkai in pilgrim's garb, the Hōkyōin sutra repository, the contorted maple with udderlike growths which women touch in order to be blessed with milk, and the old ginkgos and Chinese black pines. The walk brings many low-key pleasures, including a stretch of the Kamakura Kaidō (one of the main roads out of Kamakura when that city was the political hub of Japan), a shrine where legend says that Yoshitsune's wife died, the old Zama Shrine, Ryūgen'in (a temple with a curious Benten statue and a nasty legend of human sacrifice), and ancient burial caves. Notice, if you can, all the water-related legends, explained in Japanese on signs along the route. The time to visit is May 4 or 5, to enjoy the children's *sumo* and the huge kites flown over the floodplain of the Zama River.

TRANSPORTATION
Odakyū line from Shinjuku to Zama (about 50 minutes, ¥430). Take the express from Shinjuku to Sagami Ōno and change there for the local train to Zama on platform 2.

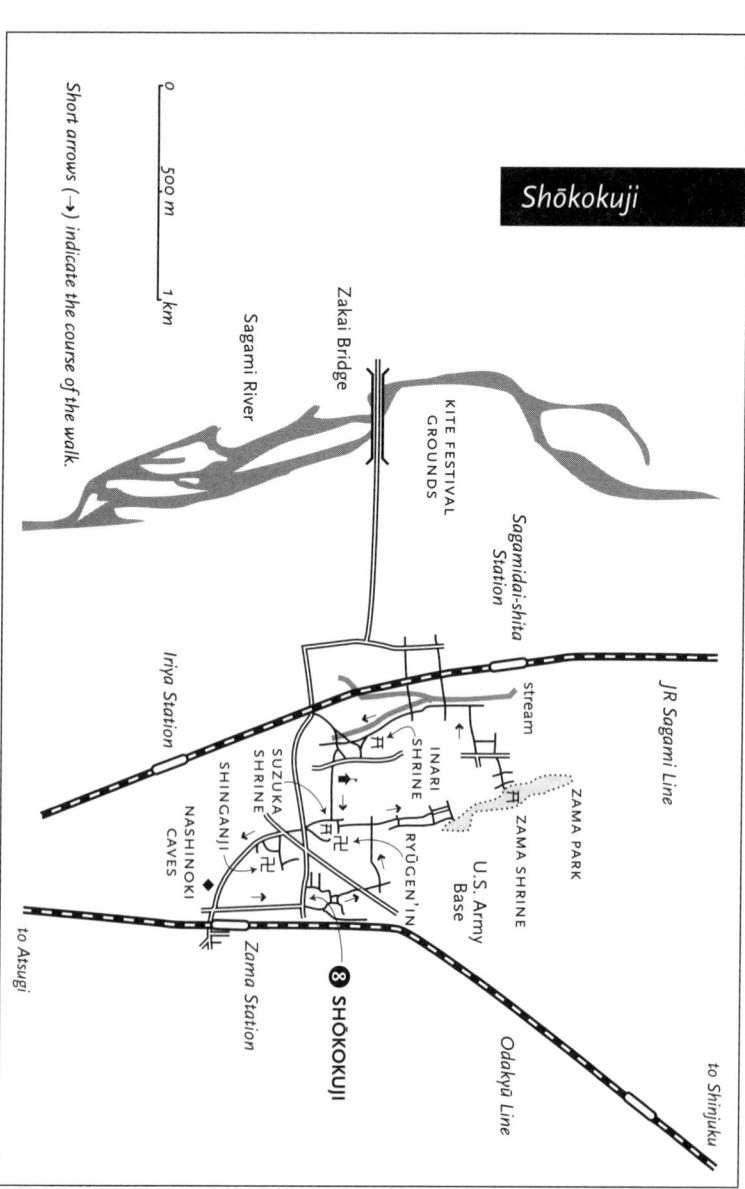

CHAPTER 8

USEFUL KANJI

Ryūgen'in	龍源院
Sagami Ōno	相模大野
Shinganji	心岩寺
Shōkokuji	星谷寺
Suzuka Shrine	鈴鹿明神
Zama	座間
Zama Park	座間公園
Zama Shrine	座間神社

JIKŌJI
Mount Kasa *** (4 hours 30 minutes)

Jikōji is located on a remote forested mountainside in the village of Tokikawa. Founded in 673, it was one of the earliest and grandest Buddhist temples in Kantō, with seventy-five residences for priests when the temple was at the height of its prosperity. Minamoto Yoritomo and members of many Bandō *musha* clans prayed here. Even today, the temple dominates the entire mountainside. See the pagoda inside the Kaizandō (the hall dedicated to Dōchū, who founded the temple proper in 770), the oldest bell in Kantō (forged in 1245), the ilex tree said to have been planted by Ennin between 824 and 834, the thatched Kannon hall with its horse *ema*, and especially the superb treasure house with its statues of Aizen, Suwa, Zaō, En no Gyōja, Daikokuten, Kannon, and Shōsō Monju, the artifacts of esoteric mountain priests, the ornately illustrated early thirteenth century *Lotus Sutra*, and the *Heart Sutra* from 871, the oldest extant sutra in Kantō. The thousand-armed Kannon is revealed to the public on April 17 and the second Sunday of April each year. The walk leads through forestry plantations to the tea fields of Nanae and then climbs steeply up the road to the peaks of Kengamine and Dōdaira. The final two hours from Mount Dōdaira to Mount Kasa and Kaiya lead through beautiful mixed woods and pretty farms.

TRANSPORTATION
Outbound:
Tobu Tōjō line from Ikebukuro to Ogose, changing trains at Sakado (¥670). JR Hachiko line from Ogose to Myōkaku. Then take the Tokikawa Son'ei Bus (☎ 0493-65-1535) from Myōkaku to Nishidaira (10 minutes, ¥180). Morning buses at 8:10 (weekdays

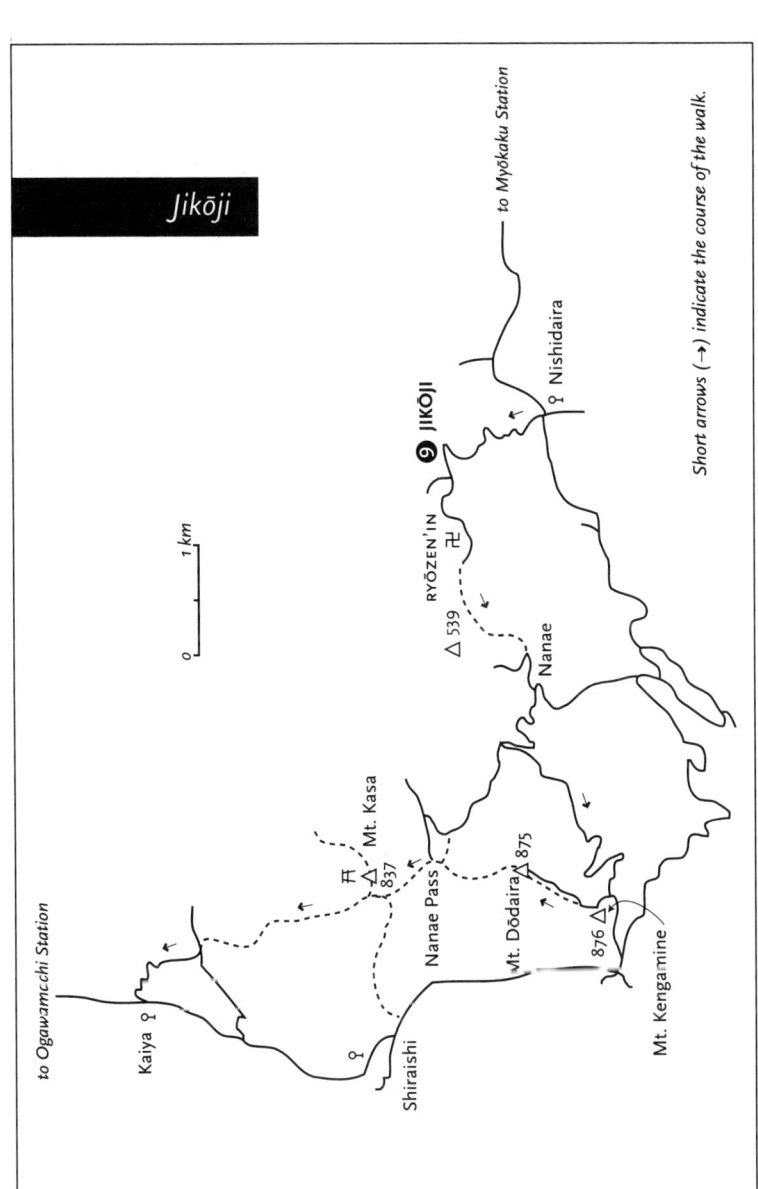

only), 9:17 10:38, 11:42. JR Hachiko line trains are infrequent. At present, the 7:00 am from Ikebukuro connects with the Hachiko line train from Ogose in time for the 9:17 bus.

Return:

Tōbu Bus from Kaiya to Ogawamachi (30 minutes, ¥420; ☎ 0493-72-0076).

ACCOMMODATIONS

In Tokikawa:

Ki no Mura (☎0493-67-0850). Bungalows and campsite near Nanae. Open May to September. Easy access by village bus for Takenotani from Myōkaku or Nishidaira.

Hot-spring hotels in Ogose (bus to Kuroyama from Ogose station):

Kuroyama Kosenkan (☎ 0492-92-2226),

Kuroyama Onsen Tojokaku (☎ 0492-92-2356),

Ogosekan (☎ 0492-92-6111).

USEFUL KANJI

bus stop	バス停
Jikōji	慈光寺
Kaiya	皆谷
Kuroyama	黒山
Mount Dōdaira	堂平
Mount Kasa	傘山
Mount Kengamine	剣ヶ峰
Myōkaku	明覚
Nanae	七重
Nishidaira	西平
Ogawamachi	小川町
Ogose	越生
Ryōzen' in	霊山院
Sakado	坂戸

SHŌBŌJI — 10
Woods and Warlords

The trip to Shōbōji has something for everyone, with the choice of a day suitable for families with small children or a pleasant walk through the historic Hiki hills. The temple itself stands against a cliff in the middle of an oasis of greenery, with the low hills of Higashi Matsuyama and Ranzan spreading out in a long row behind. But here you are closer to the plain than at Jikōji, and the ravages of development are also clear to see.

The day trip for the family can all be contained within the close vicinity of Shōbōji. After viewing the temple, first cross the road to the Peace Museum of Saitama (Saitama Heiwa Shiryōkan; ☎ 0493-35-4111) and Monomiyama Park. The museum is closed Mondays, days after national holidays, and New Year's Day; admission is ¥100. The collection is devoted to the early part of the Shōwa period (1926–89) in Japan, from the invasion of Manchuria to the atom bombs, with the special focus on Saitama Prefecture. Saitama was on the receiving end of about forty air raids during World War II. More than two hundred people died in the last raid, on the city of Kumagaya, the day the war ended. But the museum also takes care to show the lifestyle of the people of those times, not just the suffering. Besides the exhibits, the museum has many videos, a library, and a lookout tower.

Then walk a hundred meters downhill from the museum to the outstanding Saitama Children's Zoo (Kodomo Dōbutsu Shizen Kōen; ☎ 0493-35-1234; closing days same as the Peace Museum). This forty-two-hectare zoo is quite unlike any other I have seen in Japan, with wide open spaces, no signs forbidding walking on the grass or playing ball, and lots of space for the animals, too. The zoo

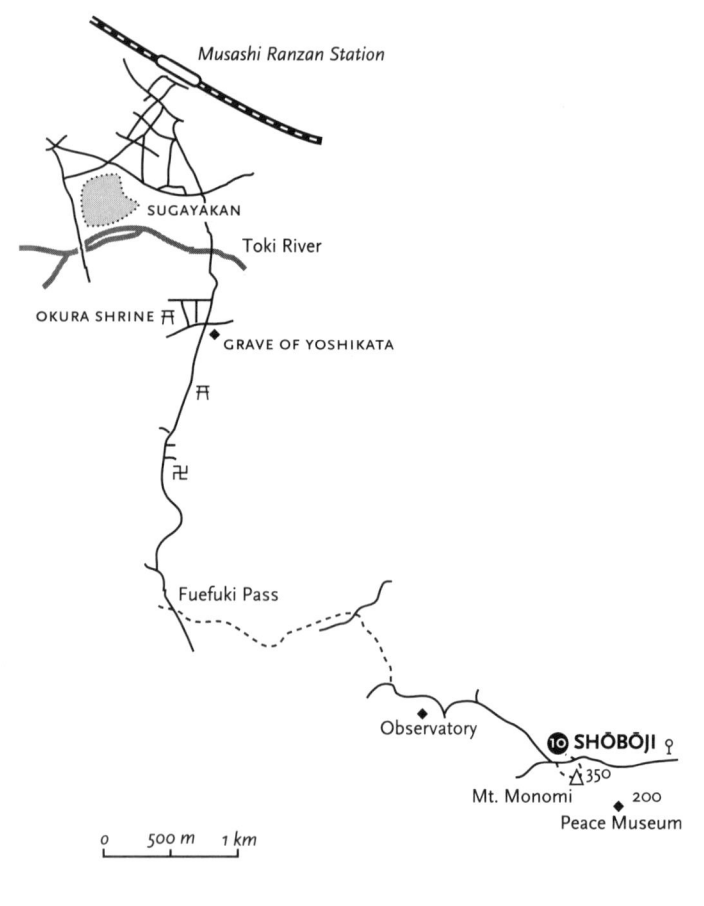

CHAPTER 10

has wisely chosen quality instead of quantity. Visitors can stroll among the kangaroos and monkeys and even view koalas (donated by Queensland in 1986) in the open. There is also pony riding, a dinosaur park, an adventure playground, and a big children's castle with many attractions inside. Admission is ¥400, with an additional ¥100 for the castle. You will not need to visit anywhere else all day. The bus stop (one stop back from the temple) for buses to Takasaka is just outside the main gate.

For those who select the walk, the first half is a stroll through mixed woods. The scenery is tame, but the trees are full of birds and insects. There are views if you look: on a clear day, you can see most of the great volcanoes of the Kantō area, including Tsukuba, Nantai, Tanigawa, Akagi, Haruna, and even the tip of Fuji. This walk also has the advantage that the hills are low and the ridge is virtually flat: it will please those who don't like their trails too steep.

The sign at Mount Monomi, near the start of the walk, carries a haiku by an unnamed poet describing the area:

The pheasant cries
 The best ninety-nine valleys
  In Bandō

The walk descends from the hills at Fuefuki Pass, once a key strategic point in the Kantō region. The armies of Sakanoue Tamuramaro, the Minamoto, the Nitta, and the Uesugi all swept across here. The name Fuefuki, or "flute-playing," comes from a tradition that Prince Munenaga played his flute here by moonlight to relieve the tensions of battle. That was in 1352, when Nitta Yoshimune was defeated at the pass by the forces of Ashikaga Takauji.

The road down more or less follows the route of the upper Kamakura Kaidō, one of three key roads in the Kantō of the Kamakura shoguns. The walk down is dull today, but there is plenty to see at the bottom, including the sites of two castles (one with its trenches and embankments magnificently preserved), a history museum, and an ancient burial mound.

THE TEMPLE

Shōbōji is a couple of minutes up the road from the bus stop for Daitō Bunka University, opposite the entrance to Monomiyama Park. The way to the temple is through the pedestrian tunnel on the right.

You emerge from the tunnel right beside the Kannon hall. The old approach to the temple winds up the quiet valley to the right. It is still more impressive to approach the temple from that side: the road leads straight as an arrow to Shōbōji at the valley's head. Only those who are ruled by bus routes must slink in from behind. You might wander down a little way. A bustling temple town used to stand at the bottom, and its shell, including former pilgrims' inns, can still be seen. The main temple is also at the foot of the slope.

Shōbōji, also known as Iwadono Kannon (for its principal deity), was founded in 718 by an ascetic called Itsukai. The famous seventh-century ascetic En no Gyōja is also said to have used the site as a retreat. Soon after the temple was founded, however, a terrible dragon wreaked havoc in the district. The great warrior Sakanoue Tamuramaro (758–811) happened to be passing through, and prayed at Iwadono Kannon for guidance. A great snow fell, covering the ground except in one warm place. Thus Tamuramaro discovered the dragon's lair and overcame the beast. Local people still give thanks to Tamuramaro at Shōbōji on June 1 each year. Shōbōji prospered under the patronage of Minamoto Yoritomo and Masako, but the buildings from that period were lost in the sixteenth century in the battles that the Hōjō fought around Takasaka.

The temple still has plenty of attractions, starting with the fine old trees in the temple precincts. Notice the huge ginkgo tree and the rows of statues in the cliff face, which mostly represent the deities of temples of the Shikoku pilgrimage. Shōbōji has a thatched belfry, a one-hundred-Jizō hall and a Yakushi hall. The main hall stands against the cliff. The bell was cast in 1322. The thousand-armed Kannon in the main hall appears to date from the Kamakura period. The main hall itself was rebuilt in 1886.

Descend to the *niōmon* by the steps and return to the tunnel by the path up the side. The walk starts from the entrance to Monomiyama Park.

THE WALK ** *(3 hours)*

Mount Monomi ("the mountain for viewing things") is only 135.6 meters high. It takes just a minute to reach the lookout point at the top. Monomi has pretty red pines, maples, and azaleas. The view of the Tanzawa Mountains, Chichibu, Gunma, and the Kantō Plain is good in winter, but entirely obscured by trees in summer. Don't worry, for you get some better scenery later on, or from the lookout tower of the Saitama Peace Museum if you prefer.

Take the path by the steps of the lookout point signposted for Fuefuki Pass. Turn left onto the road at the bottom (you see Mounts Haruna and Akagi on the right, Fuji on the left) and right a couple of minutes later up the quiet road through Shimin no Mori (Citizens' Forest).

The mixed woods of pine and oak continue to the pass. The main route stays on this narrow road but three short courses have also been laid out through the woods. You will find a map five minutes along the main route, at the entrance to the first of the shorter courses. Each of these takes ten to twenty minutes to the end and back. Fossils of shells and sharks' teeth have been found in this area.

Continuing along the road, a few minutes later you reach the monitoring antennas of the NASDA Space Center. Here, too, the view is good towards Chichibu and Fuji. You can view the center's exhibition hall, but phone in advance (☎ 0492-96-1611).

Stay with the frequent signs to Fuefuki Pass. After crossing a largish road, the final fifteen minutes to the pass are mostly along an

SHŌBŌJI

unpaved trail. A rest house and benches are placed at the pass. This ends the nature trail; now the walk descends to Ranzan in the footsteps of the Bandō warriors.

The way across Fuefuki Pass was used by armies from the Nara period on, linking Ashigara and Kamakura in the south with Gunma and Niigata in the north. The east-west route across the pass also has a history: it is known as the pilgrim's way, for this was the route that Kannon pilgrims took between temples nine and ten on the Bandō route.

Turn right. The modern road is sadly dull for the first fifteen minutes, despite a forlorn attempt to liven it up with cherry trees. Things start getting better when you reach the farms at the bottom. Passing a temple and a shrine, you come to a large sign beside what can only be described as a ditch. But this is a ditch with a history. Legend relates how Sakanoue Tamuramaro divorced his wife at this place. The story goes that while Tamuramaro was preparing to vanquish the Iwadono dragon, his wife grew so anxious that she hastened from Kyoto to be with him. The manly general was furious at being fussed over by a woman while on duty, and divorced her forthwith. It is told that even today newlywed couples avoid crossing the bridge for fear of bad luck.

Notice the wayside stones outside the temple a minute later on the left. The one by the gate has a relief of Shōmen Kongō, the god of the Kōshin faith. The natural rock just beyond is also a Koshin stone. The other two beside it are a Rokujūroku Kuyō Kannon (sixty-six-offerings Kannon) and a Batō Kannon (horse-headed Kannon). Inside, the temple has a huge number of Jizō statues.

At the crossroads just after, turn right. Go right again thirty meters later, and again immediately, following the signs to what looks like a white hut at the back of a private house. Don't worry; you are allowed in. The five-story stone pagoda inside is the grave of Minamoto Yoshikata, the younger brother of Yoshitomo (and uncle of Yoritomo), who was killed in 1155.

Yoshikata was another Minamoto who died at the hands of his relatives. His nephew, Yoshihira (Yoritomo's elder brother), invaded from Sagami in the south and defeated Yoshikata in battle here on August 16, 1155. Yoshihira was only fifteen at the time. This exploit earned the boy warrior the appellation Akugenta, or Yoshihira the Bad, and is recounted as the battle of Okura in the epic *Heike Monogatari*. Yoshihira was executed five years later in the wake of the Heiji Disturbance.

Yoshikata's two-year old son was rescued from the slaughter at Okura by the nearby Hatakeyama clan. He was sent to Nagano and grew up to be Minamoto Yoshinaka (better known as Kiso Yoshinaka) who, with Yoritomo and Yoshitsune, was one of the three great Minamoto generals of the *Heike Monogatari*. He also had a classic Nō play, *Kiso*, written about him. It was Yoshinaka who took Kyoto for the Minamoto in 1183. Yoritomo, however, found Yoshinaka too independent and sent Yoshitsune and Noriyori after him. Yoshinaka was defeated in the ensuing battle and killed soon afterwards.

Return to the crossroads and keep straight (left coming down from the pass). A large Batō Kannon stele stands on the right a minute from the crossroads, and behind it on the corner a plan of Yoshikata's old castle, Okurakan. The main site of Okurakan was where the pretty Okura Shrine is now, a couple of hundred meters further up the road on the right. Again, there are plenty of signs. Although some trenches and earthworks survive, it is probable that they date from a later period. This site was used as a military base by a long series of warlords.

Return to the crossroads, and this time continue left. The road soon crosses the Toki River at a bridge called Gakkōbashi, a popular spot for picnics and fishing. Cherry trees line the path along the bank.

Crossing the river, keep straight for another five minutes and turn left at the T-junction onto the bypass. Just as the walk seems to be winding down, you now come to the highlight. Five minutes along the bypass, there are signs right to Musashi Ranzan station and straight on to the Prefectural History Museum (☎ 0493-62-5896). First, go straight.

The entrance to the museum is three minutes further on the left. But this isn't only a museum. It is thought to be the site of Sugayakan, the castle of Hatakeyama Shigetada (1164–1205). A descendent and ally of the Taira family, Shigetada later switched sides and fought heroically for Yoritomo at the decisive battle of Dannoura in 1185. Shigetada was himself killed in battle by the Hōjō when he rose to protest the assassination of his son. Shigetada was an old-school hero: a story tells how once, fearing for the safety of his horse on a precipitous slope, he carried it over his shoulder!

The castle has been turned into a huge and beautiful woodland park. Many of the trenches and embankments have been preserved so the visitor can enjoy a fascinating scramble through history. A large statue of Shigetada stands above one of the earthworks. Much later, in 1488, rival members of the Uesugi clan fought a great battle on this site. Records tell how seven hundred men and several hundred horses died in the carnage. As with Okurakan, the moats and earthworks we see today probably date from that later period.

You can also walk back down to the river through the park and around the corner to smaller parks devoted to fireflies (Hotaru no Sato) and the big Ōmurasaki butterfly (Ōmurasaki no Mori), the designated national butterfly of Japan. The adult Ōmurasaki can be seen from late June to early August. Both parks lie on the outer boundary of the castle.

Don't neglect visiting the Prefectural History Museum to see the fascinating collection of local artifacts ranging from Jōmon-period pottery and medieval armor to everyday utensils of the early twentieth century. Admission is ¥50. Videos can also be viewed on request. Ask the attendant to show you the video of Fuefuki Pass (Fuefuki Tōge) for a history of the Kamakura Kaidō, or the one about Hatakeyama Shigetada. Both are twenty minutes long.

Leave the park by the entrance and follow that sign to the station. An old burial mound stands on the left a minute from the junction. It is thought to date from the late seventh century. Go left at the T-junction soon afterwards and take the next right for Musashi Ranzan station.

TRANSPORTATION

Outbound:
From Tokyo: Tōbu Tōjō line from Ikebukuro to Takasaka (55 minutes, ¥600). Bus from Takasaka to Hatoyama New Town, alighting at Daitō Bunka University (10 minutes, ¥170).
Return:
From Musashi Ranzan to Ikebukuro: Tōbu Tōjō line (¥670).

USEFUL KANJI

Fuefuki Pass	笛吹峠
Hatoyama New Town	鳩山ニュータウン
Higashi Matsuyama	東松山
Hotaru no Sato	蛍の里
Mount Monomi	物見山
Musashi Ranzan	武蔵嵐山
Ōkurakan	大蔵館
Ōkura Shrine	大蔵神社
Ōmurasaki no Mori	大紫の森
Prefectural History Museum	県立歴史資料館
Shōbōji	正法寺
Sugayakan	菅谷館
Takasaka	高坂

ANRAKUJI — 11
Ancient Graves and Mount Ponpon

The Ara River, like the Tone, has undergone dramatic changes during the past five hundred years. It used to be a tributary of the Tone, flowing out to Tokyo Bay on the course of the present Sumida River. Today, the Tone joins the Watarase instead, and both flow east to Chōshi, far beyond even the Watarase's former course. The Ara, meanwhile, was diverted west by the Tokugawa authorities to join the Iruma, which connects with the Sumida much closer to Tokyo Bay.

Anrakuji, the temple of the Yoshimi Kannon, stands on one of the low hills at the very edge of the Chichibu range, close to the Ara River's new course from Kumagaya to Kawagoe, linking it with the Iruma. The new course is not entirely artificial—it makes use of the valley of the former Wada Yoshino River—but is still testimony to the huge scale of the river control projects of the past few centuries.

The walk takes you along the border between the wooded hills and the paddies of the plain. The first half stays mostly on top of these tiny hills; the second strikes out on the Ara embankment across the open plain. Points of historical interest include the site of Matsuyama Castle and a group of ancient hillside burial caves known as Yoshimi Hyakketsu. The trail begins in the city of Higashi Matsuyama, but mostly lies within the township of Yoshimi.

THE TEMPLE

Anrakuji has a quiet location set back from the road. Climbing the short flight of steps to the *niōmon*, you first come to the main hall. A great Amida cast in 1790 is seated in front. A pagoda and a Daishi hall dedicated to Kūkai are on the right; the belfry and a Jizō hall

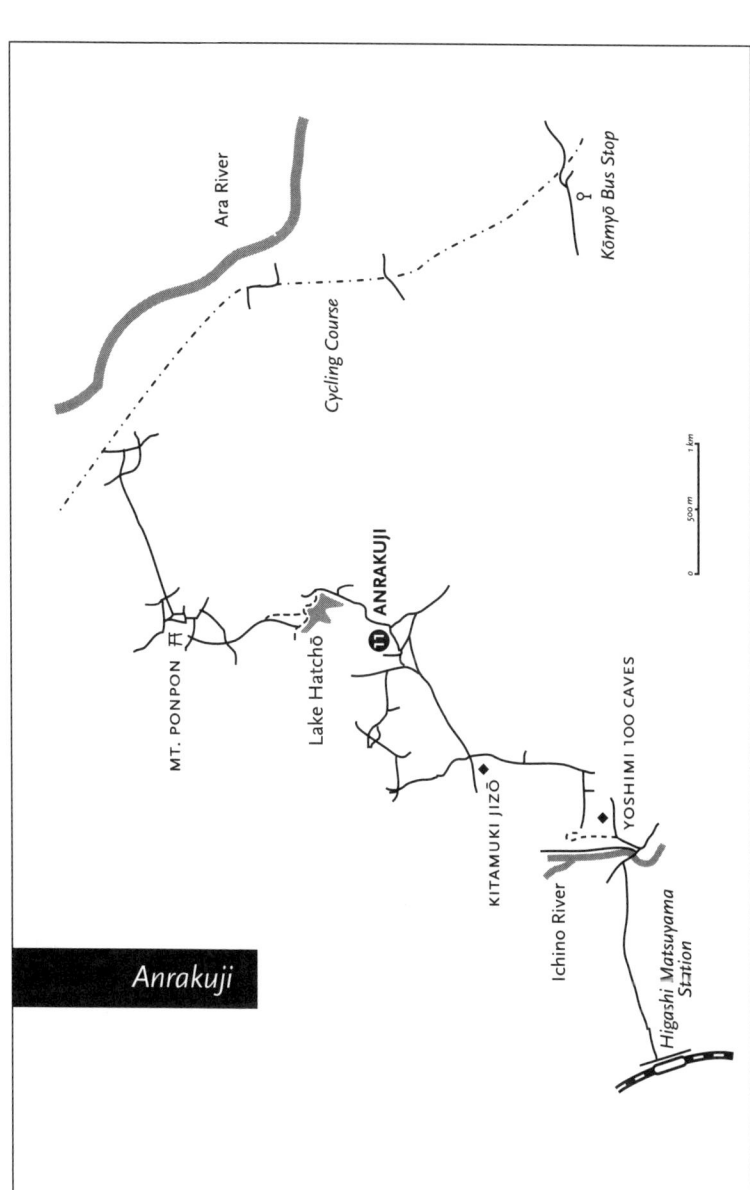

ANRAKUJI

among the trees behind. Other small halls are also scattered around the precincts.

Legend relates that the Shō Kannon image was carved by Gyōki, who gave it to the local lord. When the lord moved to another district, the statue refused to budge. The lord had it sealed inside a cave.

The temple itself was supposedly founded in 806 by Sakanoue Tamuramaro, the general who subjugated the Ezo throughout northern Japan. The Ezo were the original inhabitants before the Yamato race arrived. Tamuramaro is also, as an adjunct to his conquests, credited with spreading the Kannon faith in this area. When he opened the cave, the Kannon glowed. Tamuramaro thought that it resembled the cave of the sun goddess Amaterasu described in the *Kojiki*, the ancient chronicle of Japan.

Much later, a new hall and pagoda were erected by Minamoto Noriyori, Yoritomo's younger half-brother who had a castle a few minutes walk from here. Noriyori had come to Anrakuji as a child-priest, spared like Yoritomo and Yoshitsune after Yoshitomo's defeat in the Heiji Disturbance. He later became lord of the district. Noriyori fought for Yoritomo in Kinki and Kyūshū in the 1180s, but Yoritomo had him executed in 1193.

Noriyori's hall and pagoda were lost during the fighting for Matsuyama Castle between the Uesugi and the Hōjō. The present pagoda and main hall were built in the seventeenth century.

The tiger inside the main hall, by the way, has a history of sneaking out at night and wreaking havoc in the neighborhood. Happily, it now appears to have settled down.

The Yoshimi Kannon is displayed on June 18. Worshipers start arriving from before dawn to buy little cakes (*mayoke dango*) that ward off evil influence.

THE WALK ** *(3 hours)*

The walk starts from beneath the great red *torii* gate on the east side of Higashi Matsuyama station, leading straight down the main street of this little city towards the wooded hill beside the Ichino River where Matsuyama Castle once stood. It takes twenty minutes to reach the river.

First turn right on the far side of the bridge. A small post fifty meters from the bridge indicates the entrance to Matsuyama Castle. The castle was built in the fifteenth century and fell in 1590. It was a natural fortress, protected by the swamps of the Ichino River and commanding one of the roads between Kamakura and Kōzuke. This naturally made it a target for all comers, so the castle had changed hands several times before allies of Hideyoshi took it in 1590, the year that Odawara fell.

Unlike castle parks in most cities, this hillside has been restored to nature. Visiting in early October, the paths were an arachnophiliac's dream and hiker's nightmare. It takes three minutes to walk to the small shrine at the top and the monument a few steps beyond. This is, however, the kind of place where you may want to scramble about for some time.

Returning to the entrance, turn back past the bridge. You come to an extraordinary cliff on the right filled with manmade caves. Look closely, and you notice that it has the facade of a Western-style hotel. This is the Gankutsu Hotel (Cave Hotel), the weird product of a twentieth-century hobbyist's fantasy. The caves were originally quarried as a natural refrigerator. Visitors are no longer allowed inside. The rusting playground in front adds the finishing touch to a very eerie place.

A few steps further, also on the right, the former rear gate of the castle is now a fascinating Kannon temple. The statues in the caves at the foot of the gate represent the eighty-eight temples of Shikoku. The Iwamuro Kannon is enshrined inside the gate. You can reach it up the narrow wooden steps.

The road opposite leads in another hundred meters to Yoshimi Hyakketsu ("the hundred holes of Yoshimi"), a designated National Treasure that dates from around 1,300 years ago. Perhaps these manmade caves are a legacy of the Ezo. A hot spring hotel stands beside the entrance. Non-staying guests can have a bath for ¥980.

Admission to Yoshimi Hyakketsu itself is ¥150. A huge cave has been dug out beneath the tufa hill with many smaller holes up the hillside. Paths lead through the big cave and up past the holes to the top. Cherry trees are everywhere. The big cave is not ancient. It was built as an underground shelter during World War II, destroying some of the ancient excavations in the process.

The smaller caves look a bit like the cliff dwellings of some primitive peoples, but their size suggests that they must have been burial chambers. More than two hundred chambers have been discovered, together with tools and human remains. They are also known as a habitat of another National Treasure, luminous moss, which suggests some connection with the legend of the Yoshimi Kannon related above. The early studies of the caves were partly instigated by Edward Morse, the American who did so much scientific and archaeological research in Meiji Japan.

Turn right out of Yoshimi Hyakketsu to join the Yoshimi Furusato Hodō (Yoshimi Hometown Hiking Course). You pick up the signs to Kitamuki Jizō and Yoshimi Kannon from the corner of the next car park. The path climbs up through the woods around the edge of the Hyakketsu park to emerge in a peaceful farming district. There are several turns but the signs are easy to follow. Watch for the many wayside stones. Keep straight by the six-handed god, Shōmen Kongō of the Kōshin faith, where the signpost is a little confusing.

You reach Kitamuki Jizō in fifteen minutes from Yoshimi Hyakketsu at a five-way junction. The Jizō image is on the near left-hand corner. Yasaka Shrine stands on the opposite side of the road. Cross the road and follow the signs up the lane to the left of the shrine for the route across the hills to the Yoshimi Kannon. You must turn right at a post five minutes up this road, then right once more immediately. Again, there are various twists and turns through woods and past farms but you will not get lost. You reach Anrakuji in twenty minutes from Kitamuki Jizō.

CHAPTER 11

After visiting the temple, turn left out of the *niōmon* up the narrow lane around the temple wall. You cross a low hill to come out in about five minutes at the pretty Hatchō Lake. This large irrigation reservoir was built in the Edo period. The promenade around the lake is popular with fishermen. Boat rentals are available. This park, too, has many cherry trees.

Take the promenade around the right side of the lake, following the signs for Kuroiwa Ketsugun, a second set of ancient hillside burial chambers. The path hugs the lakeshore for several minutes before climbing a short valley to the caves. About fifty have been excavated, but the hillside is thought to contain around five hundred. You are not allowed inside. Then continue up the valley, following the signs to Mount Ponpon (Pomponyama). Again, there are twists and turns through woods and farms but the signs are clear.

Mount Ponpon is a surprise. From this side, it looks completely flat, but you must recall that you are on top of a ridge. Mount Ponpon is the affectionate name given to the Takao Hikone Shrine. The rocks behind, when viewed from the plain, do look like something of a peak. Likewise, the rocks command an excellent view of the Ara River and the Kantō Plain. Two old Kōshin stones stand at the top. Records tell how the flood waters of the Ara came right up to these rocks in the Edo period. And Ponpon? That is the sound you hear if you stomp around the roots of the old pine trees.

Now turn right out of the shrine gate following the signs to the River Ara. The Yoshimi Furusato Hiking Course crosses the rice paddies at the bottom and ascends the embankment two kilometers away. Ignore the signs to a bus stop in between: the bus route has been discontinued.

The final hour of the walk leads along the cycle track on top of the embankment to the Kōmyō bus stop. The walk develops as a fascinating elevated panorama of rural Kantō. The cycle track, by the way, runs all of the way from Urawa to the national woodland park, Shinrin Kōen.

The extraordinary thing about this hour's walk along the embankment is that you never see the river! It is not far away, at least for the first forty minutes, but while the view to the right is interesting, that to the left is dominated by a seemingly interminable golf course (the modern version of the Yoshimi Hyakketsu). For the final twenty minutes, after crossing a road, matters improve scenically on the left as well, but the river drifts further away. Now there are fields and houses on both sides!

Turn right at the second road across the embankment to reach the bus stop in a couple of minutes.

TRANSPORTATION
Outbound:

Tōbū Tōjō line from Ikebukuro to Higashi Matsuyama (1 hour, ¥600). There is nothing to see for the first twenty minutes to the castle. Rather than walking, you can take a bus, either to Konosu Menkyo Center or Hiki Nōkyō, alighting at Hyakketsu Iriguchi.

Return:

Buses from Komyō run to Konosu on the JR Takasaki line for trains to Akabane and Ueno; back to Higashi Matsuyama; and to Kawagoe on the JR Saikyō line for Ikebukuro and Shinjuku. Konosu is closest.

ACCOMMODATIONS

Hyakketsu Onsen (☎ 0493-54-1888).
Saitama-ken Kinrō Seishōnen Friendship Heights (☎ 0493-54-2030). A public facility for young working people, but open to the general public. Near Anrakuji.

USEFUL KANJI

Anrakuji	安楽寺
Ara River	荒川
Higashi Matsuyama	東松山
Hiki Nōkyō	比企農協

CHAPTER 11

Kawagoe	川越
Kitamuki Jizō	北向地蔵
Konosu	鴻巣
Konosu Menkyo Center	鴻巣免許センター
Komyō	古名
Kuroiwa Ketsugun	黒岩穴群
Matsuyama Castle	松山城
Mount Ponpon	ポンポン山
Takao Hikone Shrine	高負彦根神社
Yoshimi Furusato Hodō	吉見ふるさと歩道
Yoshimi Hyakketsu	吉見百穴
Yoshimi Kannon	吉見観音

JIONJI — 12
In the City of Dolls

Iwatsuki, too, was a castle town and seat of government. It briefly became the capital of Saitama Prefecture in the early Meiji period, but then committed itself to obscurity when residents, fearing the consequences of development, rejected a plan to build the junction of the Tōhoku and Takasaki rail lines in the city. The junction was moved to Ōmiya and Iwatsuki became a backwater.

Nothing remains of the central parts of the castle, though there is a small park on what was once its periphery. Iwatsuki is known today as the city of dolls: the place where beautiful Nō dolls and dolls for the boys' and girls' festivals are produced. The city has nearly five hundred doll shops and workshops. The giant Tōgyoku Dolls Land beside the station will show you how to make dolls yourself.

In addition, the walk includes an Edo-period school still perfectly preserved, beautiful Ryūmonji, and at Jionji, a grave of Xuanzang, the great Chinese Buddhist scholar and traveler to India. That sounds incredible but it is true; an unlikely legacy of World War II.

For a city close to Ōmiya in the central, overpopulated part of the Kantō Plain, Iwatsuki offers a surprising range of attractions. Don't expect much from the scenery; but there is plenty to see, even so.

THE TEMPLE

Legend has it that Jionji was founded in 824 by Ennin (794–864), the priest who became the third abbot of the Tendai sect in Japan and converted the temples of Nikkō to Tendai teachings. He is supposed to have spent ten years here from 824 to 834.

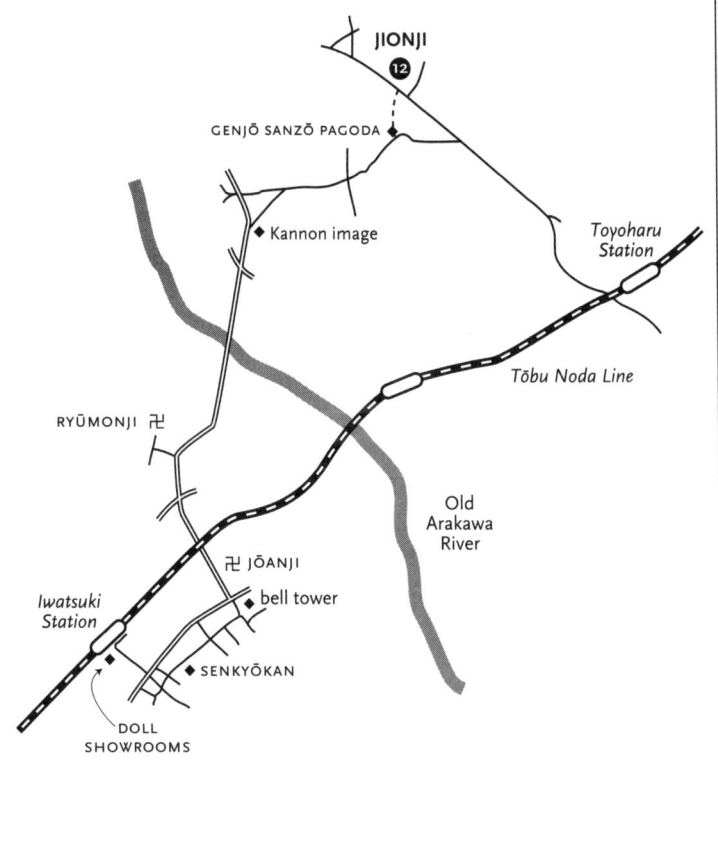

The story tells how Ennin, seeking sacred ground in Nikkō, cast seeds of damson plum to the wind. Later, when he rested at this spot, a damson plum sprouted, grew, and blossomed in a single night. He carved and consecrated a cedar thousand-armed Kannon. Ennin called the temple Jionji because the site resembled that of Daciensi (Daijionji in Japanese), at Changan, the capital of Tang-dynasty China. He set out on a pilgrimage to China himself in 838.

The relationship between Jionji, Daciensi, Iwatsuki, and Nikkō has continued in various forms all the way to modern times. Iwatsuki was a staging post on the Nikkō Onarimichi, the road which the shoguns used from Edo to Nikkō. And just before you reach the temple on the walk described below, there is a tall thirteen-story granite pagoda for the grave of Xuanzang Sanzang, the priest of Daciensi who is known as Genjō Sanzō in Japan.

Xuanzang was born in about 602. He is famous for his seventeen-year journey to India and the translation of many Buddhist works, ranking as one of the key figures in the history of East Asian Buddhism. His translation of the Heart Sutra is particularly famous in Japan. As noted in the introduction, this treatise on the wisdom of the void is one of the basic sutras used by Kannon pilgrims.

The pagoda, however, is recent. This story goes back only to the rape of Nanjing in 1942, when the Japanese army discovered Xuanzang's remains and brought a portion back to Japan. At first they were placed in the great temples of Tokyo, but the priests feared for their safety in the air raids. The ashes had to be saved from the ashes.

Jionji was chosen because Xuanzang did much of his work at Daciensi. The temple built by Ennin, author of Nyūtō Kyūhō Junrei Kōki (Record of a Pilgrimage to Tang China in Search of the Buddhist Teachings), thus become a grave of Xuanzang, the author of a record of a similar journey from China to India. The pagoda was erected in 1950. The ashes have since been further divided between Taiwan and Yakushiji in Nara. Contributions are being collected to erect a statue as well. A Genjō Sanzō festival is held on May 5 every year.

The huge main hall of Jionji was rebuilt in 1843 as one of the largest on the Bandō course. Note the fine paintings, including the huge dragon on the ceiling, and the carving of the Shichifukujin (Seven Gods of Good Fortune) beneath the roof. The Kannon image was brought from Enryakuji in Kyoto in the seventeenth century after the previous one was lost in a fire.

The other statues include the Nijūhachi Bushū (the twenty-eight attendants of the thousand-armed Kannon), Fudō Myōō, Bishamonten, Dainichi, the gods of wind and thunder, Jizō, and Daikokuten. There are separate halls for images of Amida and Jikaku Daishi (Ennin). The Amida was dedicated in 1682 to victims of a great fire in Edo. The autumn festival is held on November 16 and 17.

THE WALK * *(1 hour 15 minutes)*

First, visit the tall Tōgyoku building on the far left corner of the square outside Iwatsuki station. The second and third floors house a variety of dolls for the boys' and girls' festivals; the fourth floor, the Tōgyoku Dolls Museum. Tōgyoku will post your purchases anywhere in the world. Then cross the road to the alley opposite which leads to Tōgyoku Dolls Land (the sign is in English). This has exhibits of Nō and other dolls on the second and third floors and a room for short, practical classes on the fourth. Returning downstairs, you can also visit the workshop in the next building to see how the professionals do it. A recording explains everything in English.

Returning to the road leading from the station square, turn left at the first main junction, following the English road sign to Kasukabe. Turn right fifty meters later at Books Oshida (again, in English). This brings you into a bright little shopping street. The Iwatsuki festival is held here on the last weekend of July each year.

You now approach the former site of the castle through the old town. Take the first left (there is a large fruit shop on the corner).

JIONJI

About one hundred meters along this road, you reach a public library on the left and an old thatched building, the Senkyokan, on the right. The library has rotating displays of local treasures just inside the entrance. The Senkyokan is a domainal school from the Edo period, founded in 1799. Despite limited renovations, the building virtually retains its original appearance. It is open to the public every Saturday from 10:00 to 3:00, with no admission fee. There is not much to see inside, because the forty or so pupils sat on tatami mats. But there are some old Confucian schoolbooks, and you will be able to feel the atmosphere of the schoolroom. It must have been very cold in winter.

Continue along the same road to the end and turn left at the T-junction. You are now close to the former entrance to the castle, but there is no trace of it today. Instead, immediately on the right, you come to a tall bell tower, the toki no kane or time-keeping bell. This bell was forged in 1720 and has sounded the time ever since. It is rung twice daily, at 6:00 AM and 6:00 PM.

Stay on this road across the crossroads. You are now on the Nikkō Onarimichi, the ceremonial road taken by the shoguns from Edo to Nikkō to visit the graves of their ancestors. The Tokugawa shoguns passed this way eighteen times from 1617 until the end of their regime, in increasingly magnificent processions. They generally spent a night at Iwatsuki Castle but sometimes sheltered at Jionji, too. The Onarimichi converged with the better-known Nikkō Kaidō at Satte. One tradition tells how the Iwatsuki doll industry was founded by a sculptor who settled here after helping to build the Tōshōgū Shrine at Nikkō.

You soon reach the entrance to the large temple of Jōanji on the right. The driveway and main building are impressive, but there is not much to see in the grounds. The highlights are an Emma hall and the modern Jizō statue. You might also notice the course of a former railway line that passed between the road and the temple.

A legend tells how a beautiful cherry tree once stood by the belfry of Jōanji. One morning, a boy priest met a lovely girl beside it.

CHAPTER 12

They became close friends. The tree, however, had to be chopped down to make printing blocks for a book by Kodama Nanka, the founder of the Senkyokan school. On the day the tree was felled, the girl appeared to the boy one last time to explain that she was being sacrificed to scholarship.

Stay on the Nikkō Onarimichi past more doll shops and under the railway bridge. The road is busy in our era, too, so this part of the walk isn't much fun. You reach the entrance to Ryūmonji at a bend on the left a little under ten minutes from Jōanji.

Ryūmonji is rather special. The long driveway lined with cherry trees prepares you for the imposing peace and solitude of the temple. A fine Shōmen Kongō stele stands just inside the gate. There is a Fudō hall, plus the usual six Jizōs and, in front of the belfry, a delightful row of statues of the Shichifukujin, the Seven Gods of Good Fortune. An avenue of tall trees leads up to the main hall. Also notice the stone five-storied pagoda grave of the local warlord Ōoka Tadamitsu. Ryūmonji's prize possessions include a Kamakura-period sword that is a designated National Treasure.

The temple's main image is an unusual Amida statue showing three buddhas under a single halo. The fierce Fudō statue, also in the main hall, is known as Tenashi Fudō, the armless Fudo. It used to get out at night and terrify the populace until a samurai lopped off its arms. It has arms today, but they appear to date from the Edo period, while the rest of the statue is of Muromachi design. The temple has several other interesting paintings, prints, and statuettes.

Return to the Nikkō Onarimichi. Two minutes beyond Ryūmonji, there is a Shōmen Kongō stele on the left; then a Jizō in a shelter on the right. The road crosses the former course of the Ara River, reaching a large crossroads seven minutes beyond the bridge.

As noted in the walk for Anrakuji, the Ara was moved west when the Tone was diverted to the east. Here you are about five kilometers from the course of the old Tone at Kasukabe and some twenty kilometers from the confluence at Koshigaya.

Keep straight here, past the Seven-Eleven convenience store. There is a road to the right just afterwards, with a noodle shop on the corner. The lane you want goes off diagonally to the right just a few steps later. The telltale sign is the thousand-armed Kannon stele on the corner. This tells you that you are approaching Jionji.

Thankfully, you now get away from the traffic. In four minutes, you will cross a little star-shaped crossroads. Turn right onto the bigger road fifty meters later and keep straight at the next crossroads. This is a zone of houses, farms and many, many ornamental trees. You will be able to see the main hall of Jionji from quite a distance away.

The walk is almost done. First, you reach the thirteen-story stone pagoda dedicated to Xuanzang. The path down from behind the monument leads directly across present and former paddies to the road in front of the temple. The belfry stands by the roadside.

To reach Toyoharu station on the Tōbu Noda line, turn left out of the temple and follow the road all the way. It takes about twenty-five minutes to the railway. Jōgenji, the temple on the left five minutes down the road, has a small five-story stone pagoda erected in 1494.

TRANSPORTATION

From Tokyo via Ōmiya: JR Saikyō line to Ōmiya from Shinjuku (33 minutes, ¥440) or Ikebukuro (¥370); or JR Takasaki or JR Tōhoku lines to Ōmiya from Ueno (26 minutes, ¥440). Change at Ōmiya for Tōbu Noda line to Iwatsuki (13 minutes, ¥180).

From Tokyo via Kasukabe: Tōbu Nikkō or Tōbu Isesaki lines from Asakusa or Kita Senjū, changing at Kasukabe for Tōbu Noda line to Iwatsuki (about ¥500 total).

ACCOMMODATIONS

Azumaya Ryokan (☎ 0487-56-0159). Five minutes from Iwatsuki station.

CHAPTER 12

USEFUL KANJI

Iwatsuki	岩槻
Jionji	慈恩寺
Jōanji	浄安寺
Kasukabe	春日部
Old Ara River	旧荒川
Ōmiya	大宮
Ryūmonji	龍門寺
Senkyokan	遷喬館
Toyoharu	豊春

SENSŌJI — 13
Tokyo's Shitamachi

Asakusa, once a poor fishing village, grew to be the brilliant entertainment quarter of Edo, the city that became Tokyo. Yet Asakusa still boasts, if not quite a village, at least a small-town atmosphere. The area is a part of Tokyo's Shitamachi (literally, "Downtown") district. The term has many of the connotations of downtown in English, but in Japan is used specifically to describe this low-lying part of Tokyo.

Asakusa is lower class and lively. Homeless people sleep in the station and along the path by the river. The prices are cheap. The neighborhood has a tradition of attracting the literati, including Kawabata Yasunari and Nagai Kafū. The Yoshiwara district to the north of the temple was licensed for prostitution from the Edo period until 1958. This was the world of the Kabuki and the woodblock prints of exotic courtesans. And wherever you go, people want to strike up a conversation.

Sensōji is crowded with visitors every day of the year. It is a must on every sightseeing itinerary for the capital. Besides the temple's own festivities, the Asakusa Shrine has the huge Sanja Festival. The fireworks displays on the Sumida River are famous nationwide.

Since Asakusa is a town of the common people, it is appropriate that the walk should follow a pilgrimage popular in the Edo period: the Asakusa Shichifukujin (Seven Gods of Good Fortune) tour. The Seven Gods of Good Fortune are a mixed bag of varying ancestry. Ebisu, for example, is a native Japanese, while Daikokuten can be traced back to the Hindu god Shiva. They were promoted in the Edo years, however, as a way to keep the people happy. When pilgrims pray to the Shichifukujin, they pray for health, wealth, longevity,

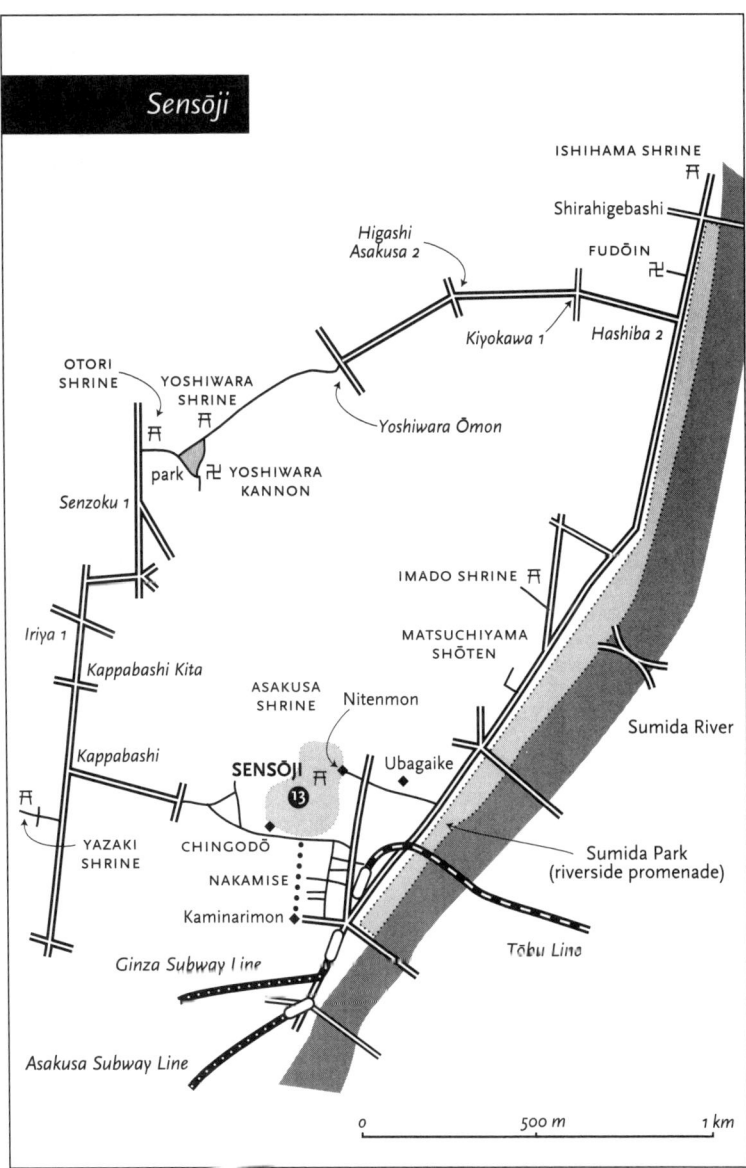

and, in short, whatever immediate benefits their hearts may desire. This walk has nine stops, not seven, as two gods are repeated along the way. It is properly performed at New Year.

The walk is interesting rather than beautiful. From the grand Sensōji to the cherry blossoms of the Sumida River, and from the quiet and diverse temples and shrines of the Shichifukujin to the former prostitution quarter of Yoshiwara, you find a Tokyo that remains in some ways close to its Edo roots.

This closeness is sometimes exaggerated. Edo was a squalid town of dense communal housing where infectious diseases were rife. Money, quick profits, exploitation, and disastrous losses in the fires, earthquakes, and typhoons that swept the city were abiding themes of Edo life. Much of that has gone, as have the grand wooden brothels of Yoshiwara. The banks of the Sumida have been concreted over. But the lower-class pride survives and so does the homely charm. You will want to go again.

THE TEMPLE

Legend traces the origin of Sensōji, also known as Asakusa Kannon, to the year 628, when fishermen netted a golden statue of Kannon. The statue was landed where the Komagata Hall now stands, beside the present Komagata Bridge and directly down the road from the temple's famous outer gate, Kaminarimon, in a straight line from Sensōji. The present approach to the temple along the street of shops known as the Nakamise is thus only half of its former length.

The early temple was restored by Ennin and later became the prayer hall of the shoguns and a hub of Edo culture. The literature says that millions of Japanese pray here each month. Judging from the perpetual crowds, that is easy to believe. The temple has a venerable history, but most of its structures are newly made from ferroconcrete. Almost everything was destroyed in the air raids of World

War II. The main hall was rebuilt in 1958, Kaminarimon in 1960, and the pagoda in 1973. The concrete is not ugly. Sensōji remains a grand and beautiful temple.

First visit the Asakusa Culture Tourist Center opposite Kaminarimon. The center has English-speaking staff and plenty of detailed literature written in several languages. Then, to the gate itself. Fūjin, god of the wind, stands in the niche on the right of Kaminarimon and Raijin, god of thunder, on the left. Two dragon gods were placed at the rear in 1978 to commemorate Sensōji's 1,350th anniversary.

Nakamise, the street of shops leading from the gate to the main hall, is a place to buy Tokyo souvenirs, traditional sweets, and accessories. Before passing through the inner gate, don't neglect to turn left a short way down Dembōin-dōri to the little temple called Chingodō. Chingodō is the *tanuki* (raccoon dog) temple. Many *tanuki* lived around Sensōji in the nineteenth century, but lost their range when walls were built around the temple in 1871. Soon, *tanuki* were being blamed for all sorts of mischief, from stealing clogs to possessing daughters. The *tanuki* temple was built in 1872 to give them, figuratively at least, a haven. Chingodō became popular with Kabuki actors and other entertainers on account of the *tanuki*'s legendary ability to change its form. The little courtyard has many *tanuki* dolls. In addition, it offers a glimpse of the seventeenth-century garden of the Dembōin guesthouse.

Return then to the inner gate, with its *niō* statues and huge straw sandals (*waraji*). Such sandals are variously associated with ascetic mountain priests and Sai no Kami, the non-Buddhist god of the road. Some Bandō pilgrims still wear waraji as an essential part of their garb.

The pagoda contains ashes said to be of Sakyamuni, the historical Buddha, presented by a Sri Lankan temple. You can take a look inside on the dates of Sakyamuni's enlightenment, death, and birth: December 8, February 15, and April 8, respectively.

Following around the courtyard from the pagoda, the small halls are dedicated to Yakushi, Fudō Myōō, Benten, Ebisu, Daikokuten, Kokuzō, and various Jizōs. The sealed gold-plated shrine inside the main hall is said to house the main image but no one has been allowed to see it for more than 1,300 years. A legend persists that some foolhardy souls did glimpse it in the Meiji era and quickly succumbed to untimely deaths.

Asakusa Shrine, to the right of the main hall, is dedicated to the fishermen who found the Kannon statue. The gate beside it, Nitenmon (built in 1618), survived the air raids. Continuing clockwise, you see a hall consecrated to Amida and a belfry, which stands atop an ancient tumulus.

Annual events at and around Sensōji:

January 1–3: Hatsumode (first temple visit of the New Year).
February 3: Setsubun (bean-scattering ceremony).
March 18: Golden Dragon Dance.
April (first or second Saturday): Sumida Park Cherry Blossom Festival beside the river. Includes *yabusame* (horseback archery; this may take place on the third Saturday in April, but check).
May (third Sat and Sun): Sanja Festival. One of Tokyo's three big festivals. Features a procession of about a hundred *omikoshi* (portable shrines).
July 9–10: Hōzuki no Ichi (Lantern Plant Market).
Late July: Fireworks on the Sumida River.
August 15: Lantern Festival.
Late August: Asakusa Samba Carnival, a recent import from Rio.
October (first or second Sunday): Edo Mikoshi Festival.
October 18: Golden Dragon Dance.
November 3: White Heron Dance.
November 15: Shichigosan Festival (for children aged 3, 5, and 7)
December 17-19: Hagoita Ichi (Battledore Market).
December 31: New Year's Eve; *jōya no kane* (ceremonial tolling of the temple bells).

CHAPTER 13

THE WALK * *(2 hours)*

The walk follows the Asakusa Shichifukujin (Seven Gods of Good Fortune) pilgrimage. The first stop on the route is Sensōji itself, where Daikokuten is enshrined. The second is Asakusa Shrine, still inside the precincts of Sensōji, just to the right of the main hall. Ebisu is enshrined there.

Leave the temple by the Nitenmon gate beyond Asakusa Shrine and continue straight towards the river. A park on the left contains several monuments and what remains of Ubagaike, a pond that once connected with the Sumida River. A legend tells of a bad old woman transformed into a dragon who finally, upon achieving enlightenment, disappeared into this pond.

Turn left up the river, either on the promenade or through the park with the cherry blossoms that runs alongside. Descend to the street at the next bridge. The third stop, Matsuchiyama Shōten, stands on a corner just a short way beyond. After the bustle of Sensōji, this small temple is a haven of tranquillity. Bishamonten is enshrined here. Ask for the English-language brochure; a famous print by Hiroshige shows how this hilltop temple above the Sumida River looked in the Edo period.

Here, too, we have a dragon legend. When the country was afflicted by drought in the reign of Empress Suiko (r. 593–628), the hill rose up in a single day, a dragon descended from heaven, and heavy rain fell. The formal name of Sensōji, Kinryūzan (the Golden Dragon), also refers to this story.

The temple today is the place to pray not only for success in business but also for sexual prowess. The pair of entwined giant radishes on the front of the main hall are a phallic image. The temple has a radish festival on January 7. The symbolism is so heavy that you might prefer not to think about what you are eating.

Stay by the riverside park as far as the sports center, then take the left fork, passing a small temple close to the corner. The fourth stop, Imado Shrine, is a short way beyond. Imado is the shrine to Fukurokuju. Very modern and simple, its courtyard has become a parking lot. Even so, quite a few *ema* with down-to-earth wishes about boyfriends and girlfriends are hung around the two sacred trees.

Return to the river and continue upstream along the promenade. It is a long way to the next bridge, Shirahigebashi, but the promenade is pleasantly constructed. The end of the promenade has no exit. Leave it by the last flight of steps more than a hundred meters before the bridge and continue on the path between the apartment blocks and the embankment.

Cross the road at the bridge. The fifth stop, Ishihama Shrine, lies on the left side of the riverside road a short way beyond. Its location today by the gas tanks, main road, and apartment blocks is almost a parody of urban bleakness, but upon entering the grounds you step into a world apart. Ishihama, the shrine for Jurōjin, is the most delightful of the nine. The highlight is the great pile of volcanic rocks on the right of the main hall, sporting banners of the White Fox God.

The real Mount Fuji can be seen from this stretch of the Sumida River. Looking closely, this little replica of Mount Fuji is a fantastic amalgam, featuring the gods of the Fuji, Inari, and Hachiman shrines; Kōshin stones with their distinctive monkeys; the Shinto deity Sarutahiko; a horse-crowned Kannon; and the god of Hakusan. The various components were gathered from elsewhere as each became displaced by construction projects.

Now return to Shirahigebashi and, recrossing the road, continue straight down the road on the other side back towards Asakusa. You quickly come to the sixth stop, Fudōin, a tiny temple down a lane to the right. Everything in this enclave is small scale, including the potted plants that line the lane in front of the houses. From the bleak world of the mountain gods, Fudōin brings you down to the Shitamachi of ordinary folk. Fudō Myōō is the main image. There is also a small Jizō hall on the right. On the Asakusa Shichifukujin circuit, this is the stop for Hotei.

Return to the road and keep going on towards Asakusa. Turn right at the junction marked Hashiba 2 in Western script (indicating that this is Hashiba 2-chōme in the block-numbering system

CHAPTER 13

used throughout Tokyo). You now have a long walk down a couple of connected shopping streets. Keeping straight all the while past the Kiyokawa 1-chōme and Higashi Asakusa 2-chōme junctions, you eventually arrive at a junction marked Yoshiwara Ōmon.

In the Edo period, the Ōmon was the only gate to Yoshiwara, the quarter set aside for licensed prostitution. The gate kept the prostitutes inside and also prevented their customers from escaping without paying. The scrawny willow is a reminder of the other willow that once stood at the gateway to the floating world. The real gate was just a short way from here. In the old days, Yoshiwara was entered across a small bridge.

The walls and the stream are gone, but immediately, upon crossing the junction, the atmosphere changes. The old buildings with their "cages" for the women were destroyed in the air raids, and it is hard to believe that this street used to be more lively than the Ginza. But smart pimps line the streets; there are many twilight establishments; and a short way down on the right you come to the ancient-looking Matsubaya (☎ 03-3874-9401), a restaurant that maintains the customs of the area with shows by *oiran*, high-class courtesans. They perform music and the dances; there is no suggestion that they also engage in the defining service of the trade. Matsubaya is popular with bus tours. It serves both traditional Japanese *kaiseki* dishes and sukiyaki. Reservations are not necessary, but it is worth inquiring in advance. Shows typically start at 7:00 PM.

Yoshiwara Shrine, the seventh stop, is the place to pray to Benzaiten. This small shrine is on the right side of the road some twenty-five minutes from Hashiba 2-chōme. It was founded in the Meiji era when the five former shrines of Yoshiwara were combined.

You next reach a tiny park on the right. This park used to have a pond. During the great earthquake of 1923, when Yoshiwara burned as it did many times in its history, many women died after jumping into the pond to escape the flames. The hospital on the corner was founded in the Meiji period to treat sexual diseases.

SENSŌJI

A few meters further on the left, the distinctive Yoshiwara Kannon, oft-mentioned in Edo-period literature, stands high atop a tall rock. This, too, was a place where distraught women prayed for protection and mercy. You have now crossed Yoshiwara from end to end.

Return to the park on the bend and leave by the lane on the other side. Turn right at the T-junction. Continue to the main road and turn right again. The eighth stop, Ōtori Shrine, is a short way up on the right. This shrine, too, is very small. Like Ishihama, the shrine has an image of Jurōjin. Ōtori Shrine is famous for its Tori no Ichi, the colorful markets held on the days of the rooster (according to the traditional zodiac) that fall in the month of November.

Now return down the main road and keep straight (not left with the main road) at the Senzoku 1-chōme junction. Go right at the next traffic lights and left at the traffic lights after that, where the road bends ninety degrees. You are now on a broad modern shopping street.

Keep going across the Iriya 1-chōme, Kappabashi Kita, and Kappabashi junctions. You will probably notice the shop selling sample plastic meals at Kappabashi. For the ninth and final stop, Yazaki Shrine, take the fourth small street to the right (opposite Ohtsuya) after Kappabashi. You first pass a temple on your right. The rather modern Yazaki Shrine stands on the next corner. Like Imado Shrine, it is a stop for Fukurokuju. A hundred paintings on the ceilings show famous historical figures on horseback.

To finish, return to Kappabashi junction and turn right down the cheerful shopping street. This leads through the heart of Asakusa, past diverse shops, bars, and a *rakugo* theater (a venue for a traditional performing art akin to stand-up comedy), back to Sensōji.

TRANSPORTATION

Asakusa, Ginza, or Tōbu lines to Asakusa. On the Ginza line, take the exit for Kaminarimon. On the Asakusa line, turn right out of exit A4 to reach the main road close to Kaminarimon. From

Tōbu Asakusa station, cross the road to the right as you exit the station and walk through the arcade to reach the Nakamise in between Kaminarimon and the main hall. Asakusa can also be reached by boat from Hinode Pier near Hamamatsuchō station on the JR Yamanote line.

ACCOMMODATIONS

Asakusa View Hotel, a large Western-style hotel, stands close to Sensōji. (☎ 03-3847-1111). There are many inexpensive hotels in the area, including capsule hotels, with rates from ¥3,000.

USEFUL KANJI

Asakusa	浅草
Asakusa Shrine	浅草神社
Chingodō	鎮護堂
Dembōin-dōri	伝法院通り
Fudōin	不動院
Imado Shrine	今戸神社
Ishihama Shrine	石浜神社
Matsuchiyama Shōten	待乳山聖天
Ōtori Shrine	鷲神社
Sensōji	浅草寺
Yazaki Shrine	矢先神社
Yoshiwara	吉原
Yoshiwara Kannon	吉原観音
Yoshiwara Shrine	吉原神社

GUMYŌJI — 14
*The Port of Yokohama * (1 hour 30 minutes)*

Gumyōji is Yokohama's oldest and best-hidden delight. Gyōki is said to have founded the temple and carved the main eleven-headed Kannon image from zelkova wood in 737, though experts believe that the statue, a National Treasure, really dates from the mid-Heian period. Unusually for the Bandō circuit, the statue is on display. See also the distinctive gate with its huge red lantern, six Jizōs and Kosodate (Child-Raising) Kannon, the statues and mandala of the main hall, and the Shōten hall with its statue of the male and female forms of Shōten (depicted as elephants) embracing. The temple serves *shōjin ryōri*, the vegetarian food of Buddhist monastics, although this must be booked in advance (☎ 045-715-0224). It costs ¥5,000 yen per person and is served to groups of five to eighty people. The walk down the Ōoka River Promenade traces the history of Yokohama to the sea. You reach the former coast of Shūkan Bay where the river branches. The land beyond was reclaimed for paddy cultivation by Yoshida Kambe in 1611–68. See the old shrines from that period, then continue down the river to Sakuragichō and the Mirai 21 (Future 21) developments around Landmark Tower (including Yokohama Maritime Museum, Yokohama Museum of Art, and Cosmo World amusement park).

TRANSPORTATION
Outbound:
From Tokyo to Gumyōji: Keihin Kyūkō line from Shinagawa to Gumyōji (¥340). There is also a Gumyōji station on the Yokohama Municipal Subway, which runs between Sakuragichō and Totsuka.

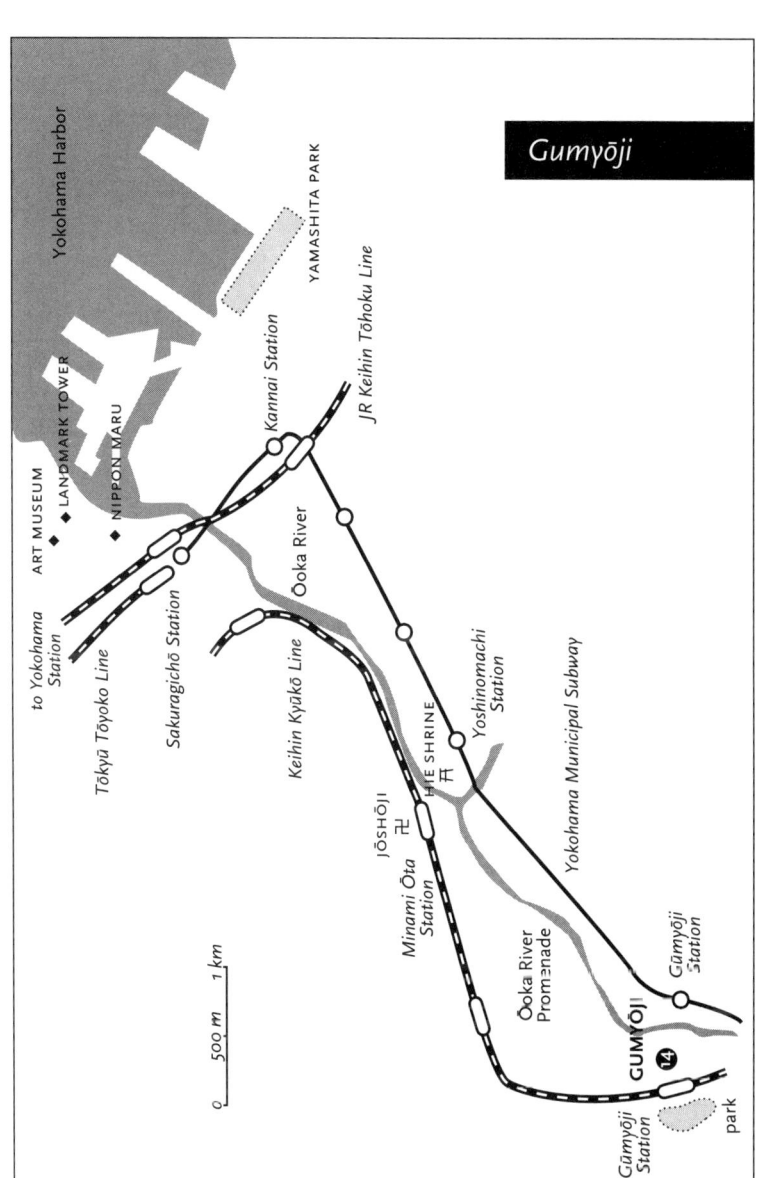

GUMYŌJI

Return:

From Sakuragicho: Tōkyū Tōyoko line to Shibuya(¥290); JR Keihin Tōhoku line to Tokyo; or Yokohama Municipal Subway to Totsuka.

Boats from the Mirai 21 pier offer harbor cruises, a shuttle to Yamashita Park, and infrequent long distance services to Hinode Pier near Hamamatsucho Station in Tokyo and Funabashi in Chiba.

ACCOMMODATIONS

Nakazato Onsen Ryokan (☎ 045 731 1454). Japanese-style hot spring inn. Behind Gumyōji Park.

USEFUL KANJI

Gumyōji	弘明寺
Hie Shrine	日枝神社
Jōshōji	常照寺
Ōoka River	大岡川
Seki Shrine	堰神社
Yokohama	横浜

CHŌKOKUJI — 15
Minowa Castle, Mount Haruna, and Ikaho Hot Spring

Only two of the Bandō temples are located in Gunma Prefecture. Despite being the base of historical leaders ranging from Nitta Yoshisada to Nakasone Yasuhiro, Gunma has always been something of a backwater in the affairs of state and culture. The traveler seeking places with tradition and unspoilt scenery will recognize this as a recommendation.

The first of two walks roams the foothills of Mount Haruna close to Chōkokuji. The rolling rural scenery is pleasantly varied. There is a lake that will delight birdwatchers. Then come the massive remains of Minowa Castle, which contain no fewer than six walking courses around the moats and earthworks.

The second walk (see the map for Chapter 16) is for mountain hikers. You must start early if you want to see the temple and do the walk on the same day. Aim to catch the first bus of the morning from Takasaki station and note the times of subsequent buses to Lake Haruna to avoid a long wait after visiting Chōkokuji.

The reward is a fabulous volcanic landscape of towering peaks, crags, and a great lake in the center of the caldera. Haruna, a composite volcano with multiple peaks, is still ranked as a live one, though the most recent eruption, at the peak called Futatsudake, occurred in the sixth century. Archaeologists are currently excavating the ruins of a village at Kuroimine that was completely buried by pumice from the eruption. The Sōma and Fuji peaks were formed around eleven thousand years ago.

After walking around the rim, you also have a delightful stroll down through natural woods of oak, alder, birch, and maple to the open air hot spring at Ikaho. The birds along the way include brown

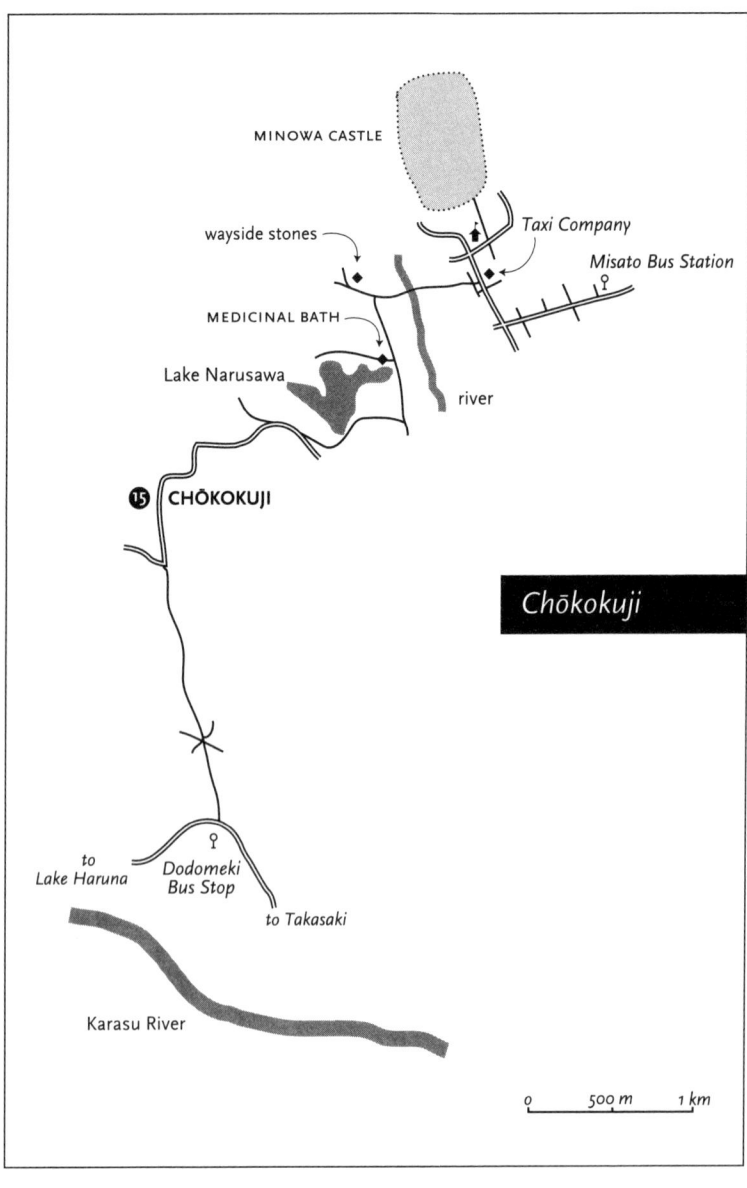

shrikes, narcissus and black paradise flycatchers, siberian blue robins, and cuckoos in summer, plus winter visitors such as long-tailed rose finches, siskins, bramblings, and hawfinches. You may see sparrow hawks and honey buzzards, too.

Unfortunately the area around Lake Haruna is overdeveloped. This ceases to mar the scenery once the path bends towards Mount Sōma.

THE TEMPLE

Chōkokuji is a small temple hemmed in between the road and the hillside. It is, however, neat and attractive, despite its unfortunate modern-day location. Entering from the front, you first see some fascinating stones at the entrance. They include a tall Twenty-Second Night pillar (commemorating a traditional vigil held on this night of each month) and a small pair of gods on a mirror-shaped stone carved in 1739. At first sight, these look like *dōsōjin*, or gods of the road, but in fact they are Ebisu and Daikokuten, two gods of wealth.

The red-lacquered *niōmon* and main hall are beautifully kept, and the hall is ornate inside. You can see the lower half of the *maedachi* Kannon (the Kannon statue that stands in front of the main image), which dates from the Kamakura period, through the altar grating. The main image itself, an eleven-headed Kannon, was carved from *kaya* wood in the mid-Heian period, making it the oldest extant statue in Gunma Prefecture. You will not be allowed to see it.

The temple flourished as a base for ascetic practices through the medieval period, but was burned in the 1560s as the army of Takeda Shingen advanced on Minowa Castle. The present hall was built in 1580. It has been renovated many times since and looks quite new.

Chōkokuji lays claim to many of the famous names of history. It is variously said to have been founded by En no Gyōja, the Nara-period ascetic, and Tokudō Shōnin, the priest of Hasedera in Yamato who created Japan's first Kannon pilgrimage route. One legend attributes the main image to Gyōki, while another says that it was discovered floating in the sea. Both Saichō and Kūkai are said to have prayed here. The temple also received the patronage of Minamoto Yoritomo and Nitta Yoshisada. In its heyday, little Chōkokuji was one of great foundations of northern Kantō.

WALK A ** *(2 hours 30 minutes)*
Chōkokuji, Lake Narusawa, and Minowa Castle

Alighting at Dodomeki, cross the road and go up the lane on the other side. A stone on the corner carries the characters for Shiraiwa Kannon. A Jizō with a red bib stands beneath a shelter a few steps up on the right.

You reach a six-way junction four minutes along the road. Kōshin, Jizō, and horse-headed Kannon stones stand on the left. The flat stone in a shelter on the fork straight ahead, beside the stone with a simple Jizō carving, is an old road marker; it is a designated Cultural Treasure of the town of Haruna. Take the right fork at this marker (the third road counting either clockwise or counterclockwise).

As the road climbs through paddies and mulberry fields, the houses get steadily fewer and the view becomes quite broad. Turn right (actually straight) at the junction with a larger road. The temple is two hundred meters further on the left.

After viewing the temple, leave by the rear entrance and continue along the same road. You reach a *dōsōjin* stele and another old road marker five minutes up the road on the left. This one is dated 1692 and was placed here for pilgrims. It reads Haruna to the left and Mizusawa to the right, the way you are going.

You enter Misato Town (the sign is in English) some five minutes from here, and six minutes later there is another junction where the sign (again in Roman letters) reads Misato Bairin. This is the entrance to the Narusawa Nature Trail, which circles the lake. Misato Bairin means Misato Plum Blossom Forest. In season, turn left here to view the blossoms. Otherwise, I suggest continuing another minute along the road to take the second entrance to the nature trail, where the route leads directly down to the lake. A map of the entire Narusawa course is posted at this second junction.

The course from the second turning descends quickly to the embankment at the lip of the lake. Lake Narusawa was created in this century as an irrigation reservoir for the paddies. Work started in 1938 and was completed in 1950. The view down the valley from the steep embankment is quite spectacular. But more than that, this quiet, little-known lake is a paradise for ducks and other wild birds.

Keep straight along the road past the school and turn left at the T-junction to return quickly to the shore. The main route to the castle continues up this road but first turn left along the shore to see a bit more of the lake. The large building close to the junction is Chikōyakuyu, a medicinal bath center. Although the facility is intended mainly for the elderly, you are welcome to drop in for a bath, and can even stay the night for the various treatments.

Returning to the main route, you should continue up the road and turn right at the next main junction. But first keep going for another fifty meters to see the fantastic collection of wayside stones at the next fork. They include a pair of *dōsōjin*, the six-handed Shōmen Kongō, a seated Amida, a Twenty-Second Night stone and a horse-headed Kannon. A maple tree rises in the center.

Retracing your steps those fifty meters, cross the bridge (there is a good view of Mount Haruna) and go straight up the hill on the other side. Keeping straight, you come to the main street of Misato (a taxi company stands on the other side of the road at the junction). Turn left here to reach another school in two minutes.

A map of Minowa Castle is posted outside the school, with your present position shown at the bottom. Beside the school, there are bus stops for Takasaki, Ikaho, and Shibukawa. The buses aren't frequent so you might target a convenient one now. Alternatively, there are many buses to Takasaki and also to Maebashi from the bus station, which is shown on the map in this book.

Enter the castle by the Kannon route, taking the lane between the school and the football fields. This leads to Hōbōji, temple number thirty-two on the former Gunma Kannon pilgrimage. Take the sign to the left a short way before the temple. Then follow the Chūō (central) course to the heart of the fortress.

Minowa Castle was built by the Nagano family in either 1512 or 1526, depending on which source you consult. The Nagano long resisted assaults by the Hōjō and the Takeda, but the castle finally fell to the huge 15,000-strong army of Takeda Shingen in 1566. Nagano Narimori died by his own sword.

Minowa Castle switched hands several times thereafter, until Tokugawa Ieyasu presented it to Ii Naomasa of Hikone in 1590. Naomasa at first implemented substantial improvements to create the castle that we see today. But soon after, in 1598, he moved his base to Wada Castle in Takasaki and Minowa fell into disuse.

At this point the author is happy to abandon you in the middle of a fascinating medieval maze. There is enough scrambling around to keep you happy here all day, and some of the earthworks are staggering even now. You know where the bus stops are, so explore!

WALK B ** (3 hours)
Mount Haruna and Ikaho Hot Spring

The walk around the rim of Mount Haruna and down to Ikaho Hot Spring is one of the scenic highlights of this book. (For the route of this walk, please refer to the map for Chapter 16.) It is best done from late October to very early November to see the autumn colors, but offers attractive views throughout the year. The course should, however, be treated with great caution in winter.

Alight at Tenjin Pass at the lip of the caldera. A Kantō Fureai no Michi sign points up the narrow lane to the right, past a tall stone lantern that was originally erected at the old pass in 1815 and moved here in 1982. You join the Kantō Fureai no Michi on its way up from Haruna Shrine just a few meters beyond the lantern. The sign to the right ("Haruna Jinja 1.9 km") is for the shrine, that to the left for Yaseone Pass. Go left.

The scenery is already spectacular, with the tall conical peaks of Haruna rising above the crater lake, the neighboring mountains, and the Kantō Plain below. The highest peak, Haruna Fuji, is the perfect cone on the far side of the lake with a cable car running up the side.

Around this time, you will curse me for all of the steps. This is a problem with the Kantō Fureai no Michi which becomes chronic in places like Haruna where most slopes are steep. For the sake of your legs, avoid the steps from the start. Use the narrow but well-trodden paths up and down the sides. The main path gets more sensible later on. The top of the first peak is reached in about ten minutes, followed by an equally steep descent on the other side. The climb then starts over again, reaching the next major peak, Tenmoku, half an hour from the bus stop. All this time, the path wends around the rim of the caldera right above the lake.

This large natural body of water is, like artificial Lake Narusawa below, an important irrigation resource. The waters of Lake Haruna were first tapped at the order of the lord of Takasaki in the early seventeenth century. The improved waterway down from Tenjin Pass was completed in 1904. The lake, as is obvious from the ridge, is also well-utilized for recreation.

Descending Tenmoku, the lake is gradually left behind as the ridge bends slowly around towards Mount Sōma. The path crosses two roads, continuing directly across each time. Now you reach the best part, for the craggy ridge that leads to the towering peak of Mount Sōma has the kind of scenery that must normally be invented by artists. Take the left fork beneath the wooden shrine gate a couple of minutes after the largest outcrop. You pick up the Kantō Fureai no Michi signs for Yaseone Pass immediately. The rest house with benches soon after has a grand view of the plain. You reach the first red gate for Sōma Shrine one minute later, and soon must climb a long flight of stone steps.

The path divides at the next gate: up to the right for the final ascent of Mount Sōma, or straight on to Yaseone Pass. If you still have the time and energy, the climb up Sōma is recommended. Most people, however, will feel that they have done enough climbing for one day. If so, turn left for the gentle path through the woods to Yaseone Pass. After all of the dramatic scenery, the quiet woods add an extra dimension to the walk.

Turn right onto the road at the pass and right again immediately, following the Kantō Fureai no Michi signs. A large map of the next leg of the Kantō Fureai no Michi stands on the corner. This is a back entrance to the Ikaho Woodland Park (Ikaho Shinrin Kōen).

The route divides five minutes from the pass: right to Futatsudake and left to Ikaho Hot Spring. Go left. The path down the wooded, boulder-strewn valley is a sheer delight. Turn right at the road at the bottom and left two minutes later at the sign for Ikaho. This is where you leave the Kantō Fureai no Michi, which continues along the road to Ikaho skating center. You should, however, first climb up fifty meters to see the Washi no Su Cave, a natural wind hole.

The route down to Ikaho follows the old road, now disused, which pilgrims from Ikaho used to climb to Futatsudake. No vehicles could possibly use it any more so the way down is perfectly tranquil. At the bottom, you can enjoy a bath in the public open-air hot spring. To enter, cross the bridge and turn right. You will see a place for drinking the hot spring waters on your left. The entrance to the public open-air bath lies fifty meters up the road. Admission is only ¥200. Beer and other refreshments are served in the bath.

Ikaho Hot Spring lies at an altitude of seven to eight hundred meters. The spring is thought to have originated with the eruption of Futatsudake around 600 AD. It was already famous in the Nara period, and appears in the famous collection of classical poems, the *Man'yōshū*. The spring has also been favored by literati of the modern era, most notably the Meiji novelist Tokutomi Roka (1868–1927) and the Taishō artist Takehisa Yumeji (1884–1934). Each has a museum dedicated to his life and works. The Yumeji museum also has a music-box museum attached. A further attraction is the former villa of the Hawaiian ambassador beside the Roka museum.

For those with less refined tastes, the sex industry thrives here. Ikaho could be described as the Yoshiwara of Gunma Prefecture, and you are likely to enjoy the sight of tattooed gangsters in the bath.

The bus stops are ten minutes further down the road. English signs point the way to Ikaho Shrine, the Street of Stone Steps (the stepped main street of this hot spring town), the ropeway (cable car) up to the skating center, and also the bus stops. The tourist information office by the Tōbu bus stop has a free English pamphlet outlining the tourist attractions, including the Ikaho Festival from September 18–20 every year.

TRANSPORTATION
Outbound:

Tokyo to Takasaki: Jōetsu Shinkansen from Tokyo or Ueno; or Takasaki line from Ueno or Ikebukuro. The Shinkansen takes 50 minutes and costs a little over ¥4,000; ordinary fare is about half of this. Express services also run from Ueno.

Takasaki to Dodomeki: Bus to Lake Haruna or Muroda via Hongō (first bus 7:40 or 7:50) from stand number 4. If taking a Muroda bus, check with the driver that you are on the right one (25 minutes, ¥450).

Takasaki or Dodomeki to Tenjin Pass: Bus to Lake Haruna. 1 hour 20 minutes from Takasaki; 55 minutes from Dodomeki. Buses to Lake Haruna leave Takasaki at 7:25 (weekdays), 8:30, 9:30 (Sundays and holidays), 10:30, 11:30 (not during winter), and 12:30.

Return:

From Misato: Buses run to Takasaki, Maebashi, Shibukawa, and Ikaho. The Takasaki service is very frequent.

From Ikaho: Tōbu buses go to Shibukawa for JR trains to Takasaki. Gunma buses go to Takasaki and Maebashi. Gunma buses stop at Mizusawa (Temple 16 on the Bandō pilgrimage route) on the way down.

ACCOMMODATIONS

Chikōyakuyu (☎ 0273-71-3372). Medicinal bath near Chōkokuji. Aimed at the elderly, it promises to restore your "life-force." You can also receive chiropractic therapy. Daytime prices for the bath are ¥1,800 from morning; ¥1,400 from 2:00 pm; and ¥700 from 5:00 pm until the bath closes at 6:30. The overnight charge with two meals starts at ¥5,000, excluding the entry fee, but this is intended for those receiving treatment.

Ikaho has sixty-four hotels and *ryokan* with prices from ¥6,000 to ¥100,000. Contact Ikaho Onsen Kankō Kyōkai (Ikaho Hot Spring Tourist Association; ☎ 0279-72-3151). ¥8,000–20,000 a night is typical. Reservations necessary.

USEFUL KANJI

Chōkokuji	長谷寺
Dodomeki	ドドメキ
Futatsudake	二ツ岳
Haruna Shrine	榛名神社
Hōbōji	法峯寺
Hongō	本郷
Ikaho	伊香保
Ikaho Shinrin Kōen	伊香保森林公園
Kantō Fureai no Michi	関東ふれあいの道
Lake Haruna	榛名湖
Lake Narusawa	鳴沢湖
Maebashi	前橋
Minowa Castle	箕輪城
Misato	箕郷
Mount Fuji	榛名山
Mount Haruna	富士山
Mount Sōma	相馬山

CHAPTER 15

Mount Tenmoku	天目山
Muroda	室田
Shibukawa	渋川
Shiraiwa Kannon	白岩観音
Takasaki	高崎
Tenjin Pass	天神峠
Washi no Su Cave	ワシノ巣風穴
Yaseone Pass	ヤセオネ峠

MIZUSAWADERA — 16
Mount Mizusawa and Ikaho Hot Spring */ ***
(Walk A: 1 hour 10 minutes / Walk B: 3 hours)

Mizusawadera is one of the most attractive temples on the Bandō circuit. The lovely Edo-period buildings stand on the wooded flanks of Mount Haruna beneath the conical Mount Mizusawa. The temple, said to have been founded during the reign of Empress Suiko (r. 593–628), is tastefully ornate. Sights include a rotating hexagonal pagoda containing Jizō statues, the *niōmon* with its statues of Sakyamuni, Monju, and Fugen, and the seven-hundred-year-old Mizusawa Kannon cedar. The main image is a thousand-armed Kannon from the Kamakura period. Also try the local delicacy outside the temple gates, the noodles known as Mizusawa *udon*.

A choice of walks is offered. The easy one is the stroll to the seventy-two-meter Funao Falls. The second is scenically excellent, commanding a grand sweep of the Kantō Plain and the surrounding peaks. Be warned, however, that the path up to Mount Mizusawa is steep and deeply eroded. Treat this one as a serious hike. The trail leads down the other side to Ikaho Woodland Park (Ikaho Shinrin Kōen), which has glorious azaleas and maples. See the Washi no Su Cave, then finish down the broad wooded trail to the open-air hot spring at Ikaho described in the second walk in chapter 15.

TRANSPORTATION
Outbound:
From Tokyo to Takasaki: see Chapter 15.
Buses from Takasaki to Mizusawa: Gunma Bus Company. North side of station, bus stand number 6. Morning buses to Ikaho at 8:50, 9:55, 11:20. Last bus 6:25 pm. Alight at Mizusawa (1 hour,

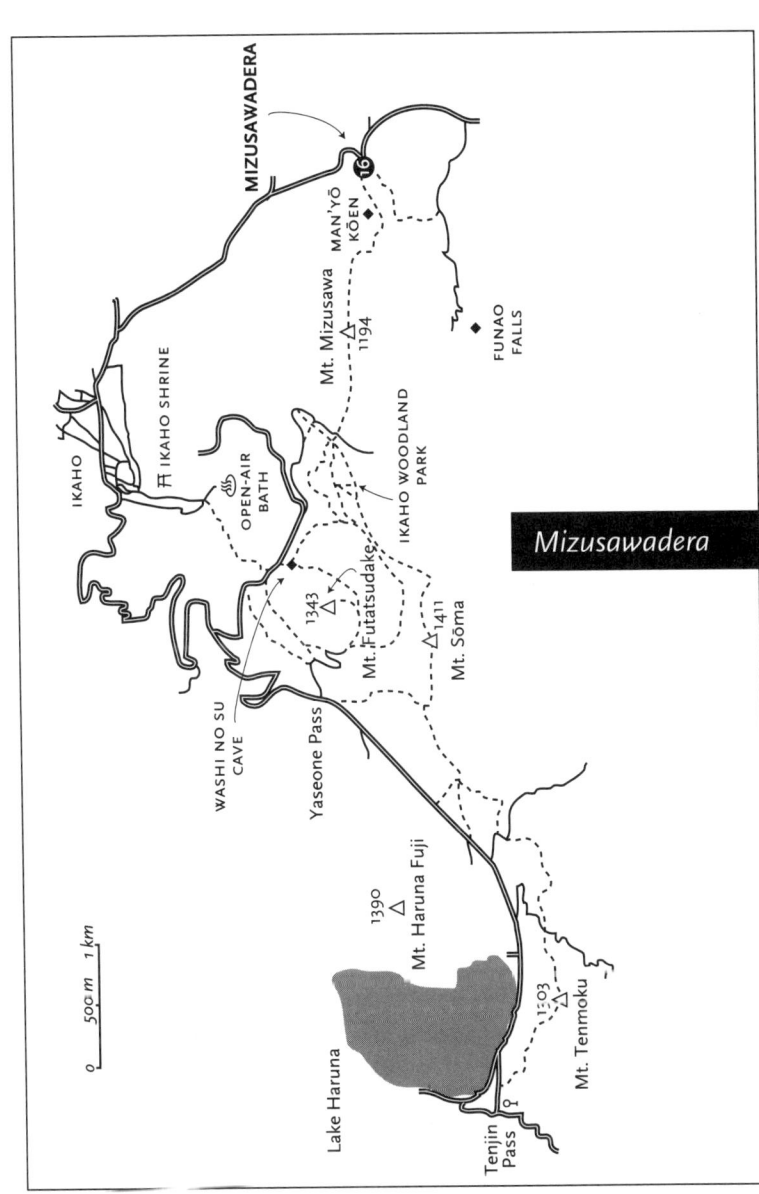

¥690). Also two buses daily from Maebashi station to Ikaho via Mizusawa at 8:15 am and 6:00 pm (45 minutes).

For the return from Ikaho, see Chapter 15.

ACCOMMODATIONS

For Ikaho, see Chapter 15. There are also quite a few "love hotels" at Mizusawa.

USEFUL KANJI

Funao Falls	船尾滝
Ikaho Hot Spring	伊香保温泉
Ikaho Shinrin Kōen	伊香保森林公園
Maebashi	前橋
Mizusawadera	水沢寺
Mount Haruna	榛名山
Mount Mizusawa	水沢山
Mount Sōma	相馬山
Takasaki	高崎
Washi no Su Cave	ワシノ巣風穴

MANGANJI — 17
Mountain Priests and Neanderthals

Manganji is special in all sorts of ways. This was not the first Bandō temple that I visited but it was the one that persuaded me to see them all. I have since heard and read others say the same.

Unlike many Bandō temples, today hemmed in by houses and roads, Manganji retains huge grounds. It has a mountain, a small waterfall, ferns, cedar woods, grottoes, paths, statues, and stones. The neighboring peaks are steep and pointed. Below, the temple village of Izuru remains just that, a temple village, albeit one that receives half a million visitors annually.

Legend declares that everybody came to this backwater: En no Gyōja, the first great ascetic; Gyōki, whose name appears so often on the Bandō course; Shōdō Shōnin, the priest who opened Nikkō; and Kūkai, the founder of the Shingon sect, who is said to have dedicated the main Kannon image.

Manganji ranks as one of the chief temples of the Chisan school of the Shingon sect, together with the famous institutions of Chishakuin in Kyoto, Shinshōji in Narita, Heigenji (Kawasaki Daishi) in Kanagawa, Yakuōin on Takao, Konkōji (Takahatasan) in Hino, and Hōshōji (Osu Kannon) in Nagoya.

The walk first ascends Mount Senbugatake at the rear of the temple for a glorious view of Mount Nantai and the Ashio Mountains. The village of Izuru lies at the southern tip of this range. Descending to the valley and crossing the next spur, it then continues down the Nagano River to Hoshino, the site of some of the oldest hominid remains in Japan. Slate tools discovered there were possibly made by Neanderthal man. These can be seen at the Hoshino Archaeological Museum together with a cluster of recon-

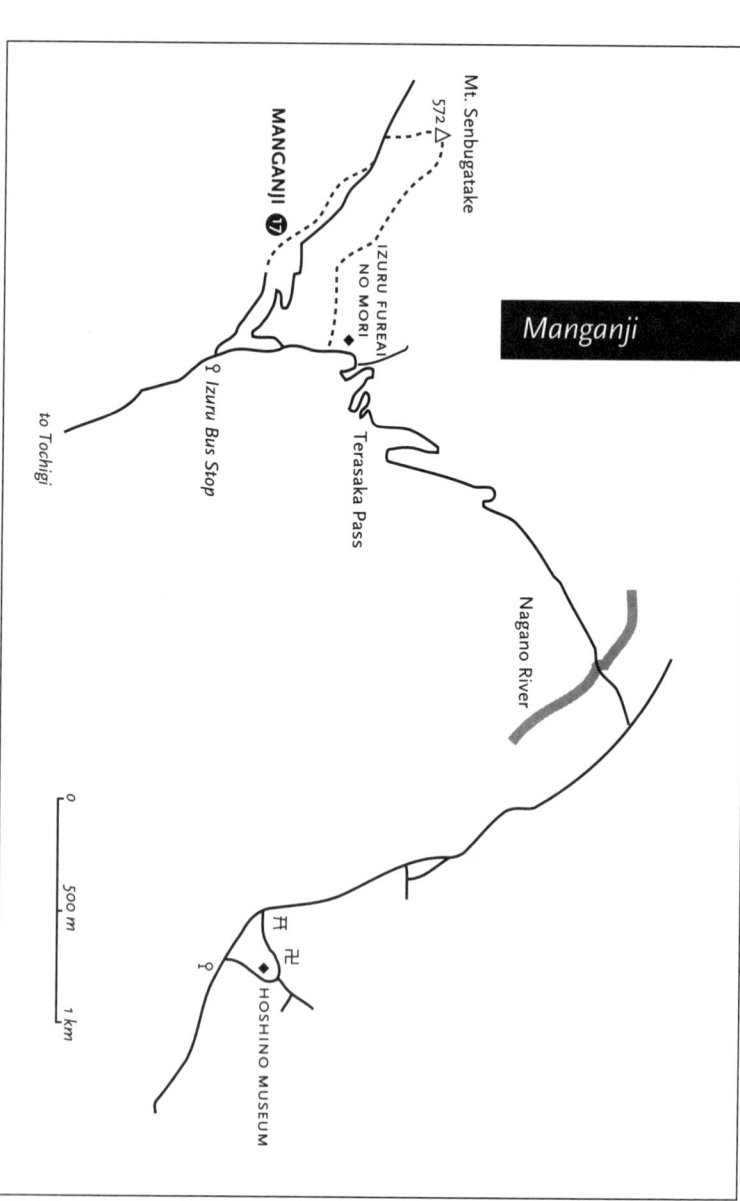

structed Jōmon-period houses dating from four to six thousand years ago.

It should be noted that the bus times are unkind at the time of writing. No problems arise if you stay at Izuru or Tochigi the night before but those taking the 10:40 AM bus from Tochigi will have to keep moving to see everything and catch the 3:26 from Hoshino. The alternative is to reach the Hoshino museum before its closing time at 4:00 PM, then take a meal at the pleasant Sato no Kura coffee house while waiting for the 6:45.

THE TEMPLE

The journey to Izuru is almost as remarkable as the temple itself. After the bus routes to Izuru and Hoshino diverge, the final six kilometers of the road pass through a ghostly landscape of quarries, where the limestone dust turns everything pale green. A seemingly endless stream of trucks loaded with the powdered rock thunders down the valley. Those with the time might choose to walk this stretch, for you will get some unforgettable photographs.

Suddenly, the bus emerges. Perhaps the village has the quarries to thank for its extraordinarily peaceful atmosphere. You pass through hell and enter sacred ground. The hills rise steeply from the plain and extend in long rows towards the bowl of Mount Yokone and the great cone of Nantai at Nikkō. The bus stops at the foot of the final approach to the temple. Several *soba* (buckwheat noodle) restaurants serve this local delicacy. Some visitors come here for the *soba* rather than the temple. A short walk uphill then brings you to the *niōmon* with its two fearsome guardian kings. The gate was built in 1735, and used to be thatched.

The modern hall beyond has overnight accommodations for two hundred, and also serves lunches. The modern belfry on the right looks like part of a Hong Kong movie set. On the left, there is a Benten pond and a pretty old hall for a stone thousand-armed Kannon.

The next flight of steps leads to the main hall, the Ōmidō. This hall, too, had a thatched roof until 1930. It dates from 1764. Fire ceremonies are held daily to purify the wishes of supplicants to Kannon. The main image is displayed only once every twelve years, in the year of the horse. The last time was in 1990, for fifty-eight days from April 7 to June 3. The next showing comes in 2002. The thousand-armed maedachi Kannon was carved from a piece of wood left over from the restoration of Sensōji in Asakusa following the Great Kantō Earthquake of 1923.

Then you must pay ¥300 to climb the valley to the Okunoin, which literally means "inner temple." Several paths crisscross the mountainside, leading to the various caves and halls. You should not enter the minor caves without a guide. The highlight is the red Okunoin perched high on the cliff above the little waterfall known as Daihi no Taki (the Falls of Great Compassion). Safe modern steps lead to the veranda and the stalagmite Kannon inside.

When En no Gyōja visited this area in the late seventh century, purple smoke, rather than the absence of green dust, was his sign that he had reached sacred ground. Climbing, he came to this cave in the cliff face, where he discovered a natural Kannon: a three-meter stalagmite resembling a rear view of the bodhisattva of mercy.

Gyōki, too, used Izuru as a retreat. Then, in the 730s, the barren wife of the governor of Shimotsuke prayed at the stalagmite for a child. After maintaining her observances for twenty-one days (three times seven, a significant combination of lucky numbers), she dreamed of something round, wrapped in threads of wisteria and placed on a lotus or a bowl. One version says that the bowl was brought by a snake; another by Kannon herself. In due course, she bore a son, Fujiito ("wisteria thread"), who in time gained fame as Shōdō Shōnin, the mountain priest whose story is intertwined with many of the templesof the Nikkō area.

Izuru was Shōdō's first retreat before he set out for Mount Yokone. He founded not only Manganji but also the major temples and shrines of Nikkō. For Shōdō, Nantai was Potalaka, the mythical paradise of Kannon in southern India. In legend, it was the view of Nantai from Senbugatake that set Shodō on his way.

Kūkai, who wrote the biography of Shōdō, is also said to have visited Izuru in 821 while tracing the saint's footsteps. The thousand-armed Kannon image in the main hall is thought to have been carved and dedicated by Kūkai at that time.

Through the middle ages, Manganji was a great center for Shugendō, an esoteric Buddhist tradition centered on ascetic practices in remote mountain areas. It was the starting point for the winter training of the Shugendō mountain priests (*yamabushi*) of Nikkō. The priests practiced for twenty-one days beneath the freezing waters of Daihi no Taki before performing their fire ceremonies on Senbugatake and entering the mountains. Ascetics still punish their bodies beneath the fall today, especially from February through April. Manganji is also temple number twenty-nine on the Shimotsuke Kannon pilgrimage.

Besides its religious history, Manganji was the scene of an armed rebellion in the nineteenth century: the Izuru Incident of 1867. The insurgency was organized as one of a series through the Kantō area to oust the shogunate, restore the emperor, and expel all foreigners. Most failed to get off the ground, but some one to three hundred samurai did gather here to declare their revolt. They were eventually surrounded by government forces, and surrendered without a fight. More than forty were executed.

THE WALK ** *(3 hours 30 minutes)*

You will require about an hour to walk up to the Okunoin. Then, continue up the valley by the path from Daihi no Taki. You quickly pass a second cave on the left, with a stalagmite thought to resemble Dainichi, then come to a forest road. Turn left onto the road and then right immediately up the path posted for Senbugatake. This is the approach to the view of Nantai that inspired Shōdō Shōnin centuries ago.

The path climbs steeply for about twenty minutes through a featureless forestry plantation. Turn right at a ridge to reach a bench with a magnificent view. Stay for a while to absorb it. Much of the Ashio range is visible. Ideally, you should be here in winter when the higher peaks are covered with snow. It is then a short walk along the ridge to the official lookout point which, curiously, commands hardly any view, and another steep twenty-minute descent to the valley.

If you don't want to bother with Hoshino, turn right at the road to reach the bus stop at Izuru in only five minutes. Otherwise, turn left for the Terasaka forest road to Hoshino. On the left, soon after, you reach the entrance to Izuru Fureai no Mori (Izuru Friendship Forest): a campsite with gardens, a playground, and a rest house that serves light meals. Keep right for the forest road, following the sign to Nagano and Hoshino. The road climbs sharply for ten minutes to Terasaka Pass, then descends for twenty-five on the other side. You will see few views through the trees, but there are few cars, either, so the walk is not unpleasant.

To keep it that way, turn right along the opposite bank of the Nagano River at the bottom. (Don't continue across to the main road.) Stay with the river as far as you can. Quite a few cherry trees line the bank. The valley is broad, with steep mountains on either side that can be impressive in the right weather. The river eventually joins the main road just before the valley narrows. The road enters Tochigi City (sign in English) soon after. Passing a small hillside shrine, a sign four minutes later points left to Hoshino Iseki (the Hoshino archaeological site).

This puts you on a narrow country lane. The first sight comes in a couple of minutes on the left. A narrow lane leads off to a little Buddhist hall called Yoshihimedō. Various wayside stones stand at the corner. The hall commemorates the wife of a fourteenth-century lord. Legend tells how she was slain here by a local man. He kindly let her stay the night at his house, but was tempted when she paid him generously for his hospitality. The man killed her at this spot the next morning, only to discover that her bag contained just dried boiled rice.

Return to the corner and continue up the lane for three more minutes. Turn right by the wall to reach, among the cherry trees, the Jōmon houses and the archaeological museum called the Hoshino Iseki Kinenkan (☎ 0282-31-0366). The museum is only open on Saturdays, Sundays, and public holidays from 10:00 to 4:00, and admission is ¥300.

The Kantō Plain has not always been its present shape. In the ice ages, the sea at times receded far beyond the current coastline. When the sea level was high, Tokyo Bay extended to the borders of Gunma and Tochigi Prefectures. In those days, the foothills at the edge of the Ashio range, where the mountains rose from marsh, offered some of the most attractive real estate in the region.

Many ancient remains have been discovered here. That, of itself, is not surprising. What is unusual is that they include stone tools that appear to be between 30,000 and 100,000 years old. Until very recently, they were the oldest such implements discovered in Japan. They may be Neanderthal. Today the oldest known remains are those at Takamori in Miyagi Prefecture, discovered in 1993. They were found in strata 500,000 years old, which places them in the era of Peking Man.

The Hoshino site also yielded no fewer than thirty-nine layers of volcanic ash. The fact that no human remains have been discovered is thought to be due to the acidity of the soil. The stone tools, clearly cut and sharpened across the grain, remain the best evidence that Neanderthal man occupied Japan.

The people of the Jōmon period, which began some ten-thousand years ago, were clearly attracted to the district for the same reasons. Besides the reconstructed straw huts, you can also see their tools, pottery, and dolls dressed in Jōmon clothing. The slightly fanciful display is rounded off with a model of Peking Man, who has nothing to do with this site.

Turning right out of the museum, you immediately reach a T-junction with another narrow lane. You can turn left at this junction to visit the Hoshino Nature Village (Hoshino Shizen Mura). Like Izuru Fureai no Mori, this is a family-oriented facility with rental tents, a short hiking course, and various "experiences" such as woodcutting, pottery, farming, and bamboo crafts. Its *katakuri* lilies are superb. They bloom around the last week of March and first week of April. Other flowers include *mizubashō* (skunk cabbage), daffodils, azaleas, hydrangeas, *mokuren* (lily-flowered magnolia), and *yamabuki* (kerria). A *soba* restaurant, Hoshi no Ie, stands 250 meters from the museum.

Turn right at that T-junction outside the museum to return to the main road. The Hoshino Iseki Mae bus stop is a minute down the road. Buses to Tochigi leave from the opposite side of the road to the bus stop sign. If you must wait, there is a coffee and souvenir shop, Sato no Kura, fifty meters further on the right. This has a broad menu of drinks, cakes, and light meals such as mushroom risotto, beef curry, and the set special called the Sato no Kura *teishoku*.

TRANSPORTATION

From Tokyo: Tōbu Nikkō Line from Asakusa or Kita Senju to Tochigi (¥920). 1 hour 15 minutes by *kaisoku* (express) or 1 hour 50 minutes by *junkyū* (limited express). Also occasional special express trains for a small additional charge. Convenient trains from Asakusa on the present timetable are the junkyū at 8:44 am and the kaisoku at 9:10. An alternative is the Tōhoku Shinkansen from Tokyo or Ueno to Oyama, changing to the JR Ryōmo line for Tochigi.

Buses from Tochigi to Izuru: Four buses daily at 6:25, 10:40, 1:00 and 4:00. (50 minutes, ¥760).

Buses from Izuru to Tochigi: 7:20, 11:55, 2:10, 5:00.

Morning buses from Tochigi to Hoshino Iseki: 6:45, 7:15, 7:50, 9:50, 11:45. (35 minutes, ¥670).

Afternoon buses from Hoshino Iseki to Tochigi: 12:46, 3:26, 6:45.

ACCOMMODATIONS

Manganji (☎ 0282-31-1717). 288 Izuru-chō, Tochigi-shi.
Izuru Sansō (☎ 0282-31-2060).
Minshuku Izuru (☎ 0282-31-1975).
Izuru Fureai no Mori and Hoshino Shizen Mura: contact the Tochigi City Tourist Association (Tochigi-shi Kankō Kyōkai; ☎ 0282-22-3535).

USEFUL KANJI

Hoshino	星野
Hoshino Iseki	星野遺跡
Hoshino Shizen Mura	星野自然村
Izuru	出流
Izuru Fureai no Mori	出流ふれあいの森
junkyū	準急
kaisoku	快速
Manganji	満願寺
Nagano	永野
Oyama	小山
Sato no Kura	里の蔵
Senbugatake	千部ヶ岳
Terasaka	寺坂
Tochigi	栃木
Yoshihimedō	よしひめ堂

CHŪZENJI — 18
Picturesque Nikkō

Chūzenji has the most beautiful location of any Bandō temple. It stands on the wooded banks of Lake Chūzenji, facing the perfect conical peak of Nantai. As noted in the last chapter, Shōdō Shōnin thought of Nantai as Potalaka, the mythical paradise of Kannon off the southern coast of India. He carved the huge Tachiki Kannon and founded the temple in 784. This glorious statue is the oldest Buddhist image in Nikkō, bearing comparison with the great Hase Kannons of Yamato and Kamakura.

Besides the pretty temple, highlights of the area include the famous Kegon Falls and stunning views of the lake and surrounding mountains from Chanokidaira and Mount Hangetsu. Two walks are described. The first offers the maximum scenic pleasure for the minimum effort. The second is the easiest modern route for walking to the lake from Nikkō and also down the other side.

One problem with Chūzenji is the access by bus. The ride from Nikkō station up the Irohazaka toll road takes just forty-five minutes on a good day, but can require three hours in high season, especially on Sundays in mid- to late-October when the leaves are turning. This does not take into account the time spent queuing, especially on the way down. There is no saying how many tourists have missed the last train back to Tokyo.

The second walk describes a way to avoid the bus as much as possible, even on a day trip. It is a hike on the grand scale. The scenery is superb, with an excellent chance of seeing monkeys and deer. Just remember to beware of bears! Lone hikers should use a bell or radio to warn any bears that you are coming. Also

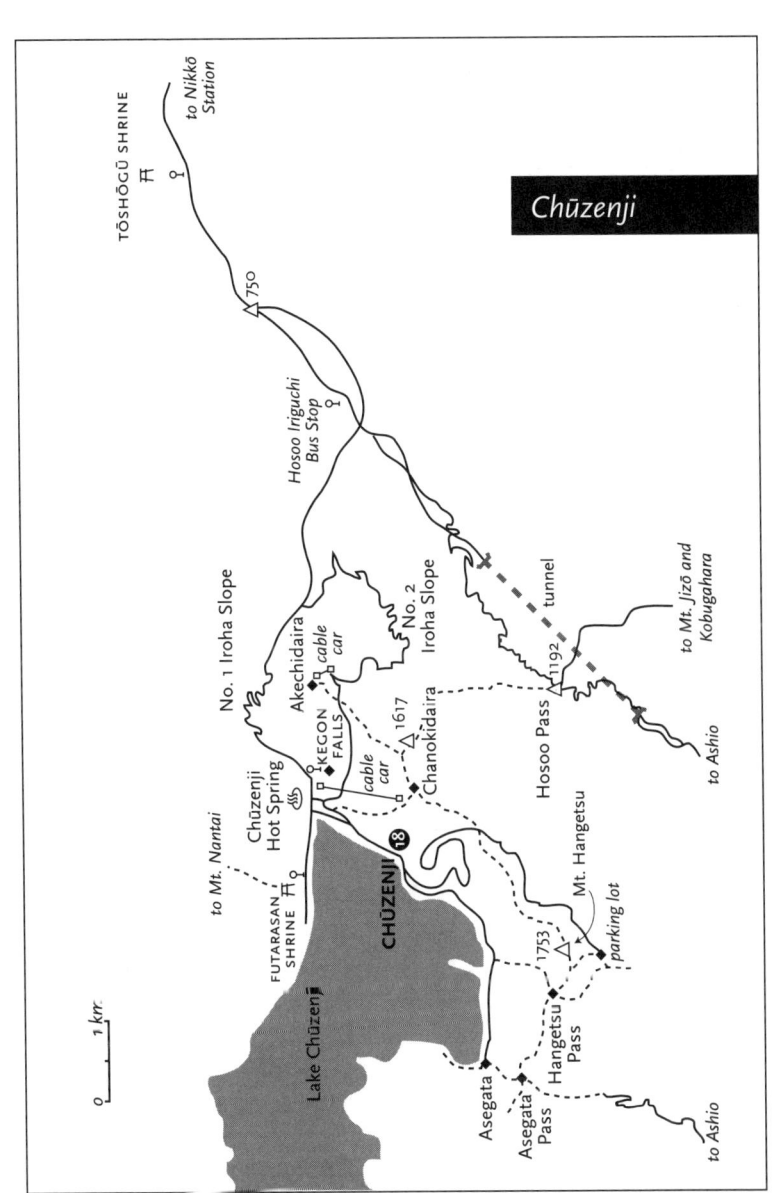

THE TEMPLE

Nikkō had two brilliant periods. The first commenced twelve hundred years ago when Shōdō Shōnin explored the mountains and established bases for ascetic practices. He founded the main temples and shrines of Nikkō, including Shihonryūji, Rinnōji, Chūzenji, and Futarasan Shrine. The ascetic mountain rites of the Nikkō *yamabushi* continued for more than a thousand years until their suppression by the Meiji government in the 1870s.

Then, in the seventeenth century, Nikkō was chosen as the site for Tōshōgū, the mausoleum of Tokugawa Ieyasu, the warlord who unified Japan and founded the Tokugawa shogunate. Nikkō was selected because it lay north from the shogunal capital at Edo (now Tokyo), and Buddhist tradition tells that northern boundaries especially must be defended against pestilence and invasion. Another factor in its selection was that the temples of Nikkō belonged to the Tendai sect, which counted among its adherents Tenkai, the great politician-priest and shogunal advisor of that era. The Nikkō Kaidō, mentioned in Chapter 12, was thus traveled by all the great men of the Edo era.

Chūzenji had a place in both eras. Tenkai was abbot of Chūzenji, and his ashes were buried beside those of Shōdō Shōnin on Kōzuke, the small island in Lake Chūzenji off the tip of the finger of land called Hatchō Dejima. You can see it quite clearly from the temple. But Chūzenji is essentially Shōdō's temple.

Shōdō Shōnin arrived in Nikkō in 766 at the age of thirty-one, discovering Lake Chūzenji the following year during his first failed attempt to scale Nantai. We know very little about his activities over the next decade and a half, but he finally reached the top of the mountain in 782. Why he found it so difficult is hard to understand.

CHAPTER 18

One local authority suggests that the mountain might have been guarded by hunters who wanted to keep it to themselves.

At any rate, Shōdō founded the temple Chūzenji two years later, on the north bank of the lake, where it stood until it was destroyed by a flood and relocated to its present site in 1902. The story of the temple's founding tells that Shōdō saw an image of Kannon reflected in the lake. He promptly carved the six-meter Tachiki Kannon from a standing Judas tree and dedicated it at the temple. An angel descended to Utagahama, the beach where the temple now stands, to sing and dance with joy. In later years, the mountain priests concluded their summer ascetic practices with twenty days of sutra-reading beside the lake at Utagahama.

Many relics related to Shōdō Shōnin are preserved at Chūzenji. The treasure house has a gold and copper axe which Shōdō used when climbing Mount Nantai as well as the bronze head of his staff. The Five Myōō (Wisdom Kings) who appeared to Shodo in a dream during his explorations of Nikkō are consecrated in the beautiful Godai hall. The temple's literature also says that the image of Daikokuten in the Hashiri Daikokuten hall is there to give thanks for the vision of Kannon in the lake which fulfilled Shodo's desires. Daikokuten, as one of of the Shichifukujin (Seven Gods of Good Fortune), is a god who fulfills desires. Significantly, Daikokuten is also the guardian deity of Saichō's temple on Mount Hiei in Kyoto, the head temple of the Tendai sect.

The many sights in the courtyard include more statues of Fudō (one of the Five Wisdom Kings) at an altar for fire purification ceremonies and spring for ablution, a Hōju Jizō (Gem Jizō) for prayers for success in trade, a six- hundred-year-old *kurobi* tree (*Thuja stan dishii*, a Japanese arborvitae), and the lovely belfry beside the main gate.

The highlight is the thousand-armed Tachiki Kannon, here gloriously on public view. The statue looks not just serene but positively happy, glowing with Shōdō's achievement. The *shakujō*, staff of the mountain priests and modern Bandō pilgrims, is held in the uppermost right hand.

The temple is open from 8:00 to 5:00 from April to October; and 8:00 to 4:00 from November to March.

WALK A ** *(2 hours 40 minutes)*
Kegon Falls, Chanokidaira, and Mount Hangetsu

This is the easy walk and it does not really matter whether you see the temple at the beginning or the end. The Chūzenji bus station is right beside Kegon Falls. The temple is a fifteen-minute walk around the lakeshore to the left.

Kegon Falls are nearly a hundred meters high. They can be viewed from above but is best seen from the observation point at the foot of the elevator. They flow over the lip of the lava flow from Nantai that created the lake. If left to themselves, the falls are expected to reach the lake in another two thousand years.

Besides their obvious beauty, the falls have also been known as a suicide leap ever since a seventeen-year-old youth plunged to his death here in 1903, decrying all hopes of salvation proferred by religion and philosophy. People still talk of the "Kegon disease" today.

Then take the six-minute cable-car ride from beside the falls to the lookout point at Chanokidaira for the best-known view of Mount Nantai and Lake Chūzenji. The cable car runs from March 18 to December 14. The Chanoki Botanical Garden at the top has some 150 species of mountain plant.

The path along the ridge to the right from here is still impassable in March due to heavy snow, but is strongly recommended later in the year. Chanokidaira has the most famous view, but Mount Hangetsu has the best. Going past two more lookout points, it takes thirty-five minutes to the next peak, Mount Tanuki; five minutes from there to the first parking lot on the toll road up Mount Hangetsu; and a further twenty-five minutes to the top of Mount Hangetsu. All the while, you have views of the lake to the right and the Ashio range to the left. You also have an excellent chance of meeting monkeys.

The lookout point at Mount Hangetsu is about five minutes beyond the peak. The view is fantastic. First, to the rear, you see past Mount Yokone all the way to Mount Fuji. The range to the right of that, leading towards Nikkō, consists of Mounts Akagi, Kesamaru, Nokogiri, Sukai, and then Nikkō Shirane. You can see Senjōgahara Marsh at the far end of Lake Chūzenji, plus Ryūzu Falls and Hatchō Dejima, with little Kōzuke Island at its tip. Then you have the lake, Mount Nantai, and Chūzenji Hot Spring as well.

To descend, continue along the unmarked trail at top of the ridge to reach Hangetsu Pass in fifteen minutes. Turning right here, it takes a further thirty minutes through the trees, with more spectacular views, to reach the lakeside road. The path is steep in places. Turn left to reach the Asegata campgrounds in fifteen minutes; or right to Chūzenji in thirty minutes.

WALK B *** *(3 hours 30 minutes)*
Hosoo Pass and Chanokidaira

To walk up to Chūzenji, take the bus for Chūzenji Hot Spring, Yumoto, or Hosoo from Nikkō station and alight at Hosoo Iriguchi (¥500). This takes around twenty-five minutes when the roads are clear; one and a half hours if not. The buses for Chūzenji and Yumoto turn right just afterwards to ascend Irohazaka but you should keep straight on via the pedestrian underpass, following the road signs for Ashio and Kiryū. Take the turning to the right marked Kyūdō, meaning Old Road. The buses to Hosoo continue a short way up this road.

As its name indicates, this is the old road across the pass to Ashio. The new road goes beneath the pass through the 2,765-meter Nisoku Tunnel. This old route, by contrast, winds up the pretty wooded slopes and gorges to the very top of the pass. Almost no traffic comes this way, so you have the road to yourself. It is your private Irohazaka, also with numbered bends. There are about thirty-five to the top. The road is particularly beautiful when the leaves are turning.

The pass is reached in a couple of hours. A large map on the left shows the hiking courses of the Zen Nikkō Kōgen Prefectural Park, which are described in my *Exploring Kiryū, Ashio, and Nikkō* (Weatherhill, 1992). For Chūzenji, however, you must turn right. Look for the tiny sign for Chanokidaira on a tree directly opposite the map. This path is easy to follow and leads through some of the prettiest mixed woods you will ever see, with grand views of the surrounding peaks. The route does get steep in places but is never dangerous or hard to see.

You know that you are reaching the top when you come to a little statue of Fudō Myōō, flames rising behind his head, perched atop a rock. Turn right at the T-junction ten minutes later for the view of Kegon Falls a couple of minutes down the path. Then return to the junction to keep right on to Chanokidaira.

The three and a half hours given above is the time from Hosoo Iriguchi to Chanokidaira. You can now descend to the Kegon Falls by cable car and walk fifteen minutes around the lakeshore to Chūzenji. Alternatively, you can walk down to the lake. The path starts at the gap in the fence just before the map in front of the cable car station. It takes about thirty minutes.

Now, suppose you want to walk down from Chūzenji as well. If returning by the route just described, be sure to catch a bus from one of the stops on the old road above Hosoo Iriguchi, as the buses coming from Chūzenji will probably be full.

Alternatively, you can walk down to the former copper-mining town of Ashio via the Asegata Pass. This walk through deer-filled forests is described in detail in *Exploring Kiryū, Ashio and Nikkō*. It takes around three hours from Chūzenji. Follow the road and then gravel track around the lakeshore (don't go up the toll road) to the campgrounds at the very end of the vehicular road. Turning left, you reach the pass with an easy ten-minute climb. Be careful not to miss your way going up; you must turn left by a great arch-like tree. Look out for the ribbons and little red and yellow squares that mark the route. If you find yourself climbing a scree slope, look again. It is then a brisk two-hour walk down to Matō station in Ashio on the Watarase Keikoku Tetsudō. The first half hour follows a well-trodden mountain path; the remainder is along a forest road.

TRANSPORTATION

Outbound:

From Tokyo: Tōbū Nikkō line to Nikkō. About 2 hours by *tokkyū* (special express; ¥1,300 plus ¥1,390 express surcharge) or slightly longer by *kaisoku* (express). Early morning *tokkyū* are direct to Nikkō. Later in the day, take the *tokkyū* for Kinugawa Onsen and change trains at Imaichi for the final ten minutes to Nikkō. Buy *tokkyū* tickets from the ticket window; tickets for other trains from the machines. Morning *kaisoku* leave Asakusa at 6:20 (arr. 8:24), 7:10 (arr. 9:12), 8:10 (arr. 10:15), and 9:10 (arr. 11:18). Morning *tokkyū* leave 7:20 (arr. 9:07), 8:00 (arr. 9:38), and 8:40 (Saturday and Sunday only, arr. 10:18) and 9:00 (arr. 10:40). The last local train back from Nikkō for Asakusa leaves at 8:47 pm (changing at Shin Tochigi).

From Nikkō to Chūzenji: bus to Chūzenji or Yumoto Onsen, alighting at Chūzenji (45 minutes if no traffic jams; can take 3 hours in high season; ¥1,100).

Return:

From Matō to Tokyo: Watarase Keikoku Tetsudō line to Aioi (just over 1 hour), then Tōbu line Ryōmo express to Asakusa (2 hours).

ACCOMMODATIONS

Nikkō has a huge number of hotels. Staff at the Nikkō Tourist Association speak English (☎ 0288-54-2496). Or visit the Tourist Information Center between the station and Tōshōgū.

CHŪZENJI

Hotels in Chūzenji Hot Spring have the bad practice of not letting rooms to lone travelers. You will need a partner if you want to stay there.

Non-hotel accommodations include several campgrounds beside Lake Chūzenji:

Senjugahama Bungalows (☎ 0288-55-0690). Reached by boat from Chūzenji Hot Spring. 5- to 6-person bungalows, ¥6,000. 6-person tents, ¥4,500 with bedding. Own tent, ¥500. July 10–August 31.

Senjugahama Kyampu Mura (☎ 0288 54 1078). Similar prices. Mid-July–late August.

Shōbugahama Kyampu Mura. Boat or bus from Chūzenji Hot Spring. Similar prices. May 1–October 31.

Asegata Kyampujo (☎ 0288 54 1111). Boat from Chōzenji Hot Spring. 6-person tents, ¥1,200. July 18–August 21. .

USEFUL KANJI	
Ashio	足尾
Chanokidaira	茶の木平
Chūzenji	中禅寺
Hosoo	細尾
Imaichi	今市
kaisoku	快速
Kinugawa Onsen	鬼怒川温泉
Kiryū	桐生
Kegon Falls	華厳滝
Kyūdō	旧道
Matō	間藤
Mount Hangetsu	半月山
Nikkō	日光
tokkyū	特急
Yumoto Onsen	湯元温泉

ŌYAJI — 19

Stone Country

The tourist who is beginning to feel that Japanese temples and Buddhist images all look alike should visit Ōyaji in the suburbs of Utsunomiya. The temple is set in a cave inhabited for eight thousand years by prehistoric man. The main image, a huge and superbly proportioned thousand-armed Kannon, was carved into the cliff a thousand years ago. Nine other equally impressive carvings adorn the rock face to one side.

Beyond the temple, the *maedachi* Kannon (the image serving as a kind of outrider for the main image) is eighty-eight feet tall. Called the Heiwa Kannon (Peace Kannon), it is a war memorial for those who died on both sides in World War II. Although not as pleasing as the older images in the cave, the Heiwa Kannon is an awesome presence in its extraordinary quarry-park.

The area around the town of Ōya is known throughout Japan for Ōya stone, a volcanic tufa formed on the ancient seabed some twenty to thirty million years ago. It has been quarried extensively since the Meiji period. The stone is light, easy to work, and highly heat resistant. It was used for the foundation stone of the Shimotsuke Kokubunji temple in 741, and for Utsunomiya Castle, the Tochigi prefectural government buildings, and the old Imperial Hotel built by Frank Lloyd Wright in Tokyo in 1922. The fact that the hotel withstood the Great Kantō Earthquake of 1923 further enhanced the stone's reputation, but these days it is mainly used for statues, ornamentation, and tombstones. Some 700,000 tons are still quarried every year.

Ōya is also the place to buy souvenir buddhas, lanterns, and toads made from the stone. The area makes much of its toads, for

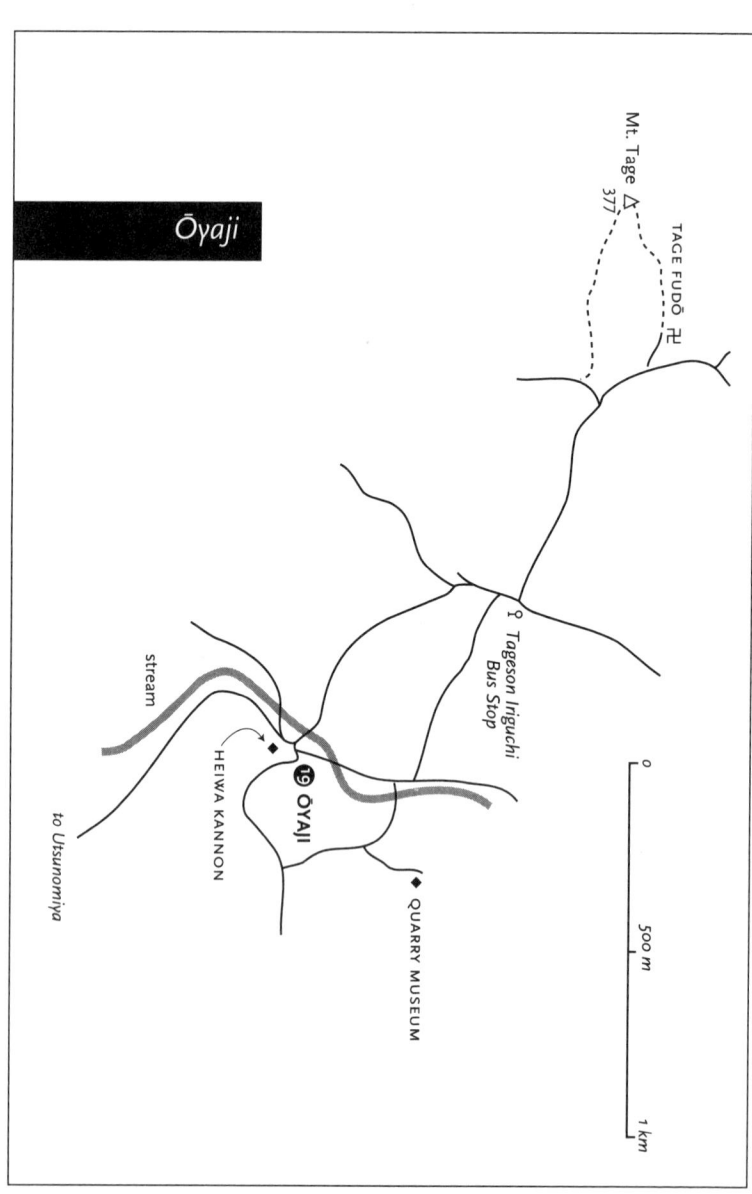

legend tells how they once saved the villagers from a terrible swarm of bees. Festivals are held in their honor in the spring and autumn each year.

Ōya is also known throughout Japan for ground subsidence. As in Paris, quarrying has been done in giant manmade caverns underground. In several infamous incidents in 1989–91, the caverns collapsed, taking fields and roads with them.

After visiting the temple, it is just a short walk to the Ōya History Museum (Oya Shiryōkan), where you can descend into one of the (still uncollapsed) caverns yourself. The walk then leads across country to Mount Tage for a visit to a colorful Fudō temple in a pretty woodland location.

THE TEMPLE

Enter Ōyaji, also known as Ōya Kannon, by the first gate on the left to reach a series of ponds. A bright red Benten hall stands on the far side. Note the equally bright white snake at its side. The snake, as noted several times already, is especially associated with this goddess of water and music. At Ōya, a legend tells how a snake once lived in these parts and occasionally released poison into the water. The pollution ended when the main Kannon image was carved.

Before continuing to the main part of the temple, you may want to climb the steps at the rear to the top of Mount Otome. Take the right-hand flight and follow the ridge around to the left. The name, Otome, means "Halt!" In earlier times, this sacred ground was off-limits to ordinary visitors. In a very tangible sense, the mountain at Ōya is itself the temple. A monument at the top commemorates the visit of the crown prince in 1900. The path offers some views of the quarries and surrounding countryside before descending again in ten minutes to the ponds.

Next, continue past the Benten pond to the main part of the temple. The concrete hall on the right is the treasure house but you need a ticket to enter, so go to the main reception window first. The combined ticket for the cave and treasure house costs ¥300. You are requested to see the cave first.

The hall has been built beneath a dramatic overhang pierced by giant holes; it looks like a Swiss cheese. Three large lanterns stand outside. The copper one on the right was cast in 1716. A small Inari shrine with foxes nestles in the cliff-face. There are many Kannon statues with bibs. Then, you notice the rows of stone five-story pagodas, each outfitted with bibs as well. The signs of popular faith are everywhere.

Entering the main hall from the right, the thousand-armed Kannon is superb. It is as if the image has been caught emerging from, or merging with, the rock face. The forty-two arms radiate in a perfect, symmetrical halo. The proportions are those of a human being, but larger than life and supremely graceful. Take your time: this is one of the highlights of the Bandō pilgrimage. No photos are allowed. It is curious to note that the carving did not always look this way. The Kannon was originally plated in gold and shone from the back of the cave. The statue has lost that former gloss but retains the dignity. Legend attributes the carving to Kūkai, who is said to have founded the temple in 810. This is probably a fiction, but the work does at least appear to date from his era. The carving was hidden from the public gaze until 1954.

Passing to the next cave, you discover nine more Buddhist images in the rockface, ranged in three groups. These trinities, known as *sanzon*, each present a buddha flanked by two attendant bodhisattvas. All are beautifully crafted.

The first trinity has Shaka (Sakyamuni), the historical buddha, in the center. Sakyamuni is usually flanked by Monju (Manjusri) on the left and Fugen (Samantabhadra) on the right. Monju is the bodhisattva of wisdom, representing the realization of buddhahood; Fugen stands for underlying principles, thought, and practice. In this case, however, the statue on the left appears to be of Kannon while that on the right looks like Jizō. They are thought to be mid- to-late Heian-period works.

CHAPTER 19

The middle group has Yakushi, the healing buddha, flanked by the sunlight bodhisattva Nikkō on the left and the moonlight bodhisattva Gakkō on the right. These are the smallest and oldest carvings, slightly predating the main Kannon image. The scars on the rock face show that these statues were once hidden behind doors. The left-hand door appears to have been removed when the Amida *sanzon* was carved.

Next comes Amida, the creator of the paradise in the West, together with his usual attendants, Kannon, the bodhisattva of mercy, on the left, and Seishi, another bodhisattva of wisdom, on the right. In Japanese Buddhism, these three are often thought to greet the souls of the newly deceased. These are the most recent carvings, dating from the late Heian or early Kamakura period.

Then it is time to visit the treasure house. As noted above, the cave was inhabited for eight thousand years, until some two thousand years ago. Various archaeological discoveries are on display: pottery shards from several periods over the past ten thousand years, including the oldest earthenware finds in Japan; a human skeleton buried at the back of the cave seven thousand years ago; grinding stones and other Jōmon-period tools; the bones of wild boar and deer, remains of ancient barbecues; and Buddhist amulets from the time when the carvings were made. Human bones of women and children have also been found, cut up and divided in just the same way as the animal bones. In prehistoric times, this was a cannibals' cave.

The temple is open from 9:00 to 4:30 from November 11 to March 10, and from 8:30 to 5:00 for the rest of the year. It closes from December 19–31 and on the second and fourth Wednesdays from January through March.

THE WALK * *(1 hour 30 minutes)*

Alighting at Ōya Kannon Mae, just beyond the large souvenir shop and drive-in, you can see the head of the giant Heiwa Kannon beyond the far side of the road. Notice also how the Ōya stone rises so suddenly from the surrounding plain. The quarrying and other developments have marred the original beauty of the area, but enough remains to appreciate how magical these pillars of stone must once have seemed.

Before proceeding to the temple at the foot of those cliffs, visit the small red hall a short way up the road on the right. The pond and cave-shrine are dedicated to a Zeni-arai Kannon, just like the Zeni-Arai Benten of Kamakura described in Chapter 4. This is a place to bless and multiply your money.

Continuing up the road, turn right where the road bends left. You come immediately to Ōyaji. After viewing the temple, leave by the *niōmon* and go through the tunnel on the right to reach the Heiwa Kannon. The plaza in front of the statue is a cubist dreamworld, for the cliffs have been cut perfectly square by the quarrymen. The effect is that of a huge movie or theater set waiting for the show to begin. The Heiwa Kannon itself has an unlovely face, but close inspection reveals a gentle, motherly expression.

The statue was sculpted under the guidance of a Professor Hida of Tokyo University of Fine Arts and Music between 1948 and 1956. A local carpenter had earlier tried to sculpt the giant Kannon on his own. When he had completed the head, however, the local authorities brought in Professor Hida to finish the job. Hida had the original head destroyed on the grounds that was insufficiently artistic. Is it divine retribution that the head is also the least pleasing part of the present statue?

Leave by the same tunnel and turn right around the foot of the mountain. Turn left five minutes later at the sign for Ōya Shiryōkan (Ōya Historical Museum; ☎ 0286-52-1232). You reach the driveway to the museum another hundred meters ahead on the right. The museum is open from 9:00 to 4:30 daily. Admission is ¥500. Before going in, notice the twenty-million-year-old fossilized tree on the left by the entrance. It was discovered in the rock at a depth of seventy-two meters. Ōya stone was formed about twenty million years ago by an undersea volcano.

At the surface, the museum has a fascinating display of old tools, clothing, and photographs of the quarrymen, together with explanations of the geology. Below the surface, you enter the giant caverns quarried from the stone. This is the underground counterpart to the park at the Heiwa Kannon. The echoes are fantastic. It is also sobering to realize that all the smooth walls were worked by hand. Quarrying still continues another thirty meters directly below.

Besides its history as a quarry, this underground cavern also served as a secret factory for Nakajima fighter planes during the World War II. Whereas other Nakajima plants like the one in Ōta were heavily bombed, this factory remained undiscovered until the Allied Occupation. The cavern also had a period as a mushroom farm, before being turned into a museum and occasional event space in 1979. A six-page English guide to the museum can be borrowed on request at the entrance.

Returning down the driveway, turn right onto the previous road. Go past the Ōya Shiryōkan bus stop, across a stream, and right at the end of the road. Take the next left, following the sign reading Tage Fudōsan past several masons' workshops. Go right at the T-junction and take the first left through a modern red gate. This is Tagesan Sandō, the main approach to the Tage Fudō temple, and it is lined with cherry trees. A small *kisuge* lily garden is located partway up on the right.

It takes about ten minutes uphill to reach the temple parking lot and three more minutes to the next gate. Tage Fudō is a popular tourist temple, so there are plenty of restaurants and shops in front. At the next gate, you have a choice: a steep flight of steps straight up, or a gentler flight to the left. I suggest you take the easier route this time.

First, notice the Ashio Daigongen hall on the left at the foot of the steps. This hall is dedicated to the god of Mount Ashio in the Tsukuba range, who is thought to cure to ailing feet and legs. Accordingly, many straw sandals have been hung in front of the hall as votive offerings. Some people even hang up ordinary city shoes. This hall is far more sensibly located than the shrine at Mount Ashio itself, which happens to be at the top of the mountain. For people with bad legs, it seems a kindness to place the hall at the foot of the steps.

Starting here, you also see a succession of thirty-six Fudō Dōji (literally, "Fudō children"), representing the thirty-six manifestations of Fudō Myōō. These playful modern statues were placed here in 1990 to celebrate the start in 1988 of a new pilgrimage course: the Thirty-Six Fudōs of North Kantō. As noted in the introduction, pilgrimages have never been so popular as now, in the late twentieth century. Seeing as the beautiful northern Kantō area is underrepresented in the Bandō circuit, you might consider this for your next challenge.

Ascending the steps through the trees and banners, you come to a Jizō hall with many very well-dressed Jizōs outside. As usual, these are dedicated to the souls of lost or aborted children. Fudō statues stand by the little waterfall.

Further up, there is a path off to the left signposted to Gotendaira Park. You will return here for the walk up the mountain. But first, continue to the belfry and the temple proper. The wooden halls to the left of the main hall are dedicated to Nyoirin Kannon and Batō Kannon. The Batō (horse-headed) Kannon is one of the thirty-three Kannons of Shimotsuke, the old name of Tochigi Prefecture. At the main reception area, charms are available for every wish for success, bounty, health, safety, and benevolence you could possibly think of.

The temple is thought to have been founded in 822, when the priest Sonchin, one of Shōdō Shōnin's disciples, dedicated a horseheaded Kannon. The Fudō enshrined at the temple was the guardian of the Utsunomiya family: the deity to whom Sōen, the family's founder, prayed during the Earlier Nine Years' War of the mid-eleventh century, in which Minamoto Yoriyoshi won control of the northeast. Sōen's reward was the province of Shimotsuke. A descendant, Utsunomiya Kintsuna, moved the statue to its present site from Katsuyama Castle in 1335. The statue bears a stamp indicating that it was repaired in October 1389.

As so often happens at sacred sites, the natural woodland has been beautifully preserved around the Tage Fudō. Mount Tage now has the only primary woodland in Utsunomiya. The species cover a wide range, from oaks and camellia to cherries, maples, and vines. Returning to the path up the mountainside, you can now enjoy the peace of the woodland and some views of the surrounding countryside. The path has unfortunately been stepped all of the way to the top, but the steps are well-spaced and gentle. It is not so different from walking on an unstepped path.

A lookout point has been erected in the clearing at the top. Someone clearly miscalculated, for even in winter the trees entirely block out the view. But scrambling around the wide mountaintop, you can find several vantage points for viewing the mountains of Nikkō and Nasu and the cities of Utsunomiya and Kanuma.

The tradition is that Sōen built Tage Castle on this hill in the period from 1058 to 1065. We do know that a descendent, Utsunomiya Kunitsuna, either built or rebuilt Tage Castle in the sixteenth century. He commanded the castle himself during the Hōjō advance into Shimotsuke in 1584, leaving a retainer in charge of Utsunomiya Castle on the plain. That invasion was repulsed by the armies of Kunitsuna and the Satake family. The castle then resisted direct siege in 1589 when assaulted by the forces of two local Hōjō allies, the Mibu and the Haga. Tage Castle was eventually abandoned in 1597. Some earthworks survive on the slopes.

Descend the mountain by the other path from the clearing, signposted Gezandō ("the way down the mountain"). This path is gentler. Turn left at the forest road to return to the road just below the Fudō temple. Then retrace your steps back past the cherry blossoms to the metal gate on the main road. A stop called Tageson Iriguchi for occasional buses to Utsunomiya stands just the other side of the road. If you are unlucky with the buses, you can wait in one of the roadside restaurants or walk back the fifteen minutes or so to Ōya Kannon, where there are two buses per hour.

TRANSPORTATION

From Tokyo: Tōhoku Shinkansen from Tokyo or Ueno to JR Utsunomiya (41 minutes, ¥4,210).

JR Tōhoku line from Ueno or Akabane to JR Utsunomiya (¥1,850)

Tōbu Nikkō line from Asakusa to Tōbu Utsunomiya (you may have to change at Shin Tochigi).

Bus from Utsunomiya to Ōya: Bus stand number 8 outside JR Utsunomiya station. Alight at Ōya Kannon Mae (25–30 minutes, ¥420). The same bus also stops at Tōbu Utsunomiya Eki Mae near Tōbu Utsunomiya station, but the stop is not as easy to find.

ACCOMMODATIONS

Banjakusō (☎ 0286-52-0524). In front of Ōya Kannon. Rock bath. Carp dishes.

INFORMATION

Ōya Tourist Information Bureau (☎ 0286-52-4733).

USEFUL KANJI

Gezandō	下山道
Gotendaira Park	御殿平公園
Heiwa Kannon	平和観音
Mount Tage	多気山
Ōyaji	大谷寺
Ōya Kannon	大谷観音
Ōya Shiryōkan	大谷資料館
Tage Fudō	多気不動
Tageson Iriguchi	多気尊入口
Utsunomiya	宇都宮

SAIMYŌJI — 20
Mashiko Pottery

Traveling to Mashiko, changing trains first at Oyama and then Shimodate for the tiny single-track Mōka Railway, it is hard to believe that you are approaching one of Kantō's most famous tourist towns. This is how it should be. When Hamada Shōji set up his kiln in Mashiko in 1924, he chose the town as a place to work close to nature. The feelings of doubt deepen as the train is reduced from two carriages to one at Mōka, and then when you get off at Mashiko station to find nothing there.

"Nothing" is an exaggeration. There is a small supermarket, a large English map, and at times a row of taxis. You will probably see other foreigners getting off, too, as Mashiko appears in every guidebook. But you have to take it on trust that this is the start of a delightful day.

Mashiko lies in the western foothills of the Yamizo range, on the borders of Ibaraki and Tochigi Prefectures. Its ceramic industry dates from the prehistoric era. Pots have been discovered from as far back as 2500 bc. Others, with distinct Korean influence, were unearthed from fifth-century burial mounds. Many rough earthenware vessels for the common people survive from the Nara period. But the modern industry began with the rediscovery of good clay by Ōtsuka Keisaburō in 1853.

Keisaburō was a farmer from a village ten kilometers to the east, not far from the pottery town of Kasama. In those days, Kasama had the only significant pottery industry in the Kantō area and a huge share of the Edo market. Just as Kasama now lies in Ibaraki Prefecture, whereas Mashiko is located in Tochigi, the two towns belonged to different fiefs in the Edo era. The lord of

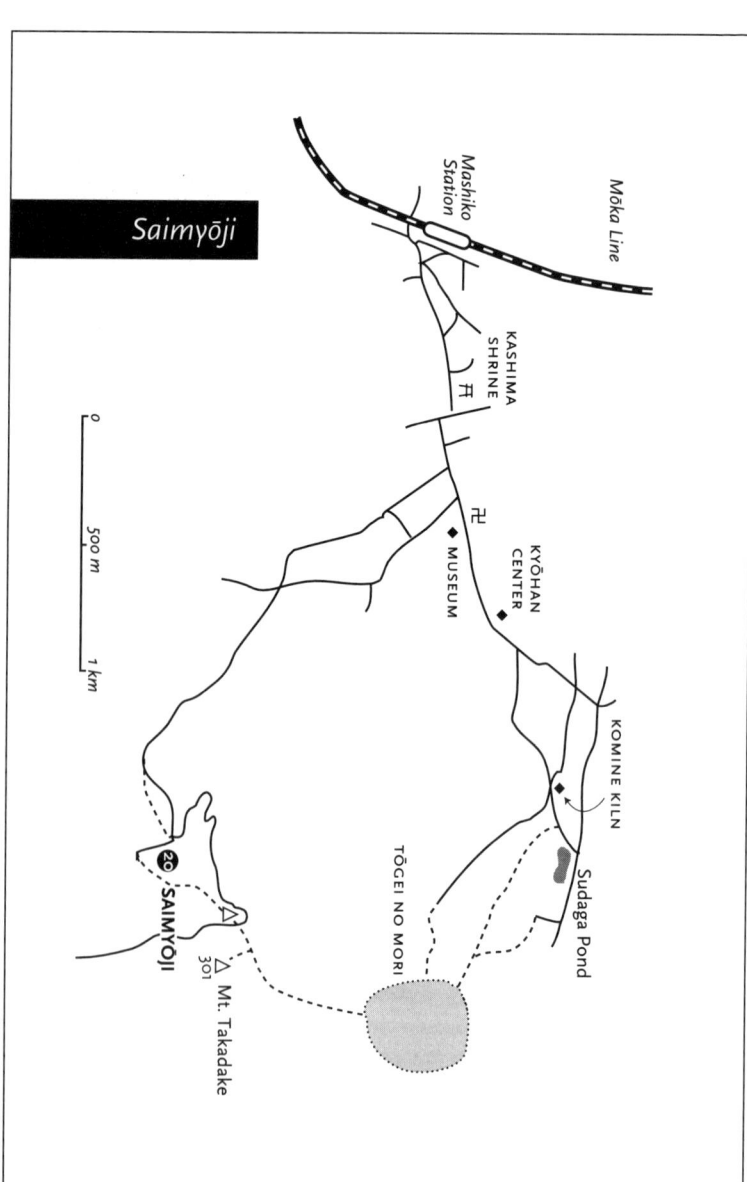

CHAPTER 20

Keisaburō's Kurobane fief was understandably delighted when the twenty-five-year-old farmer discovered clay and proposed to set up a kiln.

Capital was provided and well-paid teachers were invited, from not only Kasama but also faraway Kyoto. The work was highly derivative at first, but in time the rough features of the local clay and glazes established a distinctive Mashiko style. Huge quantities of pots and kettles were soon being shipped to Edo, carried by horse to Mōka and by boat from there down the Kinu, Tone, and Edo Rivers to the pottery markets of Nihonbashi.

The fief controlled almost all sales until its collapse in the Meiji Restoration. The potters of Mashiko then had to fend for themselves, which they did by producing for the masses. Teapots decorated with simple *sansui* (mountain and water) designs became the representative Mashiko product of the Meiji era. Americans also took note; in the late nineteenth century, one third of Mashiko's total output was exported. However, overproduction took its toll on quality, and the market had slumped badly by the turn of the century. The spread of gas in the cities was also a factor, for the ceramics could not not stand the greater heat. Pots were increasingly replaced by metal vessels.

The two big events that turned the town's fortunes around were the Great Kantō Earthquake of 1923 and the arrival of thirty-year-old Hamada Shōji the following year. The earthquake produced unlimited demand, while Hamada earned Mashiko a worldwide reputation through his art.

Hamada had studied in Kyoto with such potters as Tomimoto Kenkichi, Yanagi Muneyoshi, and Bernard Leach. He spent three years with Leach at St. Ives in Cornwall and returned to Japan determined to find a quiet, healthy haven for his work. Mashiko was still a sleepy town of thatched cottages. The clay was sound. The gently sloping hills were ideal for his kilns. It exactly fitted the bill. Hamada always stressed that beauty lay not in refinement but in purity of the heart.

The local people received this stranger coolly, uncertain what to make of his unusual wares, but began taking note as disciples started to gather, first from around Japan and then from all over the world.

Hamada used only the local clays and natural glazes. He kept his pots modest and restrained, not letting them spread on the wheel but, in his own words, controlling the shape from within. And he gave them deft, simple designs, with brushwork completed in seconds rather than minutes.

Hamada's disciples have produced a wide range of original styles of their own. All, however, are born of the local Mashiko clay and share a rustic charm much different from the glossy, intricate designs of Imari or Nabeshima ware. The Pottery Route in the center of the town is a street of pottery retailers selling everything from tea bowls and urns to pendants and *tanuki* figurines. The quality varies, but the best is very good. Expect to spend several hours just browsing from shop to shop.

Saimyōji, the temple, was founded by Gyōki in 737, in an earlier era of Mashiko pottery, though fame was still over a millennium away. For the walker, the approach to Saimyōji through the paddies, the copper-tiled and thatched temple buildings, the stroll along the ridge, plus the pottery of Mashiko all make for a fulfilling trip. You might also note that Mashiko has a big Gion festival on July 24 and a four-day pottery festival from late October to early November.

THE TEMPLE

Saimyōji stands on a quiet, densely wooded hillside now designated as the Mashiko Prefectural Nature Park. It blends perfectly with the woodland. Enter by the steep steps beneath the oak trees rather than by the gentle path around to the right. The steps used to be made of soft Ōya stone but had to be replaced due to heavy erosion. Notice the stones with Kannon images on either side of the steps and around the courtyard at the top: each represents one of the thirty-three temples of the Bandō circuit.

The *niōmon,* built in 1492, stands beside a small, quasi-Chinese three-story pagoda. The pagoda was built by the warlord Mashiko Iemune in 1537. A thatched belfry is on the left of the courtyard and a thatched Enma hall on the right. Constructed in 1714, the hall houses the only great statue of Enma in the Kantō region.

Enma, you may recall, is the lord who sits in judgment at the court of the dead, weighing our deeds and meting out sentences. As explained in the introduction, Emma holds an important place in the history of the Kannon pilgrimages, for it was he who gave the half-dead Tokudō Shōnin the thirty-three sacred seals to found the Saigoku circuit. Enma is usually depicted with a fearsome, furious face guaranteed to strike awe in the hearts of sinners. This Enma is different. Yes, he has a red face. But think of those Japanese children with broad smiles waving victory signs at the camera. That is more or less what Enma is doing. You feel like paying him a visit sometime.

A seven-hundred-year-old tree, the Saimyōji *koyamaki* (*Sciadopitys verticillata,* a type of cedar) rises to the right of the main hall, which dates from 1394. The outer chamber was built in 1691.

The story of the temple's founding tells how Gyōki carved and dedicated an eleven-headed Kannon, assisted by Ki Arimaro, a member of the warlord family that later took the name Mashiko. The temple flourished and Kūkai, too, is thought to have visited this place. The main image was recarved by Eizan in 805. The early buildings were lost, however, in great fires of 1127 and 1351.Saimyōji is also temple number thirteen on the thirty-three Kannon pilgrimage of Shimotsuke (Tochigi). With the resurgence of pilgrimages in recent years, the Shimotsuke circuit is also being revived.

The main image is revealed only once in thirty-three years, most recently in 1978. The temple also participated in a special month-long *kaichō* (public viewing of the image) in 1990 for the supposed eight-hundredth anniversary of the Bandō pilgrimage.

SAIMYŌJI

THE WALK ** *(2 hours)*

The walk follows the first half of the Kantō Fureai no Michi course from Mashiko station to Nanai. A Japanese route map for the course is displayed just next to the English map of Mashiko in the square outside the station. Plenty of maps and signs have been put up around the town, so there is no possibility of getting lost.

First, walk into the center of Mashiko. Go straight down the road opposite the station past the Mobil gas station and left up the main road. You reach a small Kashima Shrine in five minutes. A large stone to the left of the main shrine commemorates Ōtsuka Keisaburō, founder of the modern Mashiko pottery industry. Another has been erected at Saimyōji.

The Pottery Route begins five minutes from here, just after the large sign (in English) pointing right to Saimyōji. The Pottery Route continues straight ahead. You will return here at the end of the walk, so save the souvenirs till last.

First, however, walk a few steps up the Pottery Route to see the somewhat awkwardly named Museum of Pottery Furnace. This family museum gives an in-depth tour of pottery-making processes and kilns through the ages, including a reconstructed primitive kiln for the ancient *haniwa* dolls that were buried in tumuli. It also has exhibits of ceramics from all over Japan. The entrance fee of a thousand yen seems steep, but for that you get a one-hour private tour. The museum is ideal for Japanese speakers who want a quick introduction to Mashiko pottery away from the crowds.

Now return to the sign for Saimyōji. A pleasant country road winds past paddy fields and farmhouses, reaching a second English sign to Saimyōji and the Mashiko Prefectural Nature Park in ten minutes. Turn left here, also following the Kantō Fureai no Michi signs. At a bend six hundred meters from the temple, the Kantō Fureai no Michi leaves the road to climb directly up the hillside, coming out at the Saimyōji hospital. You reach the thatched roofs of Saimyōji four minutes later.

CHAPTER 20

After seeing the temple, follow the Kantō Fureai no Michi sign to Gongendaira up the wooden steps behind the main hall. Benches and a lookout post have been erected at the top. The Kantō Fureai no Michi sign indicates 1.5 kilometers to Tōgei no Mori (literally, "Ceramic Forest"). This is the start of a pretty walk along the wooded ridge.

The next peak is Mount Takadate, the highest in the range at 301 meters. One of Arimaro's descendants built a castle here in the early twelfth century, said to be the strongest of the six main castles of the Kantō region. In later years, Mashiko Masashige distinguished himself for Yoritomo at the battle of Atsukashiyama in the Ōshū campaign. Mashiko developed as a castle town for the next four centuries until the fortress finally fell in 1589.

You come to a narrow road five minutes from Gongendaira, just below the castle. Though little remains to be seen, if you want to visit the site climb the steps to the right from the small parking lot. Otherwise, take the steps to the left and turn left along the unmarked trail three minutes from the parking lot, where the path you are on turns sharply right. You quickly pick up the Kantō Fureai no Michi signs again.

Tōgei no Mori has a series of exercise devices for those who still need to work up a sweat. You emerge at a public rest house (which serves simple meals) and parking lot. Follow the Kantō Fureai no Michi sign down towards Entsūji but turn left onto the road at the big pond. Follow this road around to the right at the big Komine pottery center.

Now take the next left. A big sign in Japanese points the way to Kyōhan Center, the cooperative sales center for the Mashiko kilns. The road quickly climbs over a low hill to come out onto Pottery Route just above Kyōhan Center, only ten minutes from the pond. Allow a lot of time for Kyōhan Center and the Tōgeikan exhibition hall, which displays works by Hamada Shōji and other prominent local potters.

TRANSPORTATION

JR Tōhoku line or Tōhoku Shinkansen from Ueno to Oyama. JR Mito line from Oyama to Shimodate. 40 minutes by Shinkansen to Oyama; 18 minutes from Oyama to Shimodate. Base fare from Ueno to Shimodate: about ¥1,800. Additional Shinkansen charge: ¥1,950.

Mōka Railway from Shimodate to Mashiko (45 minutes, ¥730). In addition to regular service, the Mōka line occasionally runs a steam train as a tourist attraction. Tickets may be bought from JR East outlets beginning one month in advance. The steam train runs on many days from July through September, leaving Shimodate at 10:37 am.

ACCOMMODATIONS

Centrally located ryokan and minshuku include:

Tozansō Ryokan (☎ 0285-72-2063). By the station.

Hasegawa Ryokan (☎ 0285-72-2210).

Okadaya Ryokan (☎ 0285-72-2016). Between the station and Pottery Route.

Minshuku Toki (☎ 0285-72-3393). In the valley towards Saimyōji, but on the other side of the river.

Seizansō Ryokan (☎ 0285-72-3039). Close to Saimyōji.

Saimyōji Mitsunoi Ryō (☎ 0285-72-2957).

There are also some hot spring hotels:

Mashiko Onsen Hotel (☎ 0285-72-6310). Use a taxi.

Mashiko Unahachi Onsen (0285-72-7181). Close to Entsūji.

Mashikokan (Hotel Sunshine Kinugawa; ☎ 0285-72-7777). Close to Saimyōji, but mainly caters to groups.

For others contact Tourist Information at Mashiko Town Hall (☎ 0285-72-2111).

USEFUL KANJI

Entsūji	円通寺
Gongendaira	権現平

CHAPTER 20

Kantō Fureai no Michi	関東ふれあいの道
Kashima Shrine	鹿島神社
Kyōhan Center	共販センター
Mashiko	益子
Nanai	七井
Oyama	小山
Saimyōji	西明寺
Shimodate	下館
Tōgei no Mori	陶芸の森

NICHIRINJI — 21
Mount Yamizo—The Hard Place

Every pilgrimage has its *nansho*, the "hard place" high on a remote mountainside. Nichirinji, Temple of the Sun, is the hard place of the Bandō pilgrimage. It is the temple with stories of exhausted pilgrims who die or get lost on the road. Nichirinji stands on Mount Yamizo, the highest mountain in Ibaraki Prefecture, on the border with Tochigi and Fukushima Prefectures. You are now at the far edge of Kantō from Ashigara Pass, for Fukushima lies in the Tōhoku region.

Even by modern transportation, Nichirinji is remote. You ride the pretty Suigun line up the Kuji River to the border station at Hitachi Daigo. Passengers going on to Kōriyama in Fukushima must usually change trains here, as if entering another country. A bus takes you past thatched farmhouses, apple orchards and fields of tea, *wasabi* radishes and *konnyaku* (devil's tongue), high up narrow country lanes to the foot of the mountain. The temple is a stiff ninety-minute climb from the bus stop at Jaketsu (Snake's Lair).

The rewards of a visit to Mount Yamizo are the pleasures of the countryside. Try the local *kushidango* (sweet dumplings on sticks) or, if you visit between late July and September, the skewered *ayu* (sweetfish). On Yamizo itself, you can drink the water of some of Japan's most delicious springs and stroll in woods of oak, birch, maple, and beech. The view from the lookout point at the top encompasses Nasu, Nikkō, much of the rest of Kantō, nearby parts of Tōhoku, and even faraway Mount Fuji.

You can make this a day trip, stay at a campground on the mountain, or relax at a hot spring hotel in Hitachi Daigo or Fukuroda, one stop before Hitachi Daigo. If staying the night, visit the stunning

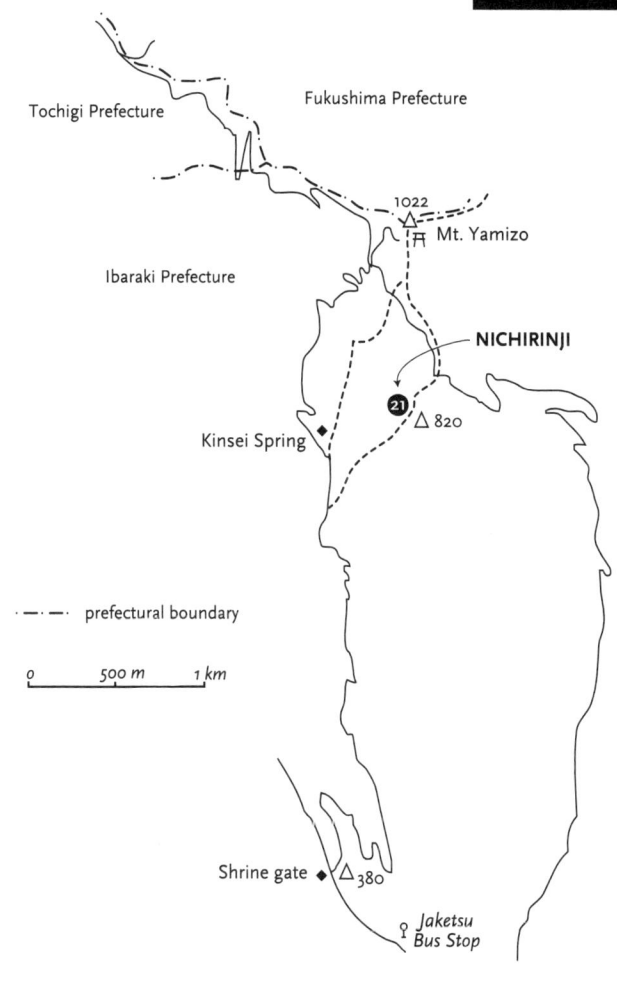

Fukuroda Falls near Fukuroda Hot Spring. Besides, Hitachi Daigo has a big fireworks and lantern festival on August 13, during the Bon Festival, when countless illuminated lanterns are released on the Kuji River. The lanterns represent ancestral spirits returning to the netherworld after their sojourn in this.

THE TEMPLE

The story of Nichirinji's founding tells how Kūkai was passing this way from Mount Yudono in the northeast to Kashima Bay. Crossing a river near Mount Yamizo, he realized that the water had a holy fragrance. When he cupped some in his hand, a sacred Sanskrit character appeared on his palm. He knew that he must be close to the pure land of Buddhism.

Kūkai inquired at a nearby homestead. The owner knew nothing about the water but told him of a mountain where clouds of five colors glistened and music was heard in the morning sun. But, the owner continued, a fierce monster called Daimōmaru dwelt at the foot of the mountain. Sometimes it appeared as a demon, sometimes as a snake. Many people used to live near the mountain but most had fled due to Daimōmaru's depredations. Kukai went to the mountain through mist and rain, chanting magical sutras, and overcame the beast. Climbing to the summit, he observed the eight (*ya*) deep valleys (*mizo*) down the mountainside that gave the peak the shape of the holy lotus, and accordingly named it Yamizo.

Now two Shinto gods, Ōnamochi and Kotoshironushi appeared, dressed in the formal robes of ancient officials, and told him that the peak was the home of the eleven-headed Kannon. They instructed him to build a Kannon hall, promising to protect it thereafter, and disappeared. Kukai carved two Kannon images, one for each of the gods he had encountered, and founded two temples. One he called Nichirinji, Temple of the Sun, and the other Getsurinji, Temple of the Moon. Besides the accommodation with older Japanese faiths, one senses a strong Daoist influence.

CHAPTER 21

Getsurinji no longer survives, though you pass close to its site on the walk down the mountain. Other legends are also told of monsters. It is related, for example, how Fujiwara Tomie built a castle in Daigo in 707 and overcame the beast of Yamizo. Tomie discovered the demon by reflecting light onto the mountain with a mirror. The story tells how light reflected from the peak like a star and from the woods like a moon.

Another legend credits the ascetic En no Gyōja with founding Nichirinji in 673, and the warrior Sakanoue Tamuramaro with founding Getsurinji. After Kūkai's visit in 807, Ennin came and built a bigger hall in 853. The temple received gifts from Minamoto Yoritomo and once had three great halls (including Getsurinji). The warlords Satake Yoshiatsu and Fujiwara Naohiro helped with a major renovation in 1537. The temple then continued to thrive as a center for the ascetic mountain practices of Shugendō through the Edo period, until the Mito clan, caught up in the spirit of Shinto revivalism that preceded the Meiji Restoration, tried to suppress Buddhism in 1832. The buildings, however, were lost in fires. The huge main hall of zelkova wood burned in 1643; then the replacement was destroyed by a fire of 1880.

Nichirinji, for all of its weighty legends, is a small temple today. The main hall is a plain white and red building. An old Kannon hall stands to the right. Also notice the large stele with a carving of Benten, and the two statues of white horses. Horses were a treasure for the people of this border village across the pass from Kuroiso in Tochigi Prefecture. Another horse statue is placed near the top of the mountain at the gate to Yamizomine Shrine. A souvenir and refreshment hall, a godsend for the weary pilgrim even now, stands to the left of the main hall.

THE WALK *** *(3 hours 30 minutes)*

Having climbed the pretty valley of the Kuji River on the train and taken the bus to the back of beyond, you alight on quite a large (but empty) road at Jaketsu, the former home of Daimōmaru. Keep going a couple of hundred meters in the same direction and turn right at the English road sign reading Mount Yamizo and Nichirinji Temple. The *torii* you see is the gate for Yamizomine Shrine at the top of the mountain. Two drive-ins on the corner sell specialities of the region, including the sweet *kushidango* and salty *ayu* mentioned above.

The essence of a successful pilgrimage is to cast aside creature comforts and discover a better self. The steep fifty-minute walk up the road through the forestry plantations on the lower slopes of Mount Yamizo offers an opportunity. The less devout may hitchhike.

The walk improves quite suddenly. A path branches off to the right at a sign for Nichirinji Bungalows. Another sign points on up the road for Nichirinji, but turn right here. The path descends steeply through mixed woods, crossing a stream in just under ten minutes, then climbs eight minutes on the other side to the temple. Turn right onto the road at the bungalows to reach the temple.

To continue, take the concrete road up from the Kannon hall. This reaches a larger road in four minutes. Cross and take the path up the other side signposted for the top of Mount Yamizo. The woods from here are superb with several old trees and lots of bamboo grass underfoot.

Turn right at the junction of paths twelve minutes from the road. Remember this junction because you must return here later. The path left, signposted to Kyūsandō and Kinseisui, is the way down.

The path branches again fifty meters higher up. The path to the right leads seventy meters to Ginseisui, one of Yamizo's five famous springs. The path up takes you the final two hundred meters to the summit.

Ginseisui is the Silver Spring. All were named by Tokugawa Mitsukuni, the renowned Mito Kōmon (see Chapter 22). In modern times, this group of five springs has been commended by the Environment Agency as one of the best one hundred in Japan. The association with metals has historical precedent. It is recorded in the ancient chronicle *Shoku Nihon Kōki* that gold from Yamizo was presented to envoys to Tang-dynasty China in 836. The gold mines thrived in the middle ages under the Satake warlords.

Continuing up, you come to the third white horse at the gate to Yamizomine Shrine and then the shrine itself. This shrine claims to have been founded by the legendary conqueror of the north, Yamato Takeru. Others credit it to En no Gyōja. It was rebuilt in 1630 by Tokugawa Yorifusa, Ieyasu's son and founder of the Mito Tokugawa line, and patronized by the Mito fief through the Edo period. Every head of the Mito clan made a point of visiting Yamizomine Shrine at least once.

The shrine's colorful Bonten Festival is held on May 3. Young men carry a bamboo image of Bonten (the Hindu god Brahma) on a cedar log to the mountain. The image is hung with products of the field and the young men feast at the top. The festival pacifies the mountain god, thus serving as a prayer for a bountiful harvest.

A castlelike structure stands behind the shrine. This is the lookout point at the top of Ibaraki's highest mountain. The peak is 1,020 meters above sea level. The building's design is fanciful, for no castle actually stood here. Admission is ¥100.

Now return to that junction with the sign for Kinseisui and Kyūsandō. The Kyūsandō is the former path used by pilgrims to Yamizomine Shrine. A steep flight of steps descends the slope known as Hatchōzaka, reaching Tessui, or Iron Spring, in six minutes. A sign left indicates that Ryūmosui (Dragon-Hair Spring) is eighty meters to the left. Keeping straight, however, the path bends sharply right just twenty meters below Iron Spring. This is the end of Hatchōzaka. You are close to the former site of Getsurinji, Temple of the Moon. Five minutes further through the woods bring you to Kinseisui, or Gold Spring, which is said to be the most delicious of all.

A minute later, you reach a final celestial body on this mountain of sun, moon and stars. A stele on the right carries the name of the bodhisattva Myōken, the deity who represents the female form of the Great Bear constellation. The Great Bear was considered the most perfect constellation because it indicates true North by pointing to the Polar Star. Myōken is thus the ruler of the stars. In Japan, Myōken is worshipped as a manifestation of Dainichi, the Great Sun Buddha of Kūkai's esoteric Shingon sect. The short path up from the stone leads to a stone shrine beneath a standing rock.

Returning and continuing along the path at the bottom, take the left fork soon after the Myōken stone. It takes another ten minutes to reach the road up from the bus stop a short way above the path to Nichirinji. Turn left and retrace your steps to Jaketsu.

TRANSPORTATION

Outbound:

From Tokyo: JR Jōban line from Ueno to Mito, then JR Suigun line from Mito to Hitachi Daigo. Around ¥3,300 plus additional express charge of ¥1,400 (Ueno to Mito).

Bus from Hitachi Daigo to Jaketsu: Jaketsu is the terminus, but the sign on the front of the bus may read Kurosawa. (45 minutes, ¥780). Morning buses at 8:03 and 10:37. For latest bus times, call Ibaraki Kōtsū (☎ 0295-72-0428). On the present timetable, day trippers must take the 6:46 local train, the 7:30 Hitachi 101 express, or the 8:00 Super Hitachi express from Ueno to meet the 9:24 train from Mito to Kōriyama (platform 1), arriving at Hitachi Daigo at 10:30 just in time for the 10:37 bus.

Return:

Buses from Jaketsu: Afternoon buses at 3:00 (weekends and holidays only), 4:15 (daily), 5:05 (Monday to Friday only; does not run on school or public holidays).

ACCOMMODATIONS

There is a tourist information office outside Hitachi Daigo station. Daigo (including Fukuroda) has thirty-one *ryokan* and *minshuku* and eleven campgrounds with bungalows. Call Daigo-machi Kankō Kyōkai (Daigo-machi Tourist Association; ☎ 0295-72-

0285) or Okukuji Daigo Kankō Telephone Service (☎ 0295-72-0992).

The municipal Yamizosan Yama no Ue campsite and bungalows (open July and August) beside Nichirinji can be booked through the Town Hall (☎ 0295-72-1111) or the Tourist Association. The camp's own number is 0295-77-0241.

Hot spring hotels near Hitachi Daigo station:

Okukuji Grand Hotel (☎ 0295-72-1134)

Kikuya (☎ 0295-72 -0037)

Hojokan (☎ 0295-72-0002)

Tamaya Ryokan (☎ 0295-72-0123)

Hashimotoya Ryokan (☎ 0295-72-0194)

Nakamura Ryokan (☎ 0295-72-0226)

Yamizo (☎ 0295-72-1511). Large inexpensive leisure center with overnight facilities.

USEFUL KANJI

Ginseisui	銀性水
Hitachi Daigo	常陸大子
Jaketsu	蛇穴
Kinseisui	金性水
Kurosawa	黒沢
Kyūsandō	旧参道
Nichirinji	日輪寺
Nichirinji Bungalows	日輪寺バンガロー
Mito	水戸
Mount Yamizo	八溝山
Myōken Bosatsu	妙見菩薩
Ryōmosui	龍毛水
Tessui	鉄水
Yamizomine Shrine	八溝嶺神社

SATAKEDERA — 22

In the Steps of Mito Kōmon

Satakedera is located in Hitachi Ōta, twenty kilometers from Mito by the little JR Suigun line. Paddies spread across the plain, vegetable farms dot the wooded escarpment above the Yamada River, and beyond rises a range of low mountains. This is rural Japan at its most luscious. Try to visit in summer when the flowers are in bloom, for the farmers love their flowers almost as much as their crops.

The first-time visitor may wonder how a Bandō temple came to be located in such a pleasant, out-of-the-way spot. The answer lies in the name of the temple itself, for the Satake were one of the most powerful of the Bandō *musha* clans. Here we are fully back in the territory of the great feudal lords.The Satake were descended from the third son of eleventh-century Minamoto Yoriyoshi, the Genji warlord who held sway over the province of Hitachi after helping to suppress the rebellion of Taira Tadatsune.

Come the twelfth century, the Satake at first miscalculated badly by failing to support Yoritomo, their distant cousin from the line of Yoriyoshi's eldest son. They were defeated by Yoritomo at Kanasago, just outside Hitachi Ōta, in November of 1180, and fled to the north. Belatedly recognizing which way the wind was blowing, Satake Hideyoshi then restored and even enhanced his position by switching sides and joining Yoritomo's Ōshū campaign of 1189. The Satake thus entered the Kamakura era, when the Bandō course was founded, as important allies of Yoritomo on Kantō's northern boundary.

Satake Sadayoshi made no mistake one-and-a-half centuries later when taking the side of Ashikaga Takauji in the overthrow of the Kamakura shogunate and subsequent battles, thus adding further

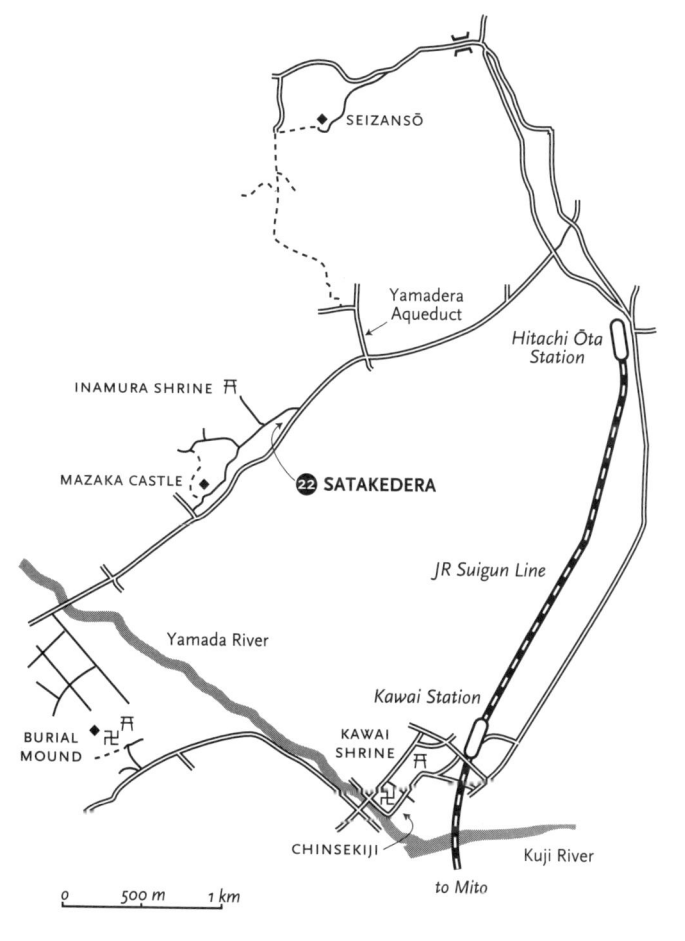

to his territory. The Satake were also richly rewarded with new land for helping Toyotomi Hideyoshi to overthrow the Hōjō in 1590. Satake Yoshishige and Yoshinobu moved their base to Mito, renovated Mito Castle and played an active part in Hideyoshi's Korean campaign. By the end of the sixteenth century, the Satake were the seventh richest warlord clan in Japan.

Having reached the heights, the Satake fortunes plumbed the depths after Hideyoshi's death in 1598. Relations with Tokugawa Ieyasu were far cooler, with the result that the Satake were not involved in the decisive battle at Sekigahara. They were abruptly expelled to Akita in 1602, and replaced in the Mito region by a branch line of the Tokugawa family. This rich rice-growing district thus retained the patronage of the powerful through the Edo era. The new Mito line was one of three minor lines descended directly from Ieyasu (the others based in Owari and Kii), kept on standby to provide heirs to the shogunate should the main line die out.

The second head of the Mito line, Tokugawa Mitsukuni (1628–1700), is better known to history as Mito Kōmon. Mitsukuni was vice-shogun but also an imperial loyalist who disapproved of the treatment of the emperor by the Tokugawa regime. He resigned his official position in 1690 in order to retire to a house in the country. He left office in conscious imitation of the renowned Chinese martyrs to good government, Boyi and Shuqi, who went into the mountains where they died after refusing an order to kill their master's rival. Mito Kōmon chose to cultivate his own rice, help the people, and compile a great history of Japan. His home, Seizansō, is the final stop of the walk.

The historical richness of this district is reflected in the walk. In addition to the several temples and shrines, it also visits a huge late-fifth- or early-sixth-century burial mound over 150 meters long. While the first half follows the Yamada River across the plain, the second leads along a quiet trail to Seizansō on the top of the wooded escarpment.

CHAPTER 22

THE TEMPLE

Satakedera has a beautiful thatched main hall with various sixteenth-century devices. It was designated as a National Treasure as early as 1906, at a time when the temple was still without a priest following the disruptions of the Meiji Restoration. But while the lovely hall has been cared for over the years, Satakedera has lost its once extensive grounds. Its present predicament, hemmed in on a sliver of land at the roadside, is reminiscent of that of Chōkokuji in Gunma.

Legend recounts that Satakedera was founded by the priest Tokuitsu in 807. Another story attributes it to Gemmitsu Shōnin in 985, in the reign of Emperor Kazan. The temple, officially called Kannonji, was originally built on a promontory above a nearby lake.

The temple's history truly starts with the arrival of the Satake. A story tells how Masayoshi, the clan's founder, chose the name Satake ("helping bamboo") after seeing some wonderful bamboo in the temple's grounds. Masayoshi gave Kannonji a rich gift of land in 1177. The temple's name was changed to Satakedera following a major restoration by the sixth Satake, Nagayoshi. In later years, Tokugawa Mitsukuni also gave the temple his patronage. Besides its place in the Bandō pilgrimage, Satakedera was made number eleven of the new thirty-three Kannon pilgrimage of Mito in the 1740s.

Sadly little remains of the former glory. Everything was destroyed by a fire in 1543. That provided the opportunity to relocate the temple to its present site in 1546. Satake Yoshiaki rebuilt it here in order to protect his northern boundary. The thatched main hall dates from that time but with substantial alterations from the Edo period. The eleven-headed Kannon is worshiped as a guardian of safe birth.

THE WALK ** *(2 hours 50 minutes)*

The walk starts from the station at Kawai, which is two stops short of the terminal at Hitachi Ōta. This little country station is unmanned, so you have to give your ticket to the driver or guard when you get off.

Turn left out of the station and keep straight across the main road, following the sign to Chinsekiji. The quiet road leads past paddies and farmhouses. Take the right fork a hundred meters from the station. Kawai Shrine, the village shrine, stands opposite the nursery school. Notice the little halls to the left of the main building that contain a lot of tiny Shichifukujin statues. Most are of Daikokuten (the one with the hammer).

Continuing, Chinsekiji is six minutes beyond the shrine at the embankment of the Yamada River, a major tributary of the Kuji. A statue of Shinran in priest's garb stands at the entrance.

Shinran (1173–1262) was the founder of the Jōdō Shin (True Pure Land) sect who followed Hōnen in the teaching of salvation through trust in Amida. Shinran taught for some twenty years in Hitachi from 1214. It was during this time that he wrote the basic Jōdō Shin text, *Kyōgyōshinshō*. Shinran, a Tendai rebel and preacher of a new popular faith, was one of the religious leaders whom the esoteric Buddhist founders of the Bandō pilgrimage were trying to resist.

Chinsekiji's main image is an Amida presented by Tokugawa Mitsukuni in 1673. The temple's name, literally meaning "pillow stone," and the story of its founding relate to a night that Shinran had to spend out in a blizzard.

When Shinran and two disciples appealed for shelter at the house of Hino Yoriaki, they were sternly refused, with the rebuke that the Buddhist's vocation is to sleep in the open without creature comforts. Shinran found a stone for a pillow and lay down to rest. However, Kannon appeared to Yoriaki that night, telling him to take Shinran in and learn from him. As a result, Yoriaki became a priest himself and founded Chinsekiji. The great monument on the stone in front of the main hall also commemorates this story, while one of the temple's treasures is the stone pillow itself, with an inscription said to have been carved by Shinran.

CHAPTER 22

Climb the embankment from Chinsekiji and turn right to cross the bridge. Then continue in the same direction along the path on top of the embankment on the far side of the river. You have the hills to the right and a broad swathe of paddies to the left. Turn left at the next bridge, Shimakuhashi, taking the road past the houses at the foot of the low hills. Keeping straight for Nakano at an English road sign, you want to turn right ten minutes from the river just opposite a large stone lantern. A wine shop is on the far corner. A white post with an arrow indicates the way to another temple, Hōkongōin.

Turn left at the next T-junction (with three Jizōs on the corner) to reach the temple gate. Hōkongōin, like Chinsekiji, is very neatly maintained. Founded as a Mizuko Jizō temple for prayers for lost babies in 1445, it was moved to this site and given its present name at the order of Tokugawa Mitsukuni in 1699. A Fudō hall and belfry stand on the right and a Daishi hall dedicated to Kūkai on the left.

The main sight is behind the temple to the left. The steps lead up to a Bonten Daigongen Shrine at the top of an ancient burial mound. Bonten is the Brahma heaven in Hindu mythology, and also the name of its king, who was adopted as a guardian deity of Buddhism. The path leads to the dip in the middle of the mound and down to the natural hill on the other side.

This is the largest of twelve mounds in the Bontenyama group. Others are scattered over quite a wide area. You can spot some in the fields. This mound is 150 meters long and probably dates from the late fifth or early sixth century. It is the second biggest in Ibaraki Prefecture. A cluster of burial caves is also found on the hillside. The large mound is thought to be the grave of Funase no Sukune, the leader who established Kuji, one of the seven domains that became the province of Hitachi. An excavation at one of the smaller mounds in 1950 unearthed three skeletons, three swords, copper bracelets and other remains.

No path is obvious, but descend directly the other side from the path up to the middle of the mound. This brings you to another

SATAKEDERA

plain of rice fields in the village of Kanasago. A broad grassy track leads across the fields towards the main road and the next bridge across the Yamada River. Follow this track, briefly going right at a large drainage channel to join a paved road.

That completes the walk on the plain. Next the route heads across the Eidai Bridge and up the escarpment to Satakedera. Turn left at the foot of the escarpment in order to climb the pretty lane between the houses and turn right at the little T-junction. A sign to the left near the top of the steep concrete road indicates fifty meters to the site of Mazaka Castle.

Mazaka was a fortress built about 1131 by the founder of the Satake family, Satake Masayoshi. Including outer fortifications, it occupied an area of nearly four thousand square meters. The main Satake family soon relocated to nearby Ōta Castle, but minor relatives remained at Mazaka until the Satake were expelled from the area in 1602. A monument in the middle of the vegetable fields marks the spot. Jōmon-period shell mounds have also been discovered on this site.

Return down the steps and continue up the road to the top of the embankment and onto the plateau. Five minutes bring you to the gate of the great Inamura Shrine, which was established from a group of ancient shrines by Mito Kōmon. It is recorded that Kōmon often came here. The older shrines claimed connections with Yamato Takeru's northern campaign. Inamura Shrine also celebrates Nigihayahi, the ancestor of Funase no Sukune. It has a remarkable location at the tip of a promontory.

Continue along the same road. The *niōmon* of Satakedera stands on the corner where the lane rejoins the main road. After viewing the temple, continue another five minutes along the same road. You pick up a sign to the left for Hakubaji and the Yamadera Aqueduct. You now find yourself on a narrow lane past farmhouses and vegetable fields. The contrast with the main road is astonishing. This feels like the heart of rural Japan.

CHAPTER 22

You soon come to a sign on the left telling you that you are passing over the Yamadera Aqueduct. This two-kilometer waterway, built in 1668 at the order of Tokugawa Mitsukuni, travels through tunnels for fully 750 meters of its course. The local people still drink from it today.

Turn left a minute later, following the sign to Hakubaji. Some farm buildings are thatched. Follow the sign pointing right three minutes later. This brings you to a long track through the trees. All habitation is left behind for twenty minutes as the path leads along the plateau. A couple of turns have to be made. Follow the signs for Seizansō and Nishiyama Kōen.

The descent to Seizansō brings you out directly behind the ticket office. Admission is ¥300. The house and garden were no doubt modest for a former vice-shogun but would do very nicely in modern Japan. They are set in a deep gulley against the wooded hillside, with bamboos at the gate. The ponds are designed in a mirror-image of the Chinese character for heart. The idea, true to Kōmon's style, is that you have to view both writing and men's motives from behind. The thatched building we see today is an early nineteenth-century restoration on a slightly smaller scale than the original, which was destroyed by fire.

Many other devices were used to create the desired ambience. A cedar was transplanted from Kumano and five willows were placed here after the five willows in the garden of Chinese poet Tao Chien (825–885). The villa also has a moon-viewing hall and a garden with various medicinal herbs.

You can also buy a statuette of Kōmon with his long sage's beard. He is a familiar character to all Japanese, whether inclined towards history or not, for his starring role in a long series of films and TV programs. In these stories, he wanders the country anonymously with just two retainers, dispensing justice and kindness wherever he goes. The pop stories are fiction, but Kōmon did have unusually free and easy contact with the common people. His reputation as a moral giant is not only modern. This saying was once current among the populace:

> *Two treasures under heaven are inexhaustible,*
> *The gold mines of Sado,*
> *And the golden gate (kōmon) of Mito.*

The 402-volume Mito history of Japan, by the way, was completed in 1906.

Leaving the house, follow the path past Mito Kōmon's rice paddy and the iris ponds to the large restaurant at the bottom. This ends the walk. You have a choice. You can call a taxi (Ekimae Taxi, ☎ 0294-72-0122; Shinsei Taxi, ☎ 0294-72-1266), or you can walk thirty minutes down the road to Hitachi Ōta station. If walking, follow the English road signs for Mito and Hitachi.

TRANSPORTATION

Train from Tokyo: JR Jōban line from Ueno to Mito. Try to get the Super Hitachi express bound for Taira at 7:00 am (just over 1 hour) for a good connection at Mito. Then JR Suigun line for Hitachi Ōta from Mito to Kawai (35 minutes). You may have to change trains at Kami Sugaya. The entire trip (one way) should cost ¥2,160 (¥3,200 with express supplement).

ACCOMMODATIONS

Business Hotel Takakura (☎ 0294-72-2511). Near Hitachi Ōta Station.

USEFUL KANJI

Chinsekiji	枕石寺
Hitachi Ōta	常陸太田
Hakubaji	白馬寺
Hōkongōin	宝金剛院
Inamura Shrine	稲村神社
Kami Sugaya	上菅谷

CHAPTER 22

Kawai	河合
Kawai Shrine	河合神社
Mazaka Castle	馬坂城
Mito	水戸
Nishiyama Kōen	西山公園
Satakedera	佐竹寺
Seizansō	西山荘
Shimakuhashi	しまくはし
Yamadera Aqueduct	山寺水道

KANZEONJI — 23
*Azaleas and Modern Art * (1 hour)*

The heyday of this temple, founded in 651 atop Mount Sashiro, passed in 1205 soon after the Bandō circuit began. First, war broke out against the priests of another temple. Then, the expansionist Utsunomiya clan stepped in, massacred the priests, and built a castle on the temple's site. After a series of bad experiences, a Kannon hall was established inside the castle in order to absolve the owners of their guilt, but it too was destroyed in the Meiji Restoration. The mob that burned the Kannon hall had intended to continue to Rakuhōji (Temple 24) on the same night, but somehow the momentum was lost. The present Kanzeonji was established in 1984 with the growing popularity of the modern pilgrimage. It still lacks a proper main hall.

There is, even so, plenty to see in the town of Kasama, which like Mashiko is a pottery town. Ōtsuka Keisaburō, founder of the Mashiko industry, learned his skills here. Ask about pottery classes at the tourist information center outside the station (where you can also rent bicycles). The town has pretty hillside paths around the site of the old castle, the great Kasama Inari Shrine (which attracts more than two million worshipers annually), the Nichidō Museum of Art, and the Nichidō Sports Car Museum. The azalea park behind Kanzeonji has 35,000 bushes of twenty-five species.

TRANSPORTATION
JR Jōban line from Ueno to Tomobe (1 hour 10 minutes by Hitachi express). Then Mito line from Tomobe to Kasama (15 minutes). Fare from Ueno to Kasama: ¥1,850. Additional express charge from Ueno to Tomobe: ¥1,340.

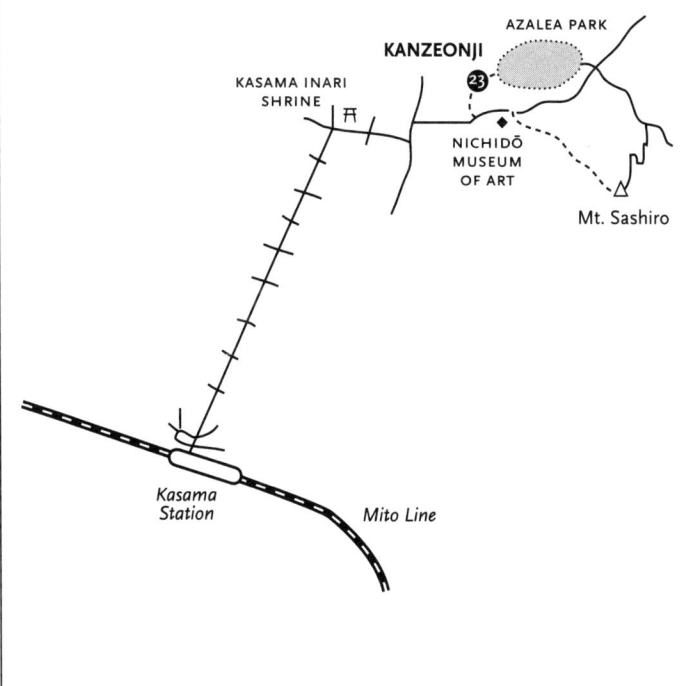

ACCOMMODATIONS

Near Kasama station:
Ryokan Inami (☎ 0296-72-0165).
Jōshūya (☎ 0296-72-0185).
Near Kanzeonji:
Hotel Yamanosō (☎ 0296 72 1221).
Hotel Izutsuya (☎ 0296-72-1101).
Ryokan Komatsukan (☎ 0296-72-0668).
Ryokan Mifune (☎ 0296-72-0569).

USEFUL KANJI

Kanzeonji	観世音寺
Kasama Inari Shrine	笠間稲荷神社
Mount Sashiro	佐白山
Sashiro Kannon	佐白観音
Sashiro Kōen	佐白公園
Tomobe	友部

RAKUHŌJI — 24
Mount Kaba

The Bandō course now follows the Tsukuba range from Kasama to Rakuhōji and on to Ōmidō on the flanks of Mount Tsukuba itself. Those who enjoy ridges with panoramic views can hardly do better, for the mountains stand out sharply from the plain. With an early start, the whole lot can be walked in a single day from Iwase station, reaching the peak of Mount Tsukuba by evening. It is far better, however, to break the walk and see some of the sights in the foothills as well. Among these, Rakuhōji, the temple of the Amabiki Kannon, is most impressive. As noted in the previous chapter, the mob had intended to burn Rakuhōji on the same night as Kanzeonji. The modern tourist can be grateful that it did not, for this is one of the Bandō pilgrimage's most beautiful temples.

The walk follows the ridge from above Rakuhōji as far as the spectacular craggy peak and shrines of Mount Kaba, then descends by the route used by worshipers to more shrines at the bottom. Mount Kaba, too, was long used by the mountain priests of Shugendō. It also gave its name to the well-known Kabasan Incident of 1884.

The Kabasan Incident arose in conjunction with the People's Rights Movement that culminated in the promulgation of the Meiji Constitution in 1889. A former samurai of Shimodate, Tomimatsu Masayasu, plotted with members of the Liberal Party to assassinate leading government officials at the ceremony for the opening of the Utsunomiya prefectural government offices. Their targets included Sanjō Sanetomi, Iwakura Tomomi and Mishima Michitsune. The conspiracy was discovered, however, and the ceremony postponed indefinitely. Armed Liberal Party members rallied to set up a base on Mount Amabiki, only to change course part way and climb

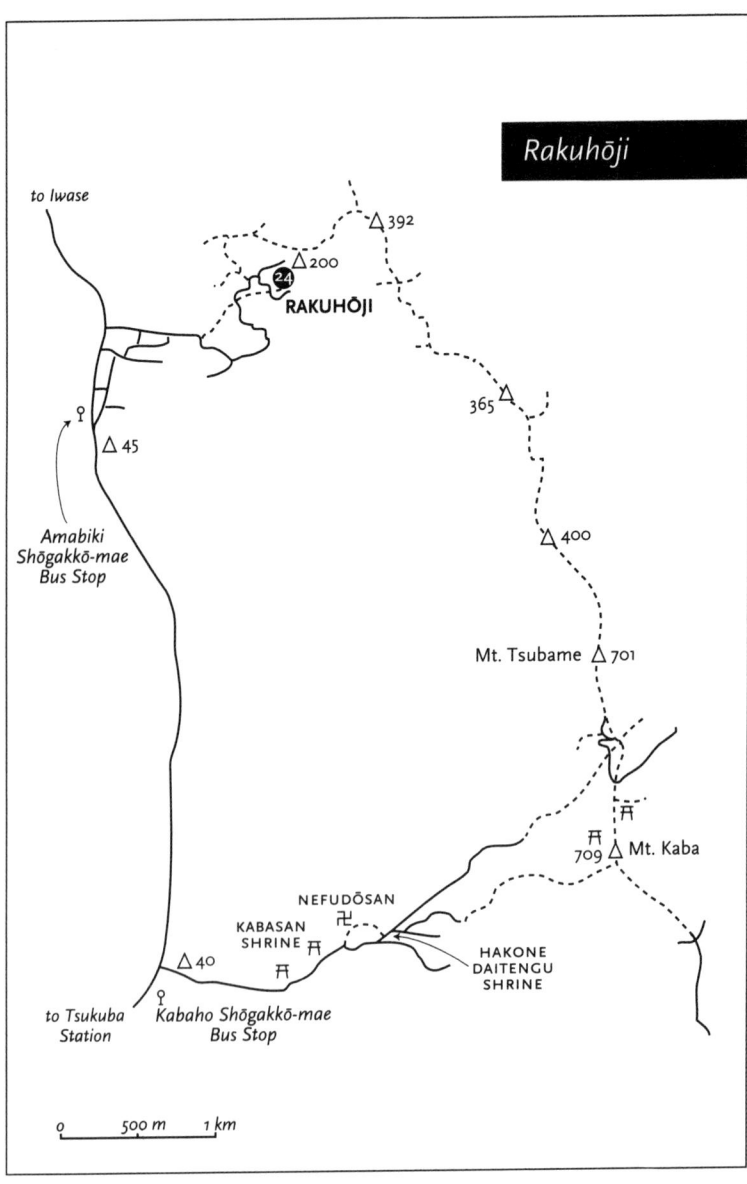

Mount Kaba instead. Eventually, like so many rebellions of the period, it all fizzled out. Most of the insurgents were arrested near Iwase as they sought to escape.

THE TEMPLE

Rakuhōji, the temple that everyone marches on and nobody reaches, has always been associated with magic. It is also known as Amabiki Kannon, which literally means "Rain-Summoning Kannon." One of the mountain priests' key functions was to pray for rain. When a great nationwide drought occurred in the summer of 821, the emperor himself asked for prayers to be raised here. Rain fell, and the delighted emperor commanded that the temple's *sangō*, or "mountain name," be changed to Amabikisan. The emperor's missive is preserved in the temple today. (A *sangō* was an alternate name for a temple taking the name of a nearby mountain; in time this custom spread to include even temples that were not situated in mountainous areas.)

Rakuhōji claims to have been founded in 586, just seven years before the accession of Shōtoku Taishi to the regency. Prayers at this temple were also efficacious for restoring the health of Empress Suiko (592–628) and ensuring safe births in the imperial family. The main image is an Enmei (Longevity) Kannon, so Rakuhōji is also a place to pray for a long life, but the prayers for safe birth are what the temple emphasizes today. Rakuhōji later received the patronage of the Kamakura shoguns, Ashikaga Takauji, and Tokugawa Ieyasu. Yoshimune, the eighth Tokugawa shogun, was particularly fond of this temple, visiting several times and also planting a cherry tree in the grounds.

The long flight of 145 steps to the *niōmon* was constructed in the early 1820s. Those who climb intoning the mantra of Kannon, *Namu Kanzeon Bosatsu*, can expect all evil to fall away among the beautiful hydrangeas on either side of the path. Come in June for the hydrangeas, in April for cherry blossoms, and for azaleas in the first week of May. The belfry is silhouetted against the sky to the right. This grand structure, built in 1830, looks out across the Kantō Plain.

The red *niōmon* was erected in 1682. Take a look at the superb carvings around the sides, made in 1704. The *niō* statues are Kamakura-period works preserved from an earlier gate of 1254.

Passing through the *niōmon*, next notice the gnarled oak on the right. The main Kannon image is said to have leapt from the temple and sheltered beneath this tree during a great fire in 1471. A small Jizō hall also stands close by. The Jizō statue was carved in 1715. Mothers pray there for the safe growth of their children.

The next flight of steps brings you to the main courtyard, distinguished by a superb two-story pagoda, actually a *tahōtō*: a tower dedicated to the buddha Tahō Nyorai (Prabhutaratna). Such a tower is mentioned in the *Lotus Sutra*. This tower used to be a three-story pagoda, but was remodeled as a *tahōtō* in 1853.

A curious story tells of a lumber dealer who planted a pine tree in front of the pagoda and prayed for wealth. Those prayers were answered by the great Meireki fire of 1657 in Edo; the fire which led to the removal of the Yoshiwara prostitution quarter to the district where we find it in the walk from Sensōji (see Chapter 13). The price of timber soared and the lucky man's fortune was made. The pine in front of the *tahōtō* is called *takara o unda matsu* ("the pine that bore wealth"). This story recalls the experience of the Mashiko potters who likewise profited hugely from the Great Kantō Earthquake of 1923. Quite a few people might go to temples in order to pray for disaster.

The main hall, built in 1710, is also beautifully crafted, with many dragon heads under the eves. Unfortunately, the main Kannon is a secret image and cannot be seen. It is said to have been carved in 810. The *maedachi* Kannon is a Kamakura-period work.

Other sights include a red and gold shrine founded in 1625 for the repose of Tokugawa Ieyasu, rebuilt in 1727; a hexagonal concrete hall housing a wooden statue of Fudō donated by Ashikaga Yoshinori in 1438, at a time of famine, pestilence, and rebellion; a Yakushi image, also in the hexagonal hall, donated by Tokugawa Yoshimune to cure his adopted daughter's eye disease; an Enma hall with both great and small *ema* votive offerings on the roof; and an eternal spring said to have gushed up when the temple was founded in 586.

The Madara Festival is traditionally held on the first Sunday of April. This fire-prevention festival commemorates a time in the middle ages when a demon called Madara helped the priests to rebuild the burned-out temple in a single week.

THE WALK *** (4 hours)

Alighting at the Amabiki Shōgakkō Mae bus stop, return a few steps in the Iwase direction to pick up the Kantō Fureai no Michi sign pointing right down a narrow lane to Amabiki Kannon. This lane leads through the small temple village with its old farms, and still the occasional thatched roof. Stay with this lane, ignoring the second Kantō Fureai no Michi sign pointing right.

Instead, go right where the lane divides five minutes from the bus stop, and right again at the junction with a bigger road five minutes after that. Take the narrow concrete road straight up the mountain where the vehicular road bends sharply right. A sign on the corner (for cars) points right to Amabiki Kannon. You will also notice a stone buddha with a red halo on the left and a cluster of stone pagodas on the right. This is the way for pilgrims who approach the temple on foot.

More stones line the way, including both Kannons and memorials to pilgrimages past. You pick up the Kantō Fureai no Michi signs again where the path crosses the road, just beneath the entrance to the hiking course. First, continue up the roughly-hewn steps on the far side of the road to an old gate, the Yakuimon, now visible below the temple. This was the gate to Makabe Castle until 1600, before becoming the outer gate to Rakuhōji.

After viewing the temple, return to the Kantō Fureai no Michi junction close to Yakuimon. The sign (on the roadside) indicates 1.8

kilometers to Mount Amabiki and 7.3 kilometers to Mount Kaba. The path rises sharply up the mountainside, with many steps but also fine views of Mount Tsukuba, the Kantō Plain, and Mount Kaba and its sister peak, the prettily named Mount Tsubame, or Swallow Mountain. You will also notice that the climb up Tsubame is going to be long and steep. Save your energy for that part of the walk.

It takes about twenty-five minutes to reach the ridge. Those who fancy a slightly easier walk can turn left here and follow the Kantō Fureai no Michi signs across the peak of Mount Amabiki back to Iwase station. It is downhill almost all the way from Mount Amabiki. The sign left indicates 0.5 kilometers to Mount Amabiki and 2.8 kilometers to Mount Ontake (a much lower peak). Go right for Mount Kaba (6.0 kilometers).

The path right winds gently up and down the ridge for forty-five minutes through bamboo grasses, mixed trees, and hydrangeas. It is well maintained, but a couple of short slopes are very steep, so you will want to wear well-soled shoes. The serious climb begins at the 3.1 kilometer sign to Mount Kaba. The slope looks innocent enough at first, but turns into another thirty-minute climb with lots of steps. Happily, the views, both on the way up and at the top, are commensurate with the effort.

Just after the peak of Mount Tsubame, you reach some benches beneath an NHK television relay tower. Here you should take the vehicular track down for several minutes. The Kantō Fureai no Michi path branches off to the right at the 0.5 kilometer sign to Mount Kaba. Keep straight for the peak of Mount Kaba (Kabasanchō) at the 0.4 kilometer sign. You now reach the Kabasan Youth Hostel and the first of a series of Kabasan shrines.

The top of Mount Kaba is covered with giant boulders and crags, giving considerable pleasure as you clamber from one shrine to the next along the ridge. The path, however, is very safe, with no cause for concern. The third shrine is the Tobacco Shrine, where smokers and local tobacco-growers give thanks. It has a smoking festival on August 20.

CHAPTER 24

The sixth shrine is the main one, the *hongū*. Large crowds gather here on the night of July 31 each year for the traditional mountain-opening ceremonies the following day. These open the mountain in the sense of allowing visits by people from the world of the living, not in the physical sense of rending it apart.

Anybody is welcome to take part in the related Zenjō ceremonies during August, which involve prayers at more than seven hundred sacred spots on the mountain. The entire procedure takes three full days but you are allowed to divide this up over a period of years. Do be aware that this is serious mountain asceticism with steep climbs up crags, using chains. There is no fixed rate for the guide (*sendatsu*) but he should be rewarded generously. If interested, contact Kabasan Jinja (☎ 0296-55-3288; in Japanese).

Legend tells that the Kabasan shrines were founded by the mythical nation-building hero Yamato Takeru, who possibly lived around the second or third centuries AD. In another story, Kūkai ended a great drought by praying for rain on this mountain. In addition, fishermen come here to pray for good catches and safety at sea.

The Kantō Fureai no Michi continues along the ridge to Ipponsugi Pass (2.1 kilometers) and Mount Ashio, with quite a bit of walking on roads. A monument to the Kabasan Incident stands just a short way beyond your present position. The more attractive option for those not continuing to Mount Tsukuba is to descend from the *hongū*, taking the sign right for Makabe and Nagaoka. Go right where the path splits, thirty meters below the ridge.

The many wayside stones, sacred boulders, and sacred trees (indicated by ropes and offerings) leave no doubt that this is a pilgrims' trail. The path descends steeply but safely through mixed woods with more views of Mount Tsukuba to the left. Above, you will see the hang gliders of Mount Ashio, one of the best-known centers for the sport in the Kantō area. Crowds of hang-glider pilots and spectators gather every weekend throughout the year. Ashio, as noted in Chapter 19, is also the mountain with a shrine for feet.

The path crosses a road seven minutes below the ridge and soon afterwards goes across the top of a quarry. Be sure not to leave the path. Also, get as far away as you can, either up or down the path, if you hear a siren announcing blasting at the quarry. In between the excitement, you might notice stones indicating the stages of the climb, for like Mount Fuji, the ascent of this sacred mountain is divided into ten sections corresponding to levels of heaven and hell in esoteric Buddhism. In this case, of course, you are descending.

Turn right where the path meets a track. Just after, you come to the extraordinary Hakone Tengu Shrine, where the long-nosed mountain goblin is joined by a plethora of statues. Perhaps this is only fair, seeing as Mount Kaba is said to be populated by forty-eight *tengu*, all governed by a great *tengu*, and more than seven hundred gods besides. You will nonetheless be astonished by the garish, modernistic layout. It is not clear at first whether you have arrived at a shop, a showroom, a shrine, or the set of a television commercial. In fact, you have reached the shrine of a secretive new religion, the Jōdo Kongō sect, which was founded in this century. The main shrine is above Yumoto in Hakone, but this is where the founder achieved enlightenment. The sect combines Buddhism and Shinto, with an emphasis on communicating with ancestors. Don't expect a friendly welcome.

From here, you can either continue down the road to the Nefudōson Shrine or take the path to the shrine from the parking lot. If taking the road, beware of lunatic truck drivers carrying heavy loads of Kaba stone. It takes five minutes to reach the shrine.

This shrine, too, is an oddity in this century, seeing as the Fudō occupying pride of place in this Shinto shrine is actually a Buddhist god. The separation of Buddhism and Shinto is far from complete even in Ibaraki, as the reader has probably sensed by now, but such outright incongruities are normally avoided. A flood washed the Fudō image down from the middle slopes of Mount Kaba and buried it at this spot. When discovered, a hall was erected in its honor. The former hall burned down in 1990, but has already been replaced.

CHAPTER 24

Taking the road down from the shrine, you soon reach the stone marking the second stage (*nigome*) of the ascent on the left, then come out among houses and farms. The first stage (*ichigome*) stone stands outside the Kabasan shrine at the foot of the mountain.

This Kabasan shrine is small, but does have a little exhibition hall for, as you may have guessed, tobacco. The centerpiece is the largest pipe in Japan, which features in the festival mentioned earlier. There is also a Tobacco Jizō modeled on a three-hundred-year-old Tobacco Jizō in Nagano, erected to the memory of one of Japan's first fatalities from this dangerous habit. The warlord Itagaki Nobukata, a general in Takeda Shingen's army and an ancestor of the Meiji politician Itagaki Taisuke, was surprised in battle while enjoying a quiet smoke.

Three minutes later, another and much larger Kabasan shrine stands on the left. This is the main shrine for one of the smaller halls at the top, the Kabasan Saenazumi Shrine. Also known as Hoshinomiya, it was a center for the mountain priests until the separation of Buddhism and Shinto.

Turn left onto the main road at the bottom. You will reach the Kabaho Shōgakkō Mae bus stop in a hundred meters. Buses on this side of the road go to Makabe and Tsukuba station; those on the far side to Iwase.

TRANSPORTATION
Outbound:

From Tokyo by train: JR Tōhoku line or Tōhoku Shinkansen to Ōyama. Then JR Mito line from Ōyama to Iwase (30 minutes). ¥1,850 (extra charge for Shinkansen, ¥1,950).

Bus from Iwase to Amabiki Shōgakkō Mae (10 minutes, ¥240). Morning buses at 6:55, 7:35, 7:55 (except Sundays), 8:25 (except Sundays), 9:40, 11:10. The bus stop is a three-minute walk from Iwase station. Turn left out of the station and follow the tracks to the first level crossing. The stop is just the other side of the railway on the left.

RAKUHŌJI

From Tokyo by bus: JR bus to Tsukubasan from the Yaesu exit of Tokyo station (1 hour 40 minutes). Morning buses at 7:15, 9:05. Bus from the terminus at Tsukubasan (Tsukuba station) to Iwase. Alight at Amabiki Shōgakkō Mae. (40 minutes, ¥680). There are no good connections; you must wait at least an hour at Tsukubasan.

Return:

From Kabaho Shōgakkō Mae to Iwase (20 minutes, ¥380). Afternoon buses about once an hour.

ACCOMMODATIONS

Kabasan Youth Hostel (☎ 0296-55-1928). On top of Mount Kaba. You can also continue along the Kantō Fureai no Michi to Tsukubasan Youth Hostel (see Chapter 25). Be warned, though, that the next few kilometers are mostly on roads.

USEFUL KANJI

Amabiki Kannon	雨引観音
Amabiki Shōgakkō Mae	雨引小学校前
Ipponsugi Pass	一本杉峠
Kabasanchō	加波山頂
Kabaho Shōgakkō Mae	樺穂小学校前
Kantō Fureai no Michi	関東ふれあいの道
Makabe	真壁
Mount Amabiki	雨引山
Mount Kaba	加波山
Mount Ontake	御嶽山
Mount Tsubame	燕山
Nagaoka	長岡
Nefudōson Shrine	寝不動尊神社
Rakuhōji	楽法寺
Tsukuba	筑波

ŌMIDŌ — 25
Mount Tsukuba ** (3 hours)

The walk on Mount Tsukuba is one of the best day hikes from Tokyo. The original temple, founded as Chūzenji in 782, is now the magnificent Tsukuba Shrine, while little Ōmidō continues the Buddhist traditions as an afterthought. Visitors to Nikkō will notice some parallels. Besides the same temple name, Chūzenji, there is a sacred bridge, Shinkyō, at the entrance to the shrine, just like Shinkyō at Tōshōgū. This shrine, too, protected the Tokugawa Shogunate. The peaks are Nantai and Nyotai, the male and female peaks, like Nantai and Nyohō at Nikkō. Tsukuba and Nikkō share a common history of ascetic mountain priests and Tokugawa patronage. While Nikkō protected the north, Tsukuba defended the east. See Ōmidō quickly, take your time at the shrine, then climb the peaks on foot or by cable car. The views are splendid. Go first to Nantai Shrine, then follow the ridge through the tunnel of *buna* oaks to Nyotai, noticing the giant crags named for the wagtail and the toad on the way. Return down the path to the right under the cable car. This winds past a series of fantastic crags (the Great Buddha, Big Dipper, Daikokuten, and Mother's Womb, where you can crawl through a tunnel for rebirth), and on through the precarious Benkei Nanamodori natural arch. It is said that even Benkei, Yoshitsune's fearless servant, would hesitate seven times before passing beneath it, as the name implies.

TRANSPORTATION
From Tokyo by train: JR Jōban line from Ueno to Tsuchiura (about 1 hour by express). Bus to Tsukuba station from stand number 5 (40 minutes, ¥850). Then bus from Tsukuba station stand number 2 to Tsukuba Shrine (10 minutes, ¥210).

Ōmidō

CHAPTER 25

From Tokyo by highway bus: JR bus from Yaesu exit of Tokyo station to Tsukubasan (1 hour 40 minutes depending on traffic, ¥1,700). Morning buses at 7:15, 9:05. 11:05. Pay on the bus or at the ticket window. The highway bus terminates at Tsukuba station. Then bus from stand number 2 as above.

ACCOMMODATIONS

Big tourist hotels next to Tsukuba Shrine:
Aokiya Tsukubasan Hotel (☎ 0298-66-0311).
Tsukuba Grand Hotel (☎ 0298-66-1111).
Youth Hostels:
Tsukubasan Youth Hostel (☎ 0298-66-0200). 1.3 kilometers from the summit on the other side. Follow the signs from the plaza at the mountaintop.
Tsukuba Sansō Youth Hostel (☎ 0298-66-0022). Beside Tsukuba Shrine.

USEFUL KANJI

Benkei Nanamodori	弁慶七戻り
cable car	ケーブル・カー
Mount Tsukuba	筑波山
Ōmidō	大御堂
summit (*sanchō*)	山頂
Tsuchiura	土浦
Tsukuba station	筑波駅

KIYOTAKIJI — 26
Pigs, Paddies, You, and Moi ** (2 hours)

Kiyotakiji means "temple of the clear waterfall." In legend, the water welled up when a thirsty god of Tsukuba pierced the ground with his halberd. Gyōki is said to have carved and dedicated a Shō Kannon statue. The temple has moved a number of times, however, and there is no waterfall there today. Sadly, there is not much temple, either, following fires in 1969 and 1973. The present tiny ferroconcrete main hall was built in 1977. The temple has no priest, but is cared for by local farmers. The attractions of the walk are the low-key things of the countryside. Wherever you turn you are likely to be looking at pig farms or rice paddies. The map shows the Kantō Fureai no Michi route from Nagai, but start from Hongō Nihonmatsu if you only want the main sights. See the little Zen temple of Kōjōan with its Muromachi-period garden, and the pagoda grave that legend says is the last resting place of the famed Nara-period poet and beauty Ono no Komachi. The Hie Shrine has horseback archery on the first Sunday of April, and a play in which an archer saves a child sacrifice from a rampaging monkey. Tōjōji is a grand old Yakushi temple, with old cedars, cypresses and oaks. The walk ends at the eclectic Yūmoa Mura, or You-Moi Village (from English you and French *moi*), with its hillside athletic course, Alice (in Wonderland) Hall of magic mirrors, dinosaurs, Ninja Hall, a museum of local implements, and a mixed outdoor bath (no swimwear). I quite enjoyed the village, actually.

TRANSPORTATION
Outbound:
JR Jōban line from Ueno to Tsuchiura (1 hour 10 minute, ¥1,090).

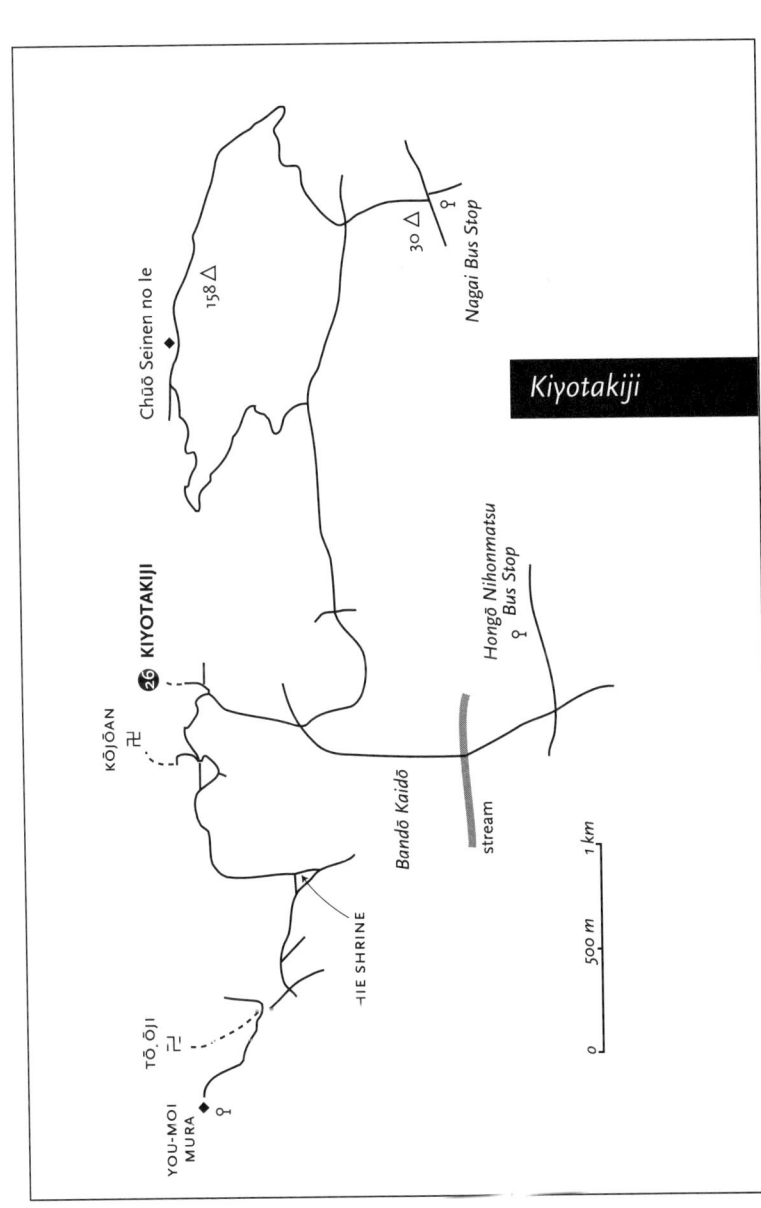

Bus to Yūmoa Mura from Tsuchiura bus stand number 5, alighting at Nagai (24 minutes, ¥420), Hongō Nihonmatsu (28 minutes, ¥530), or Yūmoa Village (35 minutes, ¥600). Buses are very infrequent. The only feasible one for the walk is at 9:00 AM on Sundays and holidays only. Catch the 8:00 Super Hitachi Express or the 7:35 slow train from Ueno to meet it.

Return:

Afternoon buses run from Yūmoa Mura to Tsuchiura at 2:01, 4:31, and 6:06 (35 minutes, ¥530). Telephone JR Bus (☎ 0298-21-5234) for details on return buses and other information.

ACCOMMODATIONS

Chūō Seinen no Ie (☎ 0298-62-3500). A public recreation facility. By far the cheapest place to stay if they will have you. Minimum of five people.

Yūmoa Mura (☎ 0298-62-3711). Overnight accommodations ¥10,000 on most days, ¥12,000 on days before holidays (includes two meals).

USEFUL KANJI

Chūō Seinen no Ie	中央青年の家
Kantō Fureai no Michi	関東ふれあいの道
Kiyotakiji	清滝寺
Hie Shrine	日枝神社
Hongō Nihonmatsu	本郷二本松
Kōjōan	向上庵
Nagai	永井
Ono no Komachi	小野小町
Tōjōji	東城寺
Tsuchiura	土浦
Yūmoa Mura (You-Moi Village)	ゆー・もあ村

ENPUKUJI — 27
Cape Inubō

Enpukuji is located in Chōshi, the port at the mouth of Bandō Tarō, the affectionate name given to the Tone River, meaning the first son of the Bandō region. The Tone's modern course reaches the Pacific close to Cape Inubō, the easternmost point of the Kantō area, at the lip of the former Katori Inland Sea. Chōshi has always been surrounded on three sides by water, and the local economy revolves around the river and the sea. This is Japan's fourth biggest fishing port and the largest in the Kantō area. Visit the fish market if you get there early in the morning.

In addition, Cape Inubō has golden beaches and a nineteenth-century English-style lighthouse. A ten-kilometer row of cliffs extends down the far side of the cape. The many seabirds include Japanese cormorants, black-tailed gulls, arctic loons, red-throated loons, and the common mew gulls. Close inshore, surfers can ride the Pacific breakers. Those who know the Japanese coast will not expect too much. The beaches are clean by Kantō standards, but far below the standards of the West. Also, no provision is made for visitors who want to enjoy the coastline on foot. But if you are looking for a day by the sea, then Cape Inubō is about your best bet.

Enpukuji is only worth a cursory visit. The temple is closely hemmed by buildings near the city center. There is little to see besides the Kannon hall. The walk, however, offers a lot of variety, from the sands of Kimigahama to the lighthouse of Cape Inubō; an aquarium and dolphin show; the lookout point on Mount Atago; and the little fishing port of Tokawa. You also get to ride part of the pretty 6.4-kilometer Chōshi Dentetsu railway around the coast.

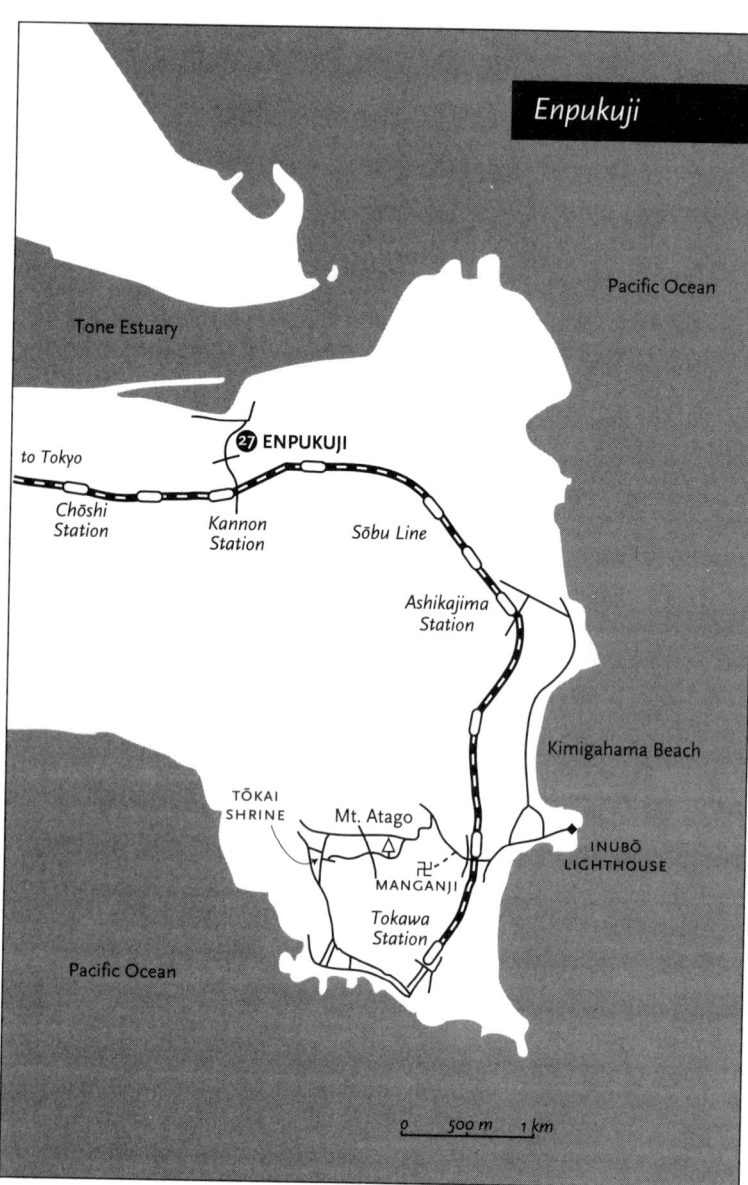

The highlight for Bandō pilgrims comes beneath Mount Atago: Manganji, a remarkable temple dedicated to the one hundred Kannons of the Bandō, Saigoku and Chichibu pilgrimages, and to the eighty-eight temples of Shikoku. Carvings of all main images are displayed, including those you cannot see at the temples themselves.

Chōshi holds its port festival on the first weekend in August, with fireworks, a procession of portable shrines, and dancing.

THE TEMPLE

Turn left out of Kannon station to reach Enpukuji, a minute down the road on the right. The temple, also known as Iinuma Kannon, is plain, and most of the precincts are given over to a nursery school. Its chief treasure is a bronze bell from the Nara period. Continue a minute or so further down the road and across the junction. The Kannon hall is on other side. Don't enter by the small red gate visible from the crossroads, but continue twenty meters down the road opposite to reach the *niōmon*.

A small row of shops leads to the giant hall. The belfry is on the right; a hall with a large buddha cast in 1714 on the left. The Kannon hall is impressive, but the once huge temple has lost its luster. All former buildings were destroyed during World War II. The temple's grounds were, of course, originally connected. The precincts formerly extended to the banks of the Tone.

Appropriately in this fishing port, the legend of Enpukuji's founding tells how local fishermen caught a Kannon statue in their nets in 724. An old man had appeared to several fishermen simultaneously in a dream and told them that he was carved from the same tree as the Kannon of Hasedera in Yamato. He had been to Ryūgū, the undersea palace of the dragon king, and wished to be raised to land. When they cast their nets, they discovered the Iinuma Kannon. Other connections with Hasedera include a shrine, which until 1869 was the hall of Ryūzō Gongen, the dragon guardian of Hasedera.

The main temple was built after Kūkai held services here early in the ninth century, and flourished as a center of esoteric Shingon practices. It came to be regarded as a defender of the province of Shimōsa and received strong patronage from the Unakami, a branch of the Chiba and Tō families, during the Kamakura period. Enpukuji also served as a major teaching temple during the Ashikaga and Tokugawa shogunates.

Chōshi thus developed mainly as a temple town until the seventeenth-century diversion of the Tone, when the river's new course provided a direct transport link to Edo. Sea products, especially sardines, and also the famous Chōshi soy sauce, could now be sent by boat to the capital.

The Matsudaira family assumed the patronage of Enpukuji in the Edo period and built a gorgeous new hall. Takayama Hikokuro, who visited in 1790, wrote appreciatively of the stone steps, *niōmon*, Fudō hall, the great golden buddha of the thirty-three buddhas hall, the two-story pagoda, Enma hall, the Ryūzō Gongen and Temman Tenjin shrines, and the great Kannon hall. But the temple suffered badly in the Meiji reforms, and what little remained was devastated by the bombs of World War II.

THE WALK * (1 hour)

Returning to Kannon station, take the train a few minutes on around the peninsula to Ashikajima. As the name suggests, *ashika* (sea lions) once lived on the beaches. Turn left out of the station and right at the T-junction. The road descends to the sea at a small headland in five minutes.

Turn right along the coast road to reach the broad sands of Kimigahama. Kimigahama is a popular surfing beach. Stroll around the bay on the sea wall or the paths laid out on the artificial beach behind. The view of the Inubōsaki Lighthouse is the one in all of the tour guides. Various short paths have also been laid out around the lighthouse at the tip of the cape. This could be a place to spend an entire afternoon sitting on the rocks beside the sea. But don't expect peace with the endless bus tours arriving at the lighthouse above.

The name Inubō (literally "howling dog") comes from a story of Yoshitsune, Yoritomo's half-brother. Yoshitsune narrowly escaped from his enemies here, but in his haste left his dog behind. The dog howled piteously for seven days and finally turned into a rock.

The lighthouse can be entered for a nominal charge. This very English-looking lighthouse was indeed built by an Englishman, Richard Brunton, in 1872. The shogunate had decided to introduce British lighthouse technology in 1866 and Brunton, who arrived two years later, is now remembered as the father of modern lighthouses in Japan. This one was also operated by British keepers until Japanese engineers could be trained. The lighthouse was badly damaged by bombing in World War II, but has since been restored to its original Meiji-era appearance. A small museum is located on the ground floor. Then, climbing to the top, look towards the craggy rocks in the center of the peninsula. They are the cliffs of seventy-three meter Mount Atago, which you will climb later for the Chikyū no Maruku Mieru Oka Tembōkan (literally, "the hall for seeing the roundness of the world"). The gaudy buildings just beneath the cliff of Mount Atago are the pilgrims' temple, Manganji.

Turning left along the road from the lighthouse, you quickly reach the Inubōsaki Marine Park. The small aquarium houses all of the creatures children most want to see: crocodiles, sharks, penguins, giant crabs, seals, eels, turtles, and piranhas. Adults will no doubt think that the tanks are much too small for the bigger creatures. There is a penguin pool and a dolphin show outside. Admission is ¥1,000.

Returning in the same direction (right out of the aquarium), go left at the first junction and then right at the next across the railway. The curious Inuboh Estacio by the railway, with its outdoor tables, is actually Inubō station on the Chōshi Dentetsu line. There are also lots of fish restaurants here, so this is a good place for lunch.

The next turning to the left leads directly up to Manganji. The brightly colored buildings beneath the little cliff look like a movie set. The architecture verges on the vulgar, but there is no denying the sincerity of the pilgrims who built it. You may love or hate this temple, but it has to be seen. Manganji was established in 1976 to give thanks for the blessings of Kannon.

Walking up towards the main hall, you first pass a Fudō hall on the right. Further, beyond the incense burners, giant footprints on the paving stones represent the great Kannon pilgrimages of Japan. The second footprint is for Bandō.

Entering the main hall by the passage to the left, the first statue is of Tokudō Shōnin, the priest of Hasedera in Yamato to whom legend attributes the founding of the Saigoku Kannon pilgrimage. Wooden statuettes of the eighty-eight images of the Shikoku pilgrimage line the long corridor. Manganji's main image is an eleven-headed Kannon. Returning down the hallway on the other side, you see the thirty-three Kannons of Saigoku, the thirty-three Kannons of Bandō, and the thirty-four Kannons of Chichibu.

Return down the road from the temple and turn left towards Mount Atago. Go left again two minutes later at the next group of signs. The road winds up around the hill, reaching the world-lookout point in five minutes. This little mountain lives up to its name. The view is fascinating all around, especially of the peninsula itself and the Tone. The river is a kilometer wide at its mouth. Also look at the ten-kilometer row of cliffs at Byōbugaura. They are not as beautiful as the cliffs at Dover, despite the comparison that is made in all of the tourist literature, but you will not see another sight like them in this part of Japan. The monument in front of the observatory is dedicated to Filipino-Japanese friendship following the tragedies of World War II. Erected in 1958, it points directly towards Mount Mayon on Luzon in the Philippines.

The people of this area were no friends of authority in the 1930s. On the night of September 6, 1930, more than 250 farmers, fishermen, priests and others gathered on Mount Atago with sticks and axes to attack the home of the mayor, the village hall, and the police station. This, the Takagami Village Incident, was sparked by the discovery that ¥20,000 from the fund for modernizing the port of Tokawa had been used for dubious purposes. It also came against a background of unusually heavy local taxation and depression in the fishing industry.

Turn right out of the observatory. The road down is more peaceful than the way up, descending through stepped vegetable fields. Go right at the first T-junction and left at the second. There is a bus stop on this corner for buses back to Chōshi station. Buses run about once every hour. The rest of the walk down to the fishing port at Tokawa coincides with this bus route, so take a close look at the schedule.

Turning left at that second T-junction, you quickly reach the side entrance to Tokai Shrine on the right. This lovely wooded shrine presents a sharp contrast to all the touristic sights so far. Provided that you are not visiting in the mosquito season, the benches are a pleasant place for a rest. The shrine was founded in 709 and moved to its present location in 1674. The deciduous woodland, untouched by human hands for three to four centuries, survives in an unusually perfect state, with several dozen tree species.

Turn left out of the main gate and follow the road down to the sea. The bus route does not descend immediately to the sea but instead runs along the main street of Tokawa just above the port. Stroll around the little port town until it is time to go home. The steep rows of fishermen's cottages have a timeless quality reminiscent of the villages of Cornwall or Brittany.

TRANSPORTATION

Take the Shiosai express on the JR Sōbu line from Tokyo (1 hour 50 minutes). Morning trains at 7:15, 10:45, and 11:45. There are also a very few slower Suigo express trains to Chōshi from Tokyo on the JR Narita line. Either way, the fare including the express surcharge is around ¥3,500.

From Chōshi, take the little Chōshi Dentetsu line two stops to Kannon station (4 minutes, ¥140).

ACCOMMODATIONS

Chōshi has many hotels, *ryokan*, and *minshuku*. Contact the Chōshi Tourist Association (☎ 0479-22-1544) or seek help at the tourist information office at Chōshi station. Convenient places include:

Near Enpukuji:
    Shingetsu Ryokan (☎ 0479-22-5454).

Near Ashikajima:
    Hamaya Hotel (☎ 0479-22-6111).
    Daitoku Hotel (☎ 0479-22-0209).
    Ashikasō (☎ 0429-22-8165).
    New Yashio (☎ 0429-24-3740).
    Kanemasa Ryokan (☎ 0429-22-6670).

Near Cape Inubō:
    Hotel Nagisa (☎ 0429-22-4855).
    Inubōsaki Royal Hotel (☎ 0429-25-1331).
    Awabiya (☎ 0429-22-1201).
    Gyōkeikan (☎ 0429-22-3600).
    Grand Hotel Isoya (☎ 0429-24-1111)
    New Taishin (☎ 0429-22-5024).
    Keisei Hotel (☎ 0429-22-8111).
    Ushioen (☎ 0429-23-5489)
    Tochigisō (0429-22-0568).

There are also eleven *minshuku* in Tokawa.

USEFUL KANJI

Ashikajima	海鹿島
Cape Inubo	犬吠崎
Chikyū no Maruku Mieru Oka	地球の丸く見える丘
Chōshi	銚子
Enpukuji	円福寺
Kannon	観音

CHAPTER 27

Kimigahama	君ヶ浜
Manganji	満願寺
Mount Atago	愛宕山
Tokai Shrine	渡海神社
Tokawa	外川

RYŪSHŌIN — 28
In the Plain of Bandō Tarō

Of the various types of dragon, the most important to those who make their living from the land is the dragon that dwells in water. Chinese and Japanese legend is rich with reference to dragons that determine the course of rivers and streams. In China, they are associated with "dragon lines" of energy that crisscross the countryside like the ley-lines of Britain. Legend also tells how the carp that swims upstream transforms into a dragon when it reaches the source. The tradition lives on in the *koinobori* (carp streamers) diplayed on Boy's Day in Japan, with the wish that boys will grow up fierce and strong.

Ryūshōin is a temple associated with *ryū*, the dragon. So, too, is Ryūkakuji, the other main temple of the walk, and in between you visit the bamboo groves of Tatsudai (Dragon Hill), *tatsu* being the other reading of the character for dragon in Japanese. A local legend tells how services were held for the corpse of a dragon god at Ryūkakuji, Ryūfukuji, and Ryūbiji. This was a plain where the rivers forever changed course. The most dramatic change, of course, was wrought by the hand of man when the Tone River was diverted to the east.

The current eastward course of the Tone only dates from 1654 and is entirely artificial. In the days when the Tone flowed into what is now Tokyo Bay, this district was marshland on the rim of the former Katori Inland Sea. The rich rice bowl we see today is the joint product of four hundred years of rigorous river control and irrigation projects and the unforeseen silting that filled in the sea. The marshland of nearby Imbanuma, and Kasumigaura to the north (Japan's second largest lake), are two of the last remaining stretches of the former sea.

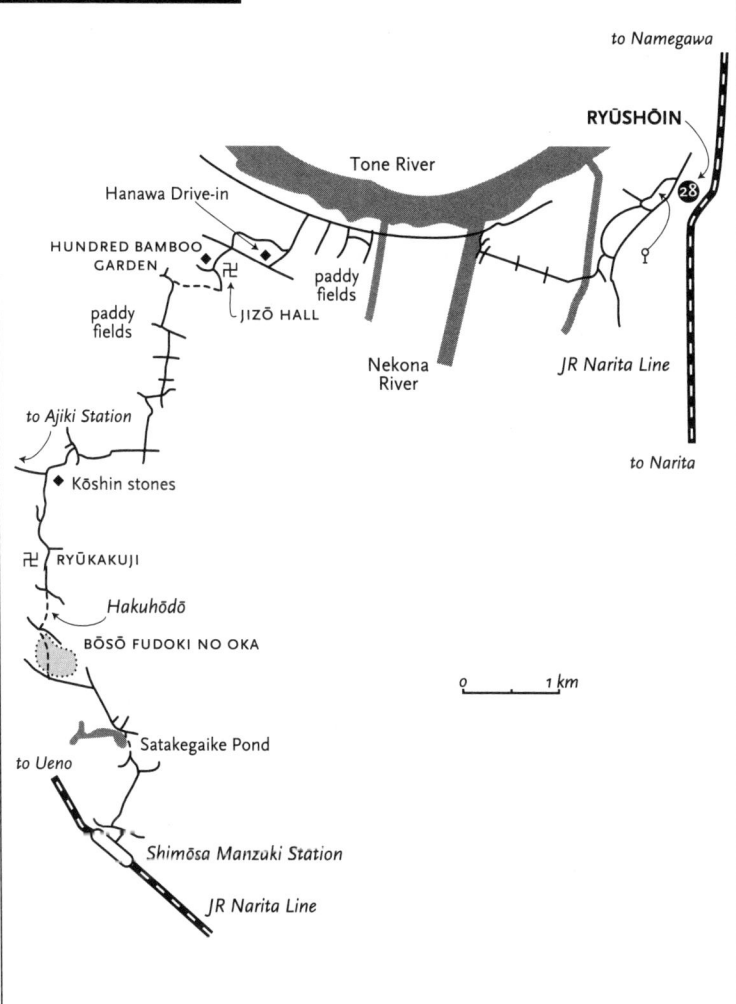

The walk is long by the standards of this book but rich in diversity, from the old temples to rivers, lakes, paddies, and low hills. The highlights are one of the three great bamboo collections of Japan; an open-air museum of old Japanese buildings; and the Ryūkakuji tumuli, a group of more than a hundred burial mounds from the sixth and seventh centuries. Airplane-lovers will also enjoy the low-flying aircraft from Narita Airport.

THE TEMPLE

The bus stops right outside the temple. Two Kantō Fureai no Michi maps are posted there, showing routes to right and left. The left-hand route is the one described in the walk below.

Ryūshōin is another temple hemmed in by a road, but the courtyard has a number of attractive sights. First, the simple thatched *niōmon* is a designated National Treasure from the early sixteenth century. The *niō* warriors guarding it are said to have saved the district from a great fire in the early eighteenth century. Ever since, the local people have shown their gratitude by hanging a huge straw rope from the gate each January 8. Sacred ropes like this are more usually associated with Shinto than Buddhism. They are often hung around holy rocks and trees.

On the left, you see a huge five-story lantern, or perhaps a lanternlike pagoda, a modern innovation in Buddhist art, and beside it a *dōsōjin* stone depicting the male and female gods of the road. The temple instructs you to pray to these gods to ward off senility, and for health, road safety, and peace in the home.

Continuing on the left, in a row, the temple has a Benten hall, a Kannon hall for prayers for safe birth and, beyond the small office, a Kūkai hall. In the center, you see a large copper sutra repository, cast in 1718; a monument to the poet Bashō; and a husband-and-wife pine tree with two trunks, one thick and the other thin.

The main hall itself was erected around the end of the seventeenth century, with a major renovation in 1968. Besides Kannon, statues of Fudō and Bishamonten can be seen inside. To the right, a group of bibbed Kōshin stones line up against the fence; and around the corner, there is a row of bibbed Kannons. Five Shinto shrines to popular gods like Inari and Tenjin are placed behind the main hall.

Ryūshōin was founded in 838. The rather complex story goes that one May the district was beset by freezing weather which destroyed most of the crops. Soon people were starving. The local lord, Oda Masaharu, distributed food and alms and prayed fervently to Kannon. A girl appeared and led him to a pond three hundred meters north of the present temple. There he saw an old priest punting a boat across the water. The old man netted a tiny Kannon statue from the pond and presented it to Oda, who consecrated the statue in a little hall. The weather was restored and the people were rewarded with a bumper harvest. The temple was then established by Ennin. The main image is only three and a half centimeters tall. It is placed in the womb of an eleven-headed Kannon and is not on public view.

THE WALK *** *(5 hours)*

The route of this fifteen-kilometer walk is far too intricate either to be described fully or to be shown precisely on the map. This does not matter, because it is thoroughly signposted. Accordingly, precise directions are given only at signs that may be confusing.

Turn right out of the gate and continue down the bus route following the sign to Ryūkakuji. Take the first left almost immediately down a narrow lane between the houses and into the paddies beyond. There are many twists and turns along tiny country lanes past pretty farmhouses. This is Chiba Prefecture at its best, with the homey, low-key atmosphere of a traditional rural community.

You reach Bandō Tarō, the great Tone River, at the confluence with the Nekona River about thirty-five minutes from the temple. Cross the Nekona and stay on the embankment beside the Tone. The Kantō Fureai no Michi follows a lane at the bottom but this seems daft, given the view from the top.

You cross a smaller tributary in about fifteen minutes. Descend a short while later at the sign indicating sixty kilometers to the sea. The Kantō Fureai no Michi now strikes back across the paddies. The sign reads 6.3 kilometers to Ryūkakuji. The Kantō Fureai no Michi turns right through the houses a short way from the river. But if you are feeling ready for lunch, keep straight on to the main road, where there are several restaurants, and turn right there instead. You rejoin the Kantō Fureai no Michi shortly where it crosses the main road. I especially recommend the meals at the Hanawa Drive-in.

After crossing that main road, or rejoining the Kantō Fureai no Michi, at the 5.1 kilometer sign for Ryūkakuji, the course ascends the small hill of Tatsudai. The hill is strikingly covered with bamboo but it is not till you reach the top that you realize you have come to one of the important bamboo collections of the world.

A thatched *soba* noodle restaurant stands on the right at a bend in the road. First follow the arrows around the side of the thatched cottage to the rear. The five-story pagoda is dedicated to the souls of all the baby bamboo that have been dug up and boiled for food. A sign informs us that in Kyoto there is even a shrine with special ceremonies for the repose of these poor little shoots.

After offering your prayers, stay with the arrows to the lane at the back, turning right and then left, to reach Hyakuchikuen—the Hundred Bamboo Garden. The garden, in fact, has more than a hundred different types of bamboo. Along with others in Kyoto and Shizuoka, this is one of the three great bamboo collections of Japan. Every species from lowly *Bambusa vulgaris* up has its place.

Return to the *soba* restaurant (this could also be a good place for lunch) and continue around the corner, following the Kantō Fureai

CHAPTER 28

no Michi sign. Notice the fine old camphor tree on the corner. In a few steps, you come to the entrance to a second collection of bamboo, the Henchikurin—the Strange Bamboo Grove. Again, you can enjoy a great range of bamboo. Some are very large.

Tatsudai, by the way, was also the site of a battle in 1581 between the three thousand soldiers of seven local lords and the thirteen-thousand-man army of Kuribayashi Yoshinaga. The defenders chose the steep-sided hill for its strategic value, but lost to the greater numbers. The Jizō hall beside Henchikurin is dedicated to the seven lords, who all fell in battle that day.

Returning once more to the Kantō Fureai no Michi, the course descends to the plain. Keep right at the junction without a sign. You quickly pick up the signs again at the bottom. Keep straight at the confusing 3.7 kilometer sign. The path now rises up another low hill and wends through vegetable fields.

The Kantō Fureai no Michi divides at the 0.9 kilometer sign. Take the sign left to Ryūkakuji. The route to the right leads to JR Ajiki station in 3.6 kilometers. Notice the row of Kōshin stones on the left soon after. These stand beside an old shell mound—a garbage dump of ancient man—that has not yet been excavated.

Ryūkakuji is half temple, half ancient remain. One of the oldest temples of the Kantō region, it was built in the seventh or eighth century in the style of Hokkiji in Nara. The story goes that a dragon lady erected the temple in a single night in 709, including a thirty-three-meter three-story pagoda. The foundation stone of that pagoda can still be seen today. (The pagoda at Hokkiji, by the way, was built in 706.) Both the stone and the Ryūkakuji's copper Yakushi image, which also dates from the early eighth century, are designated National Treasures. Today, though, only the head and neck of the statue are original; the rest is an Edo-period restoration following fire damage. A one-meter stone *shibi* (dolphin-tail; an ornament used on the ends of temple roof-ridges) has also been excavated from the site of the pagoda, and can now be seen in the grounds.

The temple does not have a proper main hall, as the previous one was lost in a fire. Ancient roof tiles and copper sutra tubes are displayed in a temporary structure. An early Meiji-period storeroom has been re-erected in one corner of the compound. It had to be saved from its original site at an imperial stock farm to make way for Narita Airport. Many Kannon and other stones may also be seen in the temple grounds, including some huge stone pagodas.

Leave by the steps beside the children's swings and continue down the road. Stay on the unpaved path along the ridge where the road descends, past more vegetable fields and then under a road tunnel. This brings you to Bōsō Fudoki no Oka (Bōsō Local Culture Park) in just over a kilometer.

The main sight at the park is the Ryūkakuji tumuli, a remarkable assembly of 113 keyhole, circular, and square burial mounds. Fifteen have been excavated so far. The Iwaya mound is the most famous: seventy-eight meters across, it is one of the largest square mounds in Japan. The entire area has been turned into a culture park, with lawns and plenty of shade. Although the scale of the tumuli is smaller, the general appearance is similar to that of the tumulus park of Kyongju in South Korea.

The route from Ryūkakuji to the park, by the way, though not so obvious today, appears to be very ancient. Known as the Hakuhōdō (Hakuhō Road, Hakuhō being a term for the early Nara period from 645–710), it follows the most direct course available, using natural features of the landscape. The most ancient temples of Chiba tend to be located close to clusters of burial mounds. Both were no doubt symbols of the power of the local lords.

Bōsō Fudoki no Oka also has a museum with displays of local history and various archaeological finds, including some beautiful clay haniwa figures. Note the old tiles from Ryūkakuji and the replica head of that temple's famous Hakuhō-period Yakushi. Older exhibits include a selection of Jōmon-period pottery. There is also a water-plant garden, and a reconstructed village from the Edo era, where the visitor can experience everything from cooking fish to rice-planting, the tea ceremony, book- and medicine-making, and work in a blacksmith's forge. You can even try on a suit of samurai armor. A free sixteen-page English booklet tells you all about it.

Three historic buildings have been relocated to the park from elsewhere: two eighteenth-century farmhouses and the Western-style auditorium of the Gakushūin (Peers' School), which was built in 1899.

Note that the museum and village are closed on Mondays (except when Monday is a national holiday). They are also closed on the days after national holidays, and from December 26 to January 4. Entry is free and, as noted, English-language pamphlets are provided. You may find the park too sterile for your tastes—the inhabited farmhouses earlier on the walk are more atmospheric—but it is nonetheless a bold and worthwhile attempt to stimulate interest in the local culture.

Pick up the Kantō Fureai no Michi signs again outside the Gakushūin building, or on the road by the Iwaya mound, and descend the hill to Sakatagaike. This pretty pond, deeply overgrown with reeds, is a haven for waterbirds. An old legend tells how a young woman and child were buried alive at this pond as human sacrifices to keep the embankments safe. A plum, which the child had been nibbling, took root at the spot. But though the tree bore fruit, the fruit were always rotten on one side.

From Sakatagaike, it is just a short walk to Shimōsa Manzaki station. (The English road sign mistakenly gives a more conventional reading of these characters, Shimofusa Matsuzaki.)

TRANSPORTATION

Outbound:

From Tokyo: Keisei line from Ueno (¥780) or Oshiage (¥700, connects with Tōei Asakusa line) to Keisei Narita station. Just under 1 hour. JR trains also run from Shinagawa and Tokyo to JR Narita station (¥1,090), three minutes walk from Keisei Narita station.

From Keisei Narita Station: Bus from stand number 1 (inside the large bus shelter) to Namegawa station or Sawara via Namegawa. Alight at Namegawa Kannon. The trip takes 30 minutes. Buses depart at least once an hour. If you must wait, take a look at the souvenir shops between the station and Narita's famous Fudō temple, Shinshōji.

Return:

From Shimōsa Manzaki to Tokyo: Unusually, you can take a train in either direction. Trains to the right (far platform) go to Ueno (you may have to change at Abiko) via the JR Jōban line. Trains to the left (near platform) go to Narita, just one stop away, where you can take the JR Sōbu line to Tokyo and Shinagawa, or the Keisei line to Ueno or Oshiage. Journey times are very similar, at a little over 1 hour either way.

USEFUL KANJI

Abiko	我孫子
Bōsō Fudoki no Oka	房総風土記の丘
Hanawa Drive-in	花輪ドライブイン
Henchikuen	変竹林
Hyakuchikuen	百竹園
Kantō Fureai no Michi	関東ふれあいの道
Namegawa station	滑河駅
Narita	成田
Tatsudai	竜台
Ryūkakuji	龍角寺
Ryūshoin	龍正院
Sakatagaike	坂田ヶ池
Sawara	佐原
Shimōsa Manzaki	下総松崎

CHIBADERA — 29
*City Parks and Museums * (less than 1 hour)*

Chibadera, so close to the center of the city of Chiba, is an oasis of shade and greenery. Perhaps you will see old men lounging beneath the massive ginkgo tree, over a thousand years old, children playing by the bell, or women at work in the garden. This is another Gyōki temple, founded in 709. The gate was built in 1841, but the main hall was lost in the World War II air raids. The present hall was completed in 1977. The growths hanging down from the ginkgo are thought of as milk-giving udders. Women used to boil and drink scrapings from them to become well-endowed themselves. Until the late Edo period, people also gathered here on New Year's Eve for Chiba Warai ("Chiba Laughter"), swapping hilarious stories of the year just finished. The walk is short but very attractive. First, visit Aoba no Mori Park, with the Chiba Sculpture Garden, Ecology Park (featuring reconstructions of the natural environments of the Bōsō Peninsula and a bird-watching zone), Japanese and French gardens, Araku burial mound (ca. 300–600 ad) and the superb Chiba Natural History Museum (for geology, flora, fauna, and history). Then see the Shichiten no Tsuka, seven mounds arranged in the shape of the Great Bear constellation, a device associated with the bodhisattva Myōken, guardian deity of the Chiba warlords. Finally, tour the castle museum and park on the site of their stronghold, Inohana Castle.

TRANSPORTATION
Outbound:
JR Sōbu line from Tokyo to Chiba (40 minutes, ¥610). Most buses from bus stand number 9 outside Chiba station stop at Chibadera (10 minutes, ¥180).

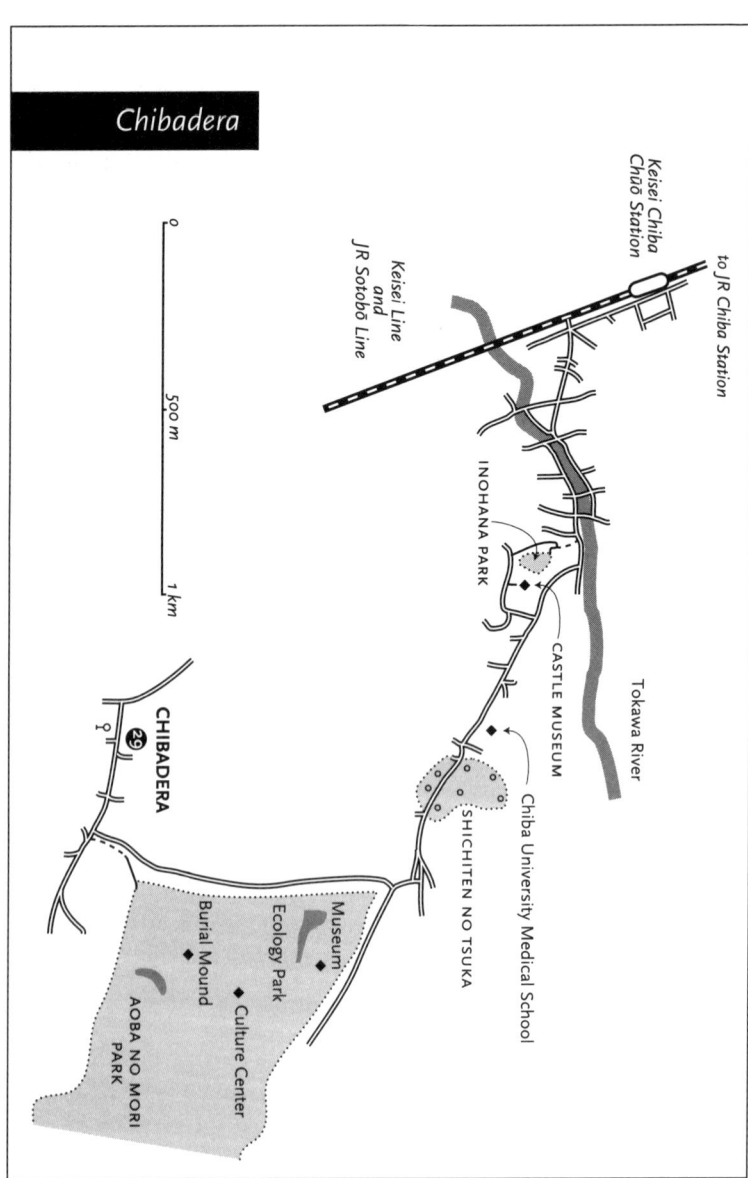

CHAPTER 29

Return:
Keisei line from Chiba Chūō station to Ueno (¥560). Change at Tsudanuma.

ACCOMMODATIONS
Hotels near Chiba station include:
Hotel Sun Garden Chiba (☎043-224-1131).
Royal Plaza Hotel (☎ 043-224-6111).
Near Chiba Chūō station:
Keisei Hotel (☎ 043-222-2111).
Near Inohana Park:
Nakajima Hotel (043-227-5315).
Kawaguchi Ryokan (☎ 043-227-0676).
Hotel New Komatsu (043-227-8585).
Yonezawa Hotel (☎ 043-222-0382) Onsen-type bath.
Ryokan Awaya (☎ 043-224-8811).
Nagatsuka Ryokan (☎ 043-222-4568).

USEFUL KANJI

Aoba no Mori Park	青葉の森公園
Chiba	千葉
Chibadera	千葉寺
Inohana Park	亥鼻公園
Seitaien (Ecology Park)	生態園

KŌZŌJI — 30
Port and Tidal Flats

Legend places the origins of Kōzōji in the reign of Emperor Yōmei (r. 585–587), when a priest, Tokugi Shōnin, found a little Kannon statue during a terrible thunderstorm. The temple has the atmosphere of an ancient pilgrim's temple, with lovely buildings, great ema, countless trinkets, and fine old *momi* firs and cedars. One, the Kamatari cedar, planted in 1526, is named for a leader of the coup d'état of 645 which paved the way for the Taika Reforms. Kōzōji plays a prominent role in the legend of his birth. This is also a temple for Mizuko Jizō. Unfortunately for walkers, it stands on the edge of the new Kazusa Academia Park, Chiba's version of Tsukuba Science City. This is still being built, so the area is about to change out of recognition. The Trans–Tokyo Bay Highway, especially, which opened in 1996, is drawing many companies to the park from Kawasaki. Take the bus back into Kisarazu and spend the day there. See the Kazusa Museum in Ōtayama Park, which displays the tools and handicrafts of country life. Many cities have museums like it, but this is the best. The park also has a burial mound and mound museum, and a thatched eighteenth-century house. Then, if visiting between April and June, go to the tidal flats at Nakanoshima Kōen or Kuzuma Kaigan where, when the tide is out, the shellfish-gathering is sure to be in full swing.

TRANSPORTATION

JR Uchibō line from Tokyo to Kisarazu (1 hour by Sazanami express, ¥1,260 plus a ¥930 express surcharge). Or take a *kaisoku* (express) on the JR Sōbu line from Tokyo to Kisarazu (1 hour 20 minutes).

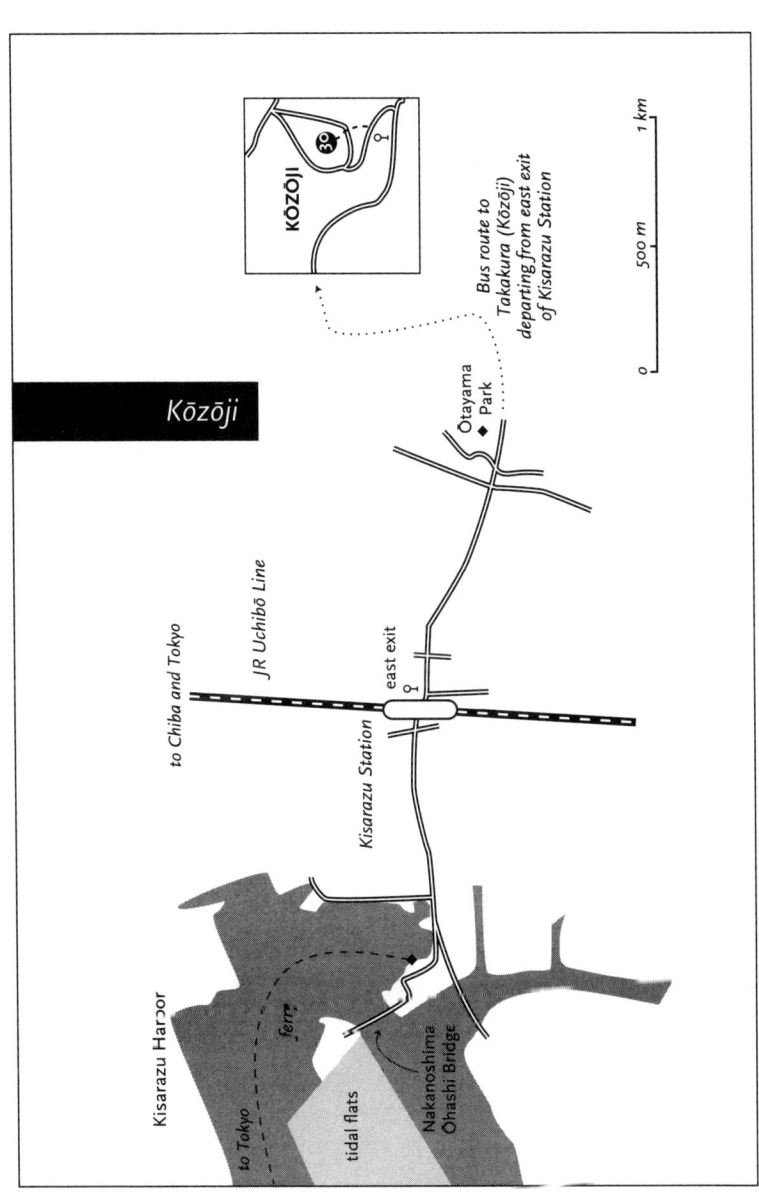

Bus from Kisarazu to Takakura, stand 6, east exit, for Takakura or Tomioka Junkan (circular route). Journey time: 15 minutes (¥440) for buses terminating at or going via Takakura on the circular route; 55 minutes (¥620) via Yokota, the long way round on the circular route. The 7:30 am Sazanami express from Tokyo meets the 8:50 bus from Kisarazu. Returning from Takakura to Otayama Park, alight at Koi no Mori. Buses on the short route from Takakura at 10:08, 11:13, 12:27, 2:50, 3:57, 5:27. Long route (via Yokota): 2:17, 4:22, 5:47.

ACCOMMODATIONS

Ryokan:
Kisarazu Onsen Hotel (☎ 0438-22-2171). Near west exit of station.
Fujiya Hotel (☎ 0438-22-2117).
Ryokan Mifuji (☎ 0438-41-2093).
Hotel Happōen (☎ 0438-23-0211). On hill in Otayama Park.
Kisarazu Bay Plaza Hotel Kangetsu (☎ 0438 22 4141). Between west exit of station and harbor.
Kappo Ryokan Ichiraku (☎ 0438-23-2221).
Kappo Ryokan Senraku (☎ 0438-22-5155).
Western-style hotels:
Kisarazu Park Hotel (☎ 0438-23-3491) Near the harbor.
Daiichi Hotel Mihoshikan (☎ 0438-25-1151) Beside the harbor.
Hotel Royal Garden Kisarazu (☎ 0438-22-7211). Three minutes from the east exit of the station.
Grand Park Hotel Kisarazu (☎ 0438-22-4123). Very close to the east exit of the station.
Hotel Ginga (☎ 0438-23-7051).

USEFUL KANJI

Kinreizuka	金鈴塚
Kisarazu	木更津
Koi no Mori	恋の森
Kōzōji	高蔵寺

CHAPTER 30

Kuzuma Kaigan	久津間海岸
Ōtayama Park	太田山公園
Takakura	高倉
Tomioka Junkan	富岡循環
Yokota	横田

KASAMORIJI — 31
The Chiba Hills ** (3 hours)

Kasamoriji is an extraordinary temple, quite unlike any other on the Bandō circuit. It is said to have been founded in 784 by Saichō, the priest who brought the Tendai sect to Japan. The main hall, which dates from around the sixteenth century, is perched on a rocky outcrop. The square roof is unique in Japan; the view from the top good; and the temple is set in a nature conservation zone with centuries-old cedars, camphors, oaks, and pines. The scene was sketched by, among others, Hiroshige II in his one hundred famous views of Japan. The sixty-one pillars that prop up the hall are all of different lengths. Inside, see the rope covered with handkerchiefs (originally neckerchiefs) that leads to the Kannon statue. Pilgrims write their prayers on the cloths they have used on the journey. Wishes, as usual, include those for everything from the health of babies to success in exams. A legend tells of how a young lady protected a roadside Kannon from the rain with an umbrella (*kasa*) and thereby (rather incredibly) won the hand of the emperor in marriage. Young women thus come here seeking to tie the knot of wedlock. The walk is a well-signposted stretch of the Kantō Fureai no Michi. The first half follows up and down a wooded ridge (with lots of steps) and the second among the rice and *wasabi* fields at the foot.

TRANSPORTATION
Outbound:

JR Sotobō line or Wakashio express (1 hour) from Tokyo to Mobara. The fare is ¥1,260, plus a ¥930 express surcharge. Bus from Mobara to Kasamori or Ushiku station, alighting at

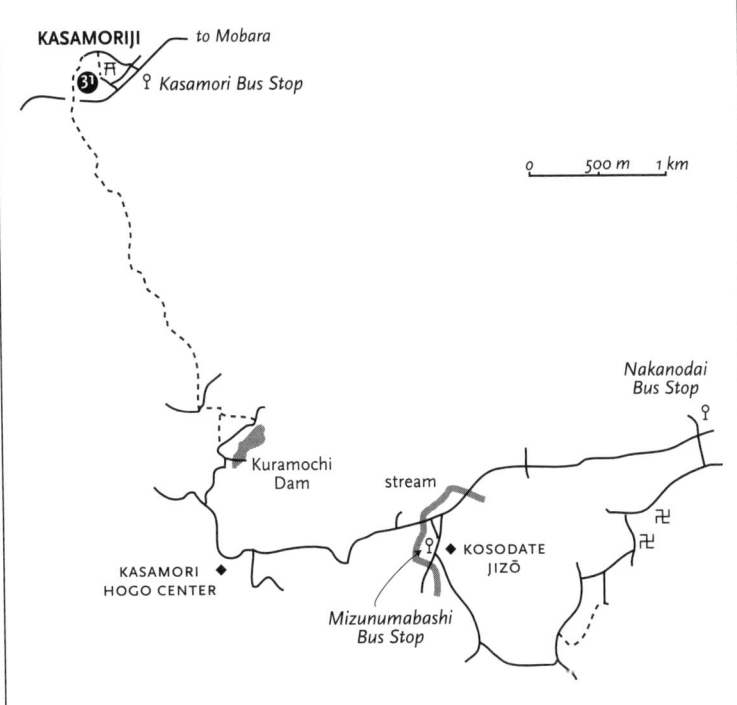

Kasamori (30 minutes, ¥500). Morning buses at 8:05, 9:40, 11:30. ¥3,000 by taxi.

Return:

Bus from Mizunumabashi to Mobara (mornings and evenings only, changing at Chōnan). Or bus from Nakanodai to Mobara (20 minutes, ¥500) at 11:48, 2:23, 5:03, and 6:18. Or Chōnan Taxi (☎ 0475-46-0003), Yutaka Taxi (☎ 0475-46-0123).

ACCOMMODATIONS

Kasamorisansō (☎ 0475-46-2096). A *minshuku* by Kasamoriji.

Kasamori Hogo Center (☎ 0475-46-2381). 4.7 kilometers from Kasamoriji, but on the course of the walk. ¥3,500–4,500 (meals extra) depending on size of party. From ¥6,300 with 2 meals. Floodlit tennis courts. Discounts for children and elderly.

USEFUL KANJI

Chōnan	長南
Jōfukuji	常福寺
Kasamori Hogo Center	笠森保護センター
Kasamoriji	笠森寺
Mizunumabashi	水沼橋
Mobara	茂原
Nakanodai	中之台
Ushiku	牛久

KIYOMIZUDERA — 32
*Deep in the Country * (1 hour 40 minutes)*

Kiyomizudera, like its Kyoto namesake, is a pretty hillside temple with lots of atmosphere and some fascinating old buildings. It stands close to the crowded summer beaches of Ōhara and Ichinomiya, but at the head of a truly quiet valley. I first visited on August 9, the day of a major annual ceremony. Two or three old ladies were selling apples and pears, and a friendly old man was serving free cups of barley tea. Externally, that was all. If, however, you are satisfied by lush green rice and the cries of cicadas and the egrets in the paddies, then you will be happy to have come. Legends variously attribute the founding of this temple to the great general, Sakanoue Tamuramaro, and the great Tendai priest, Saichō. The name is said to come from geographical similarities with the Kyoto site. It also has the same *sangō*, or mountain name, Otowasan, but no balcony like its counterpart. See the one-hundred Kannon hall with not only one hundred Kannons but also statues of the forty-seven samurai and Enma, the great judge of the dead; also the Kamakura-period eleven-headed Kannon in the Okunoin. The grand main hall was built in 1817. The walk takes in the Ibotori Fudōson at Chōyōji, a pretty Fudō temple where you can pray for wart-removal.

TRANSPORTATION
JR Sotobō Line from Tokyo to Chōjamachi. If using the Wakashio express, change at Kazusa Ichinomiya. The 7:00 am Wakashio has a good connection at Kazusa Ichinomiya, with a wait of only five minutes (1 hour 7 minutes to Kazusa Ichinomiya, and about

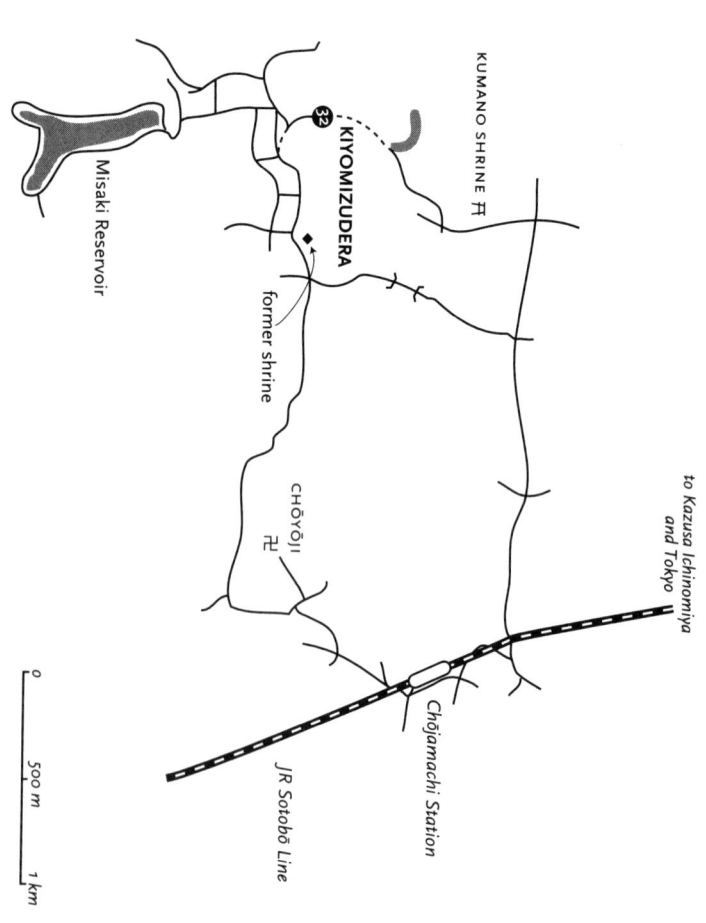

15 minutes from there to Chōjamachi; ¥1,850 plus a ¥930 express surcharge).

ACCOMMODATIONS
Minshuku Ryokan Matsunaga (☎ 0470-87-5166). Near Chōjamachi station.

USEFUL KANJI

Chōjamachi	長者町
Chōyōji	眺洋寺
Kazusa Ichinomiya	上総一宮
Ibotori Fudōson	いぼとり不動尊
Kiyomizudera	清水寺

NAGOJI
Tateyama Bay

Nagoji, the final temple of the Bandō pilgrimage, is located in Tateyama at the southern tip of the Bōsō Peninsula. This is one of Japan's representative seaside resorts. Over 1.5 million tourists visit every year to swim, lie on the beaches, and enjoy the flowers of the district's famous horticultural centers. The winters are mild, the summers hot, and the view of Mount Fuji from the bay ranks alongside that from the Ashigara Pass as the best in the Kantō area.

Unfortunately, there is a downside: the beaches are filthy; the cars get everywhere; and the coastline is overdeveloped. You may hesitate to strip and jump into the sea, tempting as that may seem at the end of a long pilgrimage. The proper technique is to focus the eyes on distant views and visit the historical sites and museums. Fortunately, Tateyama is blessed in both respects.

First, there is Nagoji, built on a low hill overlooking the sea. The temple's *sangō* (mountain name) is Fudarakusan, the Japanese derivative of Potalaka, the mountain paradise of Kannon in the sea off southern India. Nagoji lost its coast with the earthquake of 1703. The land rose and the temple was relocated. It now stands a good ten minutes from the shore. Even so, the temple commands a fine view of Tateyama Bay, the city, and Cape Suno.

After visiting pretty Nagoji, with its pagoda, cave altars, natural woodland, and lookout point, the walk leads to a spectacular cliff-face Kannon hall, where the main image is said to have been carved by Gyōki. You visit the fishing port and market of Funakata, then walk along the breakwater to a fishing museum. Finally, you ascend a hill to the municipal museum on the site of Tateyama Castle. Part of the museum is housed in the reconstructed keep of the castle.

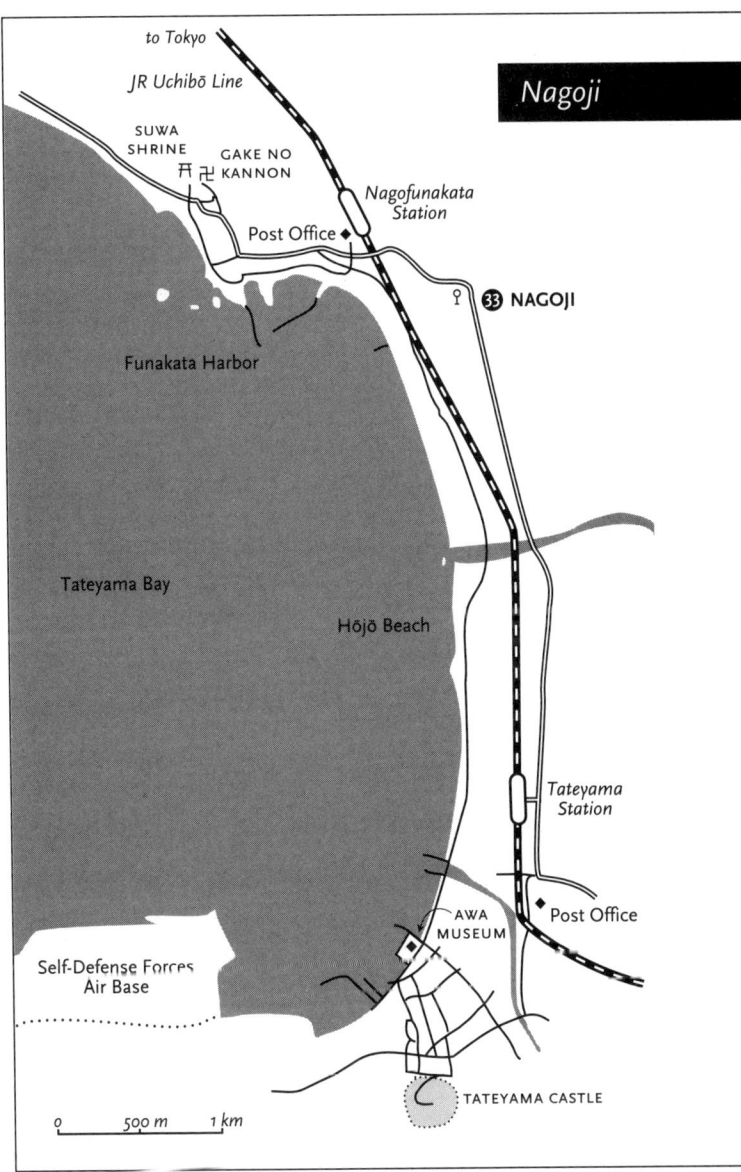

THE TEMPLE

Having started in Kamakura and passed through Edo, Yokohama, Nikkō, Utsunomiya, and Tsukuba, it may seem odd that after 1,360 kilometers the Bandō pilgrimage ends at this out-of-the-way spot on the southern tip of the Bōsō Peninsula. But those who started from the beginning will also recall the quiet simplicity of Sugimotodera. Nagoji, the last Bandō temple, is also the first of the thirty-three temples of the Awa Kannon pilgrimage.

The moment you get off the bus beneath the hillside, you sense that you have arrived at an old temple town. Nagoji, too, was founded by Gyōki. Legend tells that Emperor Genshō suffered from sickness in the Yōrō period (717–724). Gyōki, while visiting the southern Bōsō coast, found an aromatic tree floating in the sea and carved a thousand-armed Kannon from it. When he offered prayers before the image, the emperor recovered.

Ennin is also said to have come here. Minamoto Yoritomo and Ashikaga Takauji both prayed at Nagoji and the temple was especially associated with the local Satomi clan. But the last three centuries have been a tale of two natural disasters. First, Nagoji declined after the earthquake of 1703. It was only fully restored in 1922, one year before almost everything was destroyed again in the Great Kantō Earthquake of 1923.

Starting from the bus stop, enter the temple through the courtyard to the right, not up the steps to the main hall. The dignified building in the courtyard is the priest's residence, as distinct from the main hall further up the hillside. The great sago palm to the right of the temple serves as a striking reminder of the warm maritime climate at this southern tip of the Kantō area.

Take the lane up the hillside from the car park. You quickly reach a statue of Jizō and the *niōmon*. The belfry is on the left; an Amida hall on the right. Just beyond the Amida hall, you come to a two-story pagoda built in 1761. Dainichi is enshrined inside. The main hall faces over the city and Tateyama Bay. This was once listed as one of the hundred most beautiful scenes of Japan. Today, largely on account of urban development, it no longer even comes close.

A great lantern hangs inside the main hall. The main image preserves safety at sea. It cannot be seen, but a fine bronze thousand-armed *maedachi* Kannon is on display, together with votive tablets left by Bandō pilgrims who completed the course. Also notice the grotesque snake-bodied devil in the roof. The *maedachi* Kannon, which dates from the early Kamakura period, is a National Treasure.

A small Hie Shrine stands beyond the main hall to the left. To the right, you see a Daikokuten hall, then two cave shrines. The cave on the left carries the name of the eight dragon kings of the *Lotus Sutra*, who are widely regarded as gods of the sea. The cave on the right contains offerings of boat-shaped stones.

A legend is told in Musashi of how a man vowed to complete the pilgrimage to all thirty-three Kannons of Kantō but died before he even started. When his family gathered on the forty-ninth day after his death, a relative arrived who had met the dead man at Nagoji and accompanied him as far as the village gate. Amazed, they went to inspect the body and discovered a fresh pilgrim's staff by its side.

The steps to the right of the main hall ascend to a lookout point in three minutes. The woods are one of the prides of the temple. Many of the trees are generally associated with warmer climes than Kantō, including the *sutajii* (*Shiia sieboldii*), *yabu nikkei* (*Cinnamomum japonicum*) and *hime yuzuriha* (*Daphniphyllum teijsmanni*). There are also wild camellias.

To walk on over the top of the hill, descend a short way back from the lookout point and follow the unmarked path along the ridge. This descends to the road in about ten minutes. A couple of right turns bring you past the Higashi Fujinoki bus stop (which has an infrequent service to Tateyama) and then to the main Nago bus stop for buses to Tateyama and the Tokyo Bay Ferry.

NAGOJI

THE WALK * *(2 hours)*

To start the walk, continue along the main road from the bus stop for about twenty minutes. You pass under the railway in five minutes, and ten minutes later the road bends sharply to the right. Follow the English road sign to Kisarazu and Tomiura. A sign in Japanese to Gake no Kannon leads off to the right three minutes later. You are hardly likely to miss it, as the hall is visible from a long way off. This is the third Kannon of the Awa pilgrimage.

The hall of Gake no Kannon (Cliff Kannon) is truly spectacular, perched high above Tateyama Bay. Gyōki is said to have carved the main eleven-headed Kannon on the cliff in 717. You can only catch the faintest glimpse of the carving and its boat-shaped halo on the rock at the back of the hall, but you will certainly remember the location. Experts judge that the carving actually dates from the late Kamakura period. Follow the cliff to the left from Gake no Kannon to Suwa Shrine. A small Inari shrine stands at the foot of the cliff and old *yagura* (burial stupas) are carved higher up. High above, you can espy that most international of all fertility symbols, an erect penis.

Descending the steps from here and crossing the road, you quickly come to the beach. Turn left along the sands to the fishing port of Funakata. See the boats and the fishermen mending their nets, and also the first full views of Mount Fuji. The highlight, at the far side of the port, is Fureai Ichiba (Friendship Market), where the fisheries union sells a huge range of fresh and processed seafood at unbeatable prices.

From here, the walk takes the promenade along the sea wall around the bay to the city center. The views of Mount Fuji are fabulous; it looks far bigger from here than from Tokyo, because you can see right down to its base. You can also watch the old men and women foraging for seaweed. The filth of the beach, however, detracts so much from the pleasure that you might wish to take a bus part of the way. Nothing in Japan is more disappointing than the seaside.

CHAPTER 33

It takes about an hour from Funakata to reach a monument depicting two fish, on the corner of the second big stream that enters the bay. This commemorates Japan's first release of fish to the sea in 1957 in order to restore stocks depleted by overfishing and pollution. The ceremony was attended by the crown prince and fisheries representatives from all over Japan.

The Awa Museum (☎ 0470-22-8608) stands a little over five minutes further along the beach. This prefectural fishing museum is superb. A Norwegian whaling harpoon stands at the doorway. Admission is free. Museum hours are 9:00 am to 4:40 pm; it is closed New Year's, days after public holidays, and Mondays (unless Monday is a public holiday). Inside, the exhibits include 2,000-year-old dugout canoes, boats, dolls, photographs, and an extraordinary collection of old fishing and whaling utensils. The entire collection of over two thousand items is a designated National Treasure. A free English pamphlet is available.

To reach Tateyama Castle, take the road away from the beach at the traffic lights outside the Awa Museum. A Skylark restaurant stand on the corner. Continue for ten minutes along this road and turn right at the Shimochō junction (there is a sign in English). You reach the entrance to the castle park seven minutes later on the left. Shiroyama Kōen Iriguchi bus stop stands close by.

The park has a peacock garden, a Japanese garden, and areas of plum and cherry trees, camellias, and azaleas. The highlight is the imitation castle keep at the top, which also has a panoramic view. The exhibits inside are all related to a great nineteenth-century serial novel in 106 volumes, Takizawa Bakin's *Nansō Satomi Hakkenden* (Satomi and the Eight Dogs). The original Tateyama Castle was the final bastion of the Satomi, an offshoot of the Minamoto who ruled in the province of Awa for 170 years until Satomi Tadayoshi was expelled to Shimane in 1614.

The Satomi only arrived in Awa in 1441 as virtual refugees from fighting in Gunma, but quickly conquered the local lords and even expanded into Kazusa. Their big moment in history came at two battles against the Hōjō at Konodai in Ichikawa, one in 1538 and the other in 1564. The Satomi (first Satomi Yoshitaka, then his son Yoshihiro) lost both times, leaving the Hōjō in control of Ichikawa until the fall of Odawara in 1590. Today, the legend created by the novel is more famous than the warriors themselves.

The exhibits are fascinating even for non-readers of Japanese, especially the wonderfully illustrated old volumes of the novel. Certain space-age innovations include a hologram allowing one to clutch at (though necessarily miss) one of the jewels for which the protagonists had to quest. Further materials from old Tateyama can also be observed in the main hall of the museum at the bottom of the hill. If you wish, you can even try on a suit of Japanese samurai armor. The admission charge of ¥300 covers both the keep and the main museum, so hang onto your ticket.

The castle keep and museum (☎ 0470-23-5212) are open from 9:00 am to 4:30 pm. They close on days after national holidays and Mondays (unless Monday is a national holiday).

Now comes the time to complete the Bandō loop. You can take a bus from Shiroyama Koen Iriguchi to Tateyama station. But if you have time, take one all the way to the Tokyo Bay Ferry, past the point where Yoritomo landed in 1180. Crossing by ferry to Kurihama on the Miura Peninsula, return to Tokyo by the Keikyū or Yokosuka lines. The latter will carry you through Zushi, Kamakura, Kita Kamakura and Ōfuna, the stations for the first four temples of the Bandō course.

TRANSPORTATION

Outbound:

Train from Tokyo: Sazanami express on the the JR Uchibō line from Tokyo station (About 2 hours, ¥3,500 including express surcharge). Trains depart hourly on the half-hour from 6:30 am.
Bus from Tateyama to Nagoji: take the bus bound for Namuya or the Tokyo Bay Ferry, alighting at Nagoji (20 minutes, ¥200).

Return:
Bus from Shiroyama Kōen Iriguchi to the Tokyo Bay Ferry. (1 hour 30 minutes, ¥1,000). Afternoon buses at 12:50, 1:40, 2:40, 3:45 and 4:40 (weekdays), and 12:50, 2:00, 3:10 and 4:30 (Sundays and holidays).

Tokyo Bay Ferry from Kanaya to Kurihama (35 minutes, ¥490). Shuttle bus to Keikyū Kurihama station (10 minutes, ¥160). JR Kurihama station is just behind the Keikyū station.

From Kurihama to Tokyo: Keikyū line to Shinagawa (1 hour 15 minutes, ¥740), or JR Yokosuka line to Shinagawa or Tokyo (1 hour 25 minutes, ¥1,090).

ACCOMMODATIONS

There are many places to stay in Tateyama. Ask at the tourist information office outside Tateyama station (☎ 0470-22-2531), or contact the Ryokan Association (☎ 0470-22-2531).

Convenient minshuku and ryokan include:

Minshuku
In Funakata: Shiosai (☎ 0470-27-2860); Motegi (☎ 0470-27-2546); San Fraja (☎ 0470-27-5837); Okeya (☎ 0470-27-3248).
Near Nagoji: Ito (☎ 0470-27-2074).

Ryokan
In Funakata: Tateyama Mirror Beach Hotel (☎ 0470-27-5741); Island Hills Tateyama (☎ 0470-27-3211); Yamada Ryokan (☎ 0470-27-2410).
Near Nagoji: Yamatoya Ryokan (☎ 0470-27-2831).

USEFUL KANJI

Awa Museum	安房博物館
Funakata	船形
Fureai Ichiba	ふれあい市場
Gake no Kannon	崖ノ観音
Kurihama	久里浜
Nagoji	那古寺

NAGOJI

Namuya	なむや
Shiroyama Kōen Iriguchi	城山公園入口
Tateyama	館山
Tateyama Castle	館山城
Tokyo Bay Ferry	東京湾フェリー

INDEX

A
Amida, 15, 61–62
Anrakuji, 98–100
An'yōin, 49–51
Ara River, 98
Asahina Pass, 46–47
Asakusa, 114–23
Asakusa Shrine, 118
Ashigara Castle, 72
Ashigara Pass, 12, 71–72
Ashikaga Takauji, 23, 201, 248
Ashio, 156–57
Ashio, Mount, 165–66, 205
Atago, Mount, 220–21
Awa, 12, 19
Awa Museum, 251
bamboo gardens, 228–29

B
Bandō pilgrimage, 12, 14–19, 23–28
Bandō region, 12
Bandō *musha*, 19–23
Binzuru, 61
Benkei, 22, 209
Benten (Benzaiten), 60
Bonten Daigongen Shrine, 191
Bonten Festival, 183
Bōsō Fudoki no Oka (Bōsō Local Culture Park), 230–31
Botamochidera, 53
Brunton, Richard, 219
Byōbugaura Cliffs, 220

C
Chanokidaira, 154, 156
Chiba (city), 233–35
Chiba Castle, 233
Chibadera, 233–34
Chiba family, 19, 233
Chiba Natural History Museum, 233
Chiba Sculpture Garden, 233
Chiba Tsunetane, 21
Chichibu pilgrimage, 18
Chingodō, 117
Chinsekiji, 190
Chōshi, 215–23
Chōkokuji, 129–30
Chōyōji, 243

INDEX

Chūzenji (Nikkō), 15, 150–54
Chūzenji (Tsukuba), 209

D
Daibutsu (*see* Kamakura, Great Buddha of)
Daigo Hot Spring, 185
Daikōji, 51–52
Dankazura, 34
Dannoura, 21
Daruma, 69
dolls, 109

E
Ecology Park, 233
Egara Tenjin Shrine, 36–37
Engakuji, 56–57
Enma, 16, 26, 173, 203, 218, 243
Ennin, 33, 106, 108, 181, 248
En no Gyōja, 92, 129, 144, 183
Enpukuji, 217–18

F
Fudōin, 120
Fuefuki Pass, 94
Fukuroda Falls, 180
Fukuroda Hot Spring, 178, 180
Funakata, 250
Funao Falls, 138–39
Funase no Sukune, 191–92

G
Gake no Kannon, 250
Gandenji, 41–44
Genjō Sanzō (*see* Xuanzang Sanzang)
Gion Hiking Course, 53–54
Gotenba Hot Spring Hall, 74
Gumyōji, 124
Gyōki, 15–16, 33, 62, 77, 80, 83, 100, 124, 129, 141, 144, 173, 212, 246, 248, 250

H
Hakone Tengu Shrine (Tsukuba), 206
Hamada Shōji, 169–72, 175
Hangetsu, Mt., 154–55
Hannya Shingyō (*see Heart Sutra*)
Hanzōbō, 55–56
Haruna, Mt., 132–40
Hasedera (Iiyama), 77
Hasedera (Kamakura) 15, 58–61
Hasedera (Yamato) 16, 58, 217
Hatakeyama Shigetada, 96
Heart Sutra, 14, 27, 86
Heike Monogatari, 22
Heiwa Kannon, 164
Hie Shrine, 212
Hiki family, 19, 22, 52–53
Hiki Yoshikazu, 52
Hiki Yoshimoto, 53
Hinata Yakushi, 77

INDEX

Hitachi, 12
Hōjō Masako, 21–22, 49, 52, 80
Hōjō family of Odawara, 23, 66, 252
Hōjō regents, 22–23, 46, 51, 54, 56, 63–64
Hōjō Sōun, 66
Hōjō Tokimasa, 21–22, 52
Hōkaiji, 54
Hōkongōin, 191
Honkakuji, 52
Hoshino Archaeological Museum, 147

I

Ikaho Hot Spring, 134–35, 138–39
Ikaho Woodland Park, 134, 138–39
Ikego Forest, 41, 45
Imado Shrine, 119–20
Inamura Shrine, 192
Inubō, Cape, 218–19
Inubōsaki Lighthouse, 218–19
Inubosaki Marine Park, 219
Ishihama Shrine, 120
Iwatsuki, 106–13
Izuru Incident, 145

J

Jikōji, 86
Jionji, 106–9
Jizō, 14, 60
Jizōdō (Ashigara), 71
Jōanji, 110–11
Jōchiji, 64
Junisō Kajuen, 45

K

Kaba, Mt., 204–6
Kabasan Incident, 199, 201
Kabasan shrines, 204–7
Kakuonji, 55
Kamakura, 20–21, 31–40, 49–65
Kamakura, Great Buddha of, 61–62
Kamakura Museum, 36
Kamakura Shrine, 37, 54
Kannon, 12, 14–18
Kantō, 11–12
Kantō Fureai no Michi (see Chap-ters 6, 15, 16, 20, 23, 24, 25, 26, 28, 31)
Kanzeonji, 196–97
Kasama ceramics, 196
Kasa, Mt., 86
Kasama Inari Shrine, 196–97
Kasamoriji, 240–41
Katori Inland Sea, 19, 224
Kazusa, 12, 19–20
Kazusa Academia Park, 236
Kazusa Museum, 236
Kegon Falls, 154
Kenchōji, 55–56

INDEX

Kimigahama, 218
Kintarō (see Sakata Kintoki)
Kintoki, Mount, 72–73
Kintoki Shrine, 74
Kisarazu, 236–39
Kiso Yoshinaka, 21, 95
Kite Festival (Zama), 83–84
Kiyomizudera, 243–44
Kiyotakiji, 212–14
Kōbō Daishi (see Kūkai)
Kōbō, Mt., 80
Kōjōan, 212
Kōmyōji, 80
Kōtakuji Hot Spring, 77–79
Kōzōji, 236–37
Kōzuke, 12
Kūkai, 13, 43, 130, 141, 145, 173, 180–81, 218
Kuzuharagaoka Shrine, 64

L
Lotus Sutra, 14–16, 27, 86

M
Madara Festival, 203
Manganji (Chōshi), 28, 220
Manganji (Izuru), 141–45
Mashiko ceramics, 169–72, 174–75
Mashiko family, 173
Matsubaya, 121

Matsuchiyama Shōten, 119
Matsuyama Castle, 100–101
Mazaka Castle, 192
Meigetsuin, 56–57
Minamoto family, 20–23, 35
Minamoto Noriyori, 21–22, 95, 100
Minamoto Sanetomo, 18, 22, 35, 52, 80
Minamoto Yorimitsu, 70
Minamoto Yoritomo, 17, 21–22, 33–38, 43, 46–47, 49, 52, 60, 62–63, 77, 86, 92, 95, 100, 130, 181, 186, 248; grave of, 36
Minamoto Yoriyoshi, 20, 35, 186
Minamoto Yoriie, 22, 34, 52
Minamoto Yoshiie, 20
Minamoto Yoshihira, 95
Minamoto Yoshikata, 94–95
Minamoto Yoshinaka (see Kiso Yoshinaka)
Minamoto Yoshitsune, 21–22, 35, 95, 209, 219
Minowa Castle, 129, 132
Mito Kōmon (see Tokugawa Mitsukuni)
Mito Tokugawa clan, 19, 183, 188
Mizusawadera, 138–40
Mizusawa, Mt., 138–39
Monomi, Mt., 9

INDEX

Musashi, 12, 19–20
Myōhonji, 52–53
Myōken, 183–84, 233

N
Nagoji, 246–49
Nantai, Mt., 16, 144–45, 152–53, 155, 209
Narita, 224–32
Narusawa, Lake, 131
Nefudōson Shrine, 206
Nichidō Museum of Art, 196–97
Nichirinji, 18, 178–81
Nichiren, 17, 51–53
Niihari, 212–14
Nikkō, 150–58
Nikkō Onarimichi, 108, 110–11
Ninomiya Kinjirō, 68–69
Nitta Yoshisada, 23, 54, 129–30

O
Odawara, 23, 66–76
Odawara Castle, 66
Okurakan, 95
Ōmidō (Izuru), 144
Ōmidō (Tsukuba), 209–10
Ono no Komachi, 212
Ōshū campaign, 21
Ōtori Shrine, 122
Ōtsuka Keisaburō, 169, 171, 196

Ōyaji, 15, 159–63
Ōya stone, 159, 161, 165

P
pilgrimages, 12–19, 23–28
Ponpon, Mt., 103
Potalaka, 16, 144–45, 246

R
Rakuhōji, 196, 199, 201–3
Ryūkakuji, 229–30
Ryūkakuji Burial Mounds, 230
Ryūmonji, 111
Ryūshōin, 224–27

S
Sagami, 12, 20
Saichō, 240
Saigoku, 13, 16–17, 27
Saimyōji, 172–73
Saitama Children's Zoo, 89–90
Sakanoue Tamuramaro, 92, 94, 100
Sakata Kintoki, 70–71
Satakedera, 189
Satake family, 19, 23, 167, 181, 186, 188–89, 192
Satomi family, 19, 23, 248, 251–52

INDEX

Seizansō, 193
Senkyōkan, 110
Sensōji, 116–18
Seven Gods of Good Fortune (Shichifukujin), 114, 116
Shimotsuke, 12, 19
Shimōsa, 12, 19
Shinran, 17, 190
Shirahata Shrine, 36
Shizuka, 35
Shōbōji, 92–93
Shōdō Shōnin, 141, 144–45, 152–53, 166
Shōfukuji, 66–70
Shōkokuji, 83–84
Shōtoku Taishi, 15, 43–44, 80
Sugayakan, 96
Sugimotodera, 33–34

T

Tage Castle, 167
Tage Fudō, 165–66
Taira family, 20–22, 35, 62
Taira Hirotsune, 21, 46
Takagami Village Incident, 220–21
Takayama Hikokurō, 218
Takizawa Bakin, 251
Takehisa Yumeji, 134–35
Tateyama, 246–54
Tateyama Castle Museum, 251–52

Tatsudai, 224, 228–29
Ten'en, 38, 54–56
Tenjin Pass, 132
Tobacco Shrine, 204, 207
Tōjōji, 212
Tokai Shrine, 221
Tokawa, 221
Tōkeiji, 64
Tokudō Shōnin, 16, 43, 58–59, 61, 129, 220
Tokugawa Ieyasu, 23, 152, 188, 201–2
Tokugawa Mitsukuni, 188–90, 192–94
Tokutomi Roka, 134–35
Tokyo Bay Ferry, 252
Tone River, 98, 224, 228
Toyotomi Hideyoshi, 23, 66, 188
Tsubame, Mt., 204
Tsukuba, Mt., 199, 209–11
Tsukuba Shrine, 209
Tsurugaoka Hachiman Shrine, 20, 22, 35–36, 45
Tsurumaki Hot Spring, 80–82

U

Umeboshi (pickled plum) factory, 70
Utsunomiya, 159–68
Utsunomiya family, 19, 62, 166–67

X

Xuanzang Sanzang, 108–9, 112

Y

yabusame (horseback archery): at Asakusa, 118; at Kamakura, 35; at Niihari, 212
Yagumo Shrine, 53
Yamizomine Shrine, 183
Yamizo, Mt., 180–84
Yamizo springs, 182–83
Yazaki Shrine, 122
Yokohama, 124–26
Yokohama Nature Sanctuary, 39, 67
Yoshimi Hundred Caves, 101–2
Yoshiwara, 121–22
Yoshiwara Kannon, 122
Yoshiwara Shrine, 121
Yūhi Falls, 71
You-Moi Village, 212

Z

Zama, 83–85
Zama Kite Festival, 83–84
Zeni-Arai Benten, 63
Zeni-Arai Kannon, 164
Zuisenji, 37

The "weathermark" identifies this book as a production of Weatherhill, Inc., publishers of fine books on Asia and the Pacific. Editorial supervision, book and cover design: D.S. Noble. Production supervision: Bill Rose. Color separations: Oceanic Graphic Printing, Hong Kong. Printing and binding: Quebecor, Fairfield, Pennsylvania. The typeface used is Scala, with Scala Sans for display.